Women's work

Manchester University Press

Women's work:

Labour, gender, authorship, 1750–1830

Jennie Batchelor

Manchester University Press

Manchester and New York

distributed in the United States exclusively by Palgrave Macmillan

Published by Manchester University Press
Oxford Road, Manchester M13 9NR, UK
and Room 400, 175 Fifth Avenue, New York, NY 10010, USA
www.manchesteruniversitypress.co.uk

Distributed in the United States exclusively by
Palgrave Macmillan, 175 Fifth Avenue, New York,
NY 10010, USA

Distributed in Canada exclusively by
UBC Press, University of British Columbia, 2029 West Mall,
Vancouver, BC, Canada V6T 1Z2

British Library Cataloguing-in-Publication Data
A catalogue record for this book is available from the British Library

Library of Congress Cataloging-in-Publication Data applied for

ISBN 978 0 7190 8257 3 *hardback*

First published 2010

Typeset
by Florence Production Ltd, Stoodleigh, Devon
Printed in Great Britain
by MPG Books Group, UK

For Leah, Sid and Betty

Contents

Acknowledgements

Like so many of the labours described in the following pages, this book is a collaborative endeavour. Since beginning this project, I have benefited greatly from the comments and challenges offered by numerous colleagues and friends. In particular, I would like to thank David Ayers, Stephen Bending, Stephen Bygrave, Susan Carlile, Ben Dew, Gillian Dow, Rod Edmond, Abdulrazak Gurnah, Nicky Hallett, Megan Hiatt, Sarah James, Cora Kaplan, Bernhard Klein, Donna Landry, Sarah Moss, Melissa Mowry, the late Sasha Roberts, Caroline Rooney, Norbert Schürer, David Stirrup, Scarlett Thomas and Linda Zionkowski. Markman Ellis, Isobel Grundy, Cora Kaplan, Elaine McGirr and Chloe Wigston Smith found time within their hectic worklives to read versions of some of the following chapters in draft, and I know that this book has been greatly strengthened by their insights. I am especially grateful to Sarah Moss, who read several chapters several times, and who otherwise kept me on track, and to Donna Landry who undertook the Sisyphean task of reading and commenting upon the entire manuscript. Her commitment to this project goes well beyond the remit of collegiality and I am deeply indebted to her.

I would like to acknowledge the invaluable financial support of the University of Kent for a Colyer-Fergusson award and the British Academy for a Small Research Grant, which made it possible for me to work at the Huntington Library and to consult Sarah Scott's letters in the Montagu Correspondence. The completion of the book would not have been possible without a term of research leave awarded by the University of Kent. I am also grateful to all of the editorial team at Manchester University Press for their help and support throughout the publication process, and to the Press's anonymous reader for helpful comments.

Throughout the writing of this book, David Motton has continued to be a constant source of support and wisdom. I could not have written it without him.

The latter period of work on this project was bookended by the happiest and saddest of events. The arrival of our daughter, Leah Ellen Motton, just days after completing a first draft of the book, gave me an entirely new perspective on the question of women's work and taught me the joys of play. I deeply regret that my grandfather, Sidney Smith, and my grandmother, Margaret Betty Smith, will not see this book in print. I miss their company and their conversation greatly. This book is dedicated to Leah, Sid and Betty.

An early articulation of this book's project, and some of the work that appears in Chapter 2, was published as 'Woman's Work: Labour, Gender and Authorship in the novels of Sarah Scott', in *British Women's Writing in the Long Eighteenth Century: Authorship, History, Politics*, ed. Jennie Batchelor and Cora Kaplan (Basingstoke: Palgrave Macmillan, 2005), pp. 19–33. Some additional material in Chapter 2 appeared, in slightly different form, as 'Fictions of the Gift in Sarah Scott's *Millenium Hall*', in *The Culture of the Gift in Eighteenth-century England*, ed. Linda Zionkowski and Cynthia Klekar (Basingstoke: Palgrave Macmillan, 2009). Sections of these essays are reproduced here with permission of Palgrave Macmillan. Parts of Chapter 4 originally appeared in 'The Claims of Literature: Women Applicants to the Royal Literary Fund, 1790–1810', *Women's Writing*, 12: 3 (2005): 513–29. I thank Taylor and Francis for permission to reproduce this material.

Introduction: lifting the veil of 'Inchantment'

I Observe what You say, that the pursuing *this project is the only Chance You have of bringing out any thing this Year – & that with hard fagging perhaps You might do that*. I agree with You, that for *this year*, You say true – but, my dear Fanny, for God's sake, dont talk of *hard Fagging*! It was not *hard fagging*, that produced such a work as Evelina! – it was the Ebullition of true Sterling Genius! you wrote it, because you could not help it! – it came, & so you put it down on Paper – leave *Fagging*, & Labour, to him

Who, high in Drury Lane
Lull'd by soft Zephyrs thro the broken pane,
Rhymes ere he wakes, & prints before Term Ends,
Compell'd by Hunger & request of Friends.

Samuel Crisp to Frances Burney, 1779[1]

'*Fact! Fact!*' I assure you, – however paltry, ridiculous, or inconceivable it may sound. Caps, Hats, & Ribbons make, indeed, no venerable appearance upon Paper; – no more does Eating & Drinking; – yet the one can no more be worn without being *made*, than the other [can be swallowed] without being *Cooked*; & those who can niether [*sic*] pay *milliners*, nor keep '*servants*' must either toil for themselves, or go *Capless* and Dinnerless[.]

Frances Burney to Samuel Crisp, 22 January 1780[2]

To say that Frances Burney experienced the two years between the publication of *Evelina* (1778) and her final laying to rest of *The Witlings* (in 1780) as a period of highs and lows is rather an understatement. Bookended by her ecstatic journal entry of late March 1778 – that the year had witnessed 'a grand & most important Event[:] . . . the first publication of the ingenious, learned, & most profound Fanny Burney!'[3] – and her lament for the fate of the eponymous Witlings – sunk 'down among the Dead Men' after Charles Burney's and Samuel Crisp's unfavourable pronouncements upon the play – this period realized many of Burney's highest hopes for, and deepest fears about, her decision to become a professional author.[4] As her epistolary exchanges with her mentor, censor and surrogate 'Daddy', Samuel Crisp, indicate, such aspirations and anxieties emerged in the context of a much wider, and by 1780 longstanding, debate about the nature and status of authorship: what it meant to think (or to refuse to think) about writing as work. While the effects of this contestation of authorship were evidently felt by authors of both sexes, Burney's voluminous and well-documented correspondence suggests that they were experienced differently by women writers for whom the pressures exerted by literary labour were greatly intensified by their obligation to perform the cultural work of femininity. To write and to be a woman was, it seems, a Sisyphean endeavour.

Crisp's affront at Burney's (rather unladylike) troping of writing as '*hard Fagging*' in an earlier and lost correspondence reveals his uncompromising understanding of intellectual labour as a contradiction in terms. '[*H*]*ard fagging*' and immersion in the grubby worlds of labour and commerce were the activities of the 'Drury Lane' hack, and incompatible with the cultivation of works of 'genius', which seem to 'come' as gifts to authors, in Crisp's formulation of the creative process, rather than being actively worked up by them. The truly inspired artist might meet with economic success, Crisp conceded, but that success depended upon an author's leisure, their detachment from a literary marketplace that transformed authorship into a trade, the laboured and inferior productions of which satisfied the voracious appetites of readers and booksellers rather than the Muses. Rehearsing a familiar lament of eighteenth-century discussions of literary genius, Crisp argued that to view writing as work was to devalue the author's currency and to equate literature with any other mere commodity.[5] To add weight to this claim, Crisp turns to a greater authority, Alexander Pope, whose *An Epistle to Dr Arbuthnot* (1735) is cited by way of shorthand for his concerns about the deleterious effects of the commercialization and expansion of the print marketplace upon literature and the professional writer. Here, however, Crisp's model of authorship begins to unwrite itself. Equally critical of a system of aristocratic patronage that privileged rank and politics above industry and merit as it is of the professional drudge, *An Epistle to Dr Arbuthnot* displays a marked ambivalence in response to the question of writing's status as work that is characteristic of the complexity of Pope's views on textual labour.[6] If Crisp was unwilling to acknowledge these complexities, then Burney certainly was not.

Burney's letter to Crisp punctures the idealism of her mentor's views on authorship by introducing domestic labour as a key third term in the discussion of writing as work, a manoeuvre that links the debate on authorship to a wider debate on women's work with which it was intimately connected. The letter's partly tongue-in-cheek likening of authorship both to domestic labour (the making of 'Caps, Hats and Ribbons') and to service (cooking) produces various, contradictory effects. On the one hand, by presenting such activities as equivalents, Burney exposes the unfairness of Crisp's criticisms of his protégée's lack of application by emphasizing the significance and weight of the author's task in relation to the employments of the domestic drudge and the paid servant. On the other, she is able to expose as a fallacy Crisp's image of the female author as a leisured amanuensis to the Muses. '[*H*]*ard fagging*' might be considered unfeminine, but it was, after all, the reality of many women writers' lives, filled as the daily round was with 'paltry', yet demanding, tasks that competed with their professional activities, but, as a result of the perceived inconsequentiality of domestic employments and the supposed unfitness of gentlewomen for actual labour, were found to be 'inconceivable' as work in their own right.[7]

At this point, with the introduction of questions of worth in relation to work, the letter's argument about authorship takes an interesting turn. If theorizing authorship as labour ran the risk of devaluing *texts* by associating them with such flimsy and ephemeral commodities as caps and dinners, then failing to view writing as labour, Burney contended, threatened to undermine *authors* by obscuring the work, and hence the worth, invested in the creative process. Work that was culturally invisible, as demonstrated by the analogy to millinery and culinary labours (both, of course, women's work), was work that lacked economic and social value. The serious implications that Burney's playful interrogation of the relationship between women's intellectual, domestic and manual labour had for eighteenth-century women, in general, and for the eighteenth-century woman writer, in particular, form the subject of this book. Crisp's argument that neither women of a certain station nor authors should labour if they were to fulfil their respective duties to their sex and their profession may have been far from unique in the period, but neither was it wholly representative. *Women's Work* seeks to complicate the conventional narrative about labour, gender and authorship posited by Crisp and often endorsed by literary and historical scholarship, both by pointing to the vital and valued role that work of various kinds played in texts by middling and genteel women writers publishing during the later eighteenth century, and by revealing labour's centrality to these authors' self-conceptualization as women and as literary professionals.

Men's work and women's leisure

Like Burney's letter, this book is underpinned by the assumption that the questions posed by women's work in the eighteenth century were substantially different from those posed by men's work. This is not to say that men of the middling and upper ranks were wholly immune to labour's taint. That a gentleman's being compelled to undertake manual labour or paid work might produce similar unease to that provoked by the prospect of a gentlewoman having to do the same, especially in the first half of the century, has been ably demonstrated in recent studies by Judith Frank and Linda Zionkowski.[8] (The eighteenth-century novel's perennial interest in the precarious fate of second sons, especially in women's writing of the later century, attests to the longevity of at least some of these concerns.) Yet, as Sarah Jordan has explored, gentlemanly idleness was also an anxious preoccupation of eighteenth-century commentators.[9] Such contradictions surrounding gentlemanliness and work were largely, although not entirely, resolved by the growth and heightened prestige of the professions during this period. Defined by Penelope J. Corfield as 'skilled tertiary-sector occupations that are organized around a formal corpus of specialist knowledge with both a theoretical and a practical bearing', the professions – primarily the church, law, various branches of medicine and the armed services – were 'respectable calling[s] . . . fit for the elusive but desirable character of a "gentleman"'.[10] The esteem in which such occupations were increasingly held, combined with the 'specialist literature' to which they gave rise, made available a language to describe the middling sort at work (of industry, competence, vocation and professionalism) that was compatible with notions of gentility.[11] Concurrently, the gentleman's position in relation to the division of labour shifted significantly. As John Barrell has influentially argued, for many writers of at least the first half of the eighteenth century, the gentleman's social and moral authority was understood to depend upon his leisured disinterest, his ability to comprehend the workings of society (the 'equal, wide survey' which he alone could grasp) made possible by his exclusion from manual labour. From the mid-century, and particularly in the wake of the publication of Adam Smith's *The Wealth of Nations* (1776), this position of withdrawal from the division of labour became increasingly untenable. Once it became clear that 'no one was not implicated in the separation' of 'trades and occupations', the achievement of a viewpoint of 'social coherence' became an 'impossibility'.[12] Simultaneously, the valorization of labour in political economic theory of the 1760s and 1770s made participation in the division of labour morally desirable. Industriousness, expertise and specialization were to become central to the professional aspirations of the polite classes. Occupational identity began to replace traditional indicators of status, so that, by the end of the century, work was, in Clifford Siskin's words, 'rewritten from that which a true gentleman does not have to do, to the primary activity informing adult identity'.[13]

No corresponding shift occurred for women, who, as the century progressed, were increasingly expected (but often refused) to take on the attributes of leisure against which their fathers, brothers and sons were defined. Although as Corfield points out, the professions were supposedly 'meritocratic', that is to say, 'based upon skills and knowledge, not upon gender as such', the reality was that women were largely, and indeed often systematically, debarred from the professions or relegated to those 'lesser' occupations such as teaching, which were 'no more than semi-professionalized in organizational terms'.[14] Moreover, women were denied access to the vocabulary of professionalism which was increasingly central to the consolidation and prestige of the middle class. If, in the words of Thomas Gisborne, the duty of men in the 'higher and middle classes of society' was to 'benefit [their] country' by contributing to 'the diffusion of religion and virtue, [or] science and learning', then that of *all* non-labouring-class members of 'the female sex' was to confine themselves to the pleasures of 'domestic life'.[15] As Gisborne's comments imply, and as numerous social and literary historians have confirmed, in the period with which this book is concerned – roughly the second half of the long eighteenth century – gender gradually came to supplant rank or class as the most significant determinant of attitudes towards labour.

To recognize this development and its implications for thinking about gender and status in the eighteenth century is also to recognize some of the many difficulties involved in finding a suitable vocabulary (whether that of station, order, rank or class, the genteel, the polite or the middling sort, for example) with which to describe the women whom this book examines. That the language of 'rank', a marker of status that, as Stephen Wallech has argued, derived from a combination of 'an individual's personal merit and estate', was gradually superseded by that of 'class' by the early nineteenth century has become a commonplace of historical scholarship.[16] So too has the assertion that, by the turn of the nineteenth century (or at least by the passing of the 1832 Reform Act), the professional 'middle class' had risen to cultural prominence.[17] Despite these insights, the application of the language of rank and class remains deeply problematic for a number of reasons, not least because such vocabularies run the risk of anachronism or of oversimplifying the complexity of eighteenth-century notions of, and debates about, social station. Catch-all and ubiquitous designations such as the 'middle class' or 'middling sort' (the later a much more common term in the period, of course) are in danger of seeming too vague to be of meaningful significance or too inflexible to accommodate the sizeable and heterogeneous group of people who were neither of aristocratic stock nor born to labour. Moreover, questions of where to draw the lower and upper limits of such a group remain as vexed now as they did at the time. Members of the 'mechanick part of mankind', as Peter Earle has demonstrated in his study of 'middle-class' Londoners from the Restoration to the early eighteenth century, could rise to middling status through regular 'accumulation' and the 'employment of capital and labour'. Equally, gentlemen might fall into this category if they became reliant upon the profits from similar investments to those made by the 'middling sort', if they trained for a profession, or if they were forced to enter into trade.[18]

These problems multiply when women, historically often relegated to the margins of discussions of status, class and rank, are placed at their centre. For instance, if we accept Earle's view that 'middling people' were those who 'worked but ideally did not get their hands dirty' – in other words, those who were professionals or 'commercial or industrial capitalists' – then women's claim to middling status often rested on their kinship to fathers and husbands who enjoyed wider opportunities in these areas.[19] This fact, coupled with the increasingly entrenched association of femininity and leisure, had significant implications for déclassée women of higher social station. As numerous novels from the period indicate, the fall experienced by the downwardly mobile, single gentlewoman, forced to seek a living, yet all but excluded from the professions and those 'middling' trades and commercial enterprises that might prevent her from undertaking many of the more degrading forms of manual work, was great indeed. The troubling status ambiguity of fictional characters born to leisure yet compelled to work, from Camilla, heroine of Sarah Fielding's *The Adventures of David Simple* (1744), to Juliet Granville of Burney's *The Wanderer* (1814), was a recurrent theme of the eighteenth-century novel and testament to the perceived inadequacy of rigid taxonomies of social organization to reflect the diversity of individual circumstance and experience.

This diversity is amply reflected in the group of women writers (who have been variously labelled 'genteel', 'middling sort' or 'middle class') that this book explores. Sarah Robinson Scott's father, Matthew Robinson, was a member of the landed gentry, her mother, Elizabeth Drake, an heiress. Scott was well educated – in part by the Cambridge scholar Dr Conyers Middleton – and well connected through her wealthy and influential bluestocking sister, Elizabeth Montagu, although she lived (indeed she chose to live) very much on the periphery of the fashionable, bluestocking society culture over which Montagu presided. She was also, if rather briefly, connected to the court through her husband, George Scott, who was sub-preceptor to Prince George (later George III). Yet Scott's life, both before her short-lived marriage and afterwards, when she settled permanently with her companion Lady Barbara Montagu, was beset with financial concerns, and she remained precariously dependent upon allowances from family members (including the husband from whom she was separated) as well as the earnings from her writing career throughout her life.[20] In her fiction, the profits from which Scott hoped might fund various charitable projects to aid indigent and dispossessed women, Gary Kelly argues that we see a convergence of 'progressive gentry' and 'professional middle class' values.[21]

Charlotte Turner Smith was similarly born into the landed classes – her father, Nicholas Turner, held estates in Surrey and Sussex – and she enjoyed at least the beginnings of a fashionable education at a school in Kensington. But Smith's father was a gambler, and was forced to sell his Surrey estate, to mortgage other lesser properties, and to take Smith out of school. Shortly afterwards, Charlotte Turner was married off into sugar money – her father-in-law, Richard Smith, was a self-made businessman and Director of the East India Company – and she would famously spend much of her adult life trying to secure for her children the estate willed to them by their grandfather and squandered by her spendthrift husband. Benjamin Smith's gross mismanagement of his own finances and his father's estate plunged the couple into financial difficulty, and Charlotte would spend time in the King's Bench prison, an experience upon which she would later draw in her fiction and which was similarly endured by a number of the writers discussed in Chapter 4.[22] Smith famously and repeatedly declared that she had become an '*Author by profession*' unwillingly and only in order to support herself and her children in the face of a perverse 'destiny' that a woman of her station might have hoped to have avoided.[23] In the words of Edward Copeland, the impoverished Smith faced a quintessentially 'genteel dilemma' when confronted with the prospect of having to live by her pen.[24]

Unlike Scott and Smith, Mary Wollstonecraft did not belong to the propertied classes; her father was a weaver whose attempts to turn gentleman farmer in the 1760s were unsuccessful. Financially insecure, Wollstonecraft sought independence through a variety of respectable employments (she worked as a paid companion, teacher and, most unhappily, as a governess) before turning to writing as her principal source of income.[25] Notoriously, in *A Vindication of the Rights of Woman* (1792), Wollstonecraft claimed that her writing was directed at those of 'the middle class' – a term absent from the lexicon of Scott's and Smith's work – because such a group was in 'the most natural state', by which Wollstonecraft meant that they were corrupted neither by the excessive wealth of the aristocracy nor by the poverty and abjection endured by the labouring classes.[26] And yet 'middle-class' is only partly helpful for describing Wollstonecraft's own social position and political outlook, not least because she seems primarily to have used the term, as it was commonly deployed at the time, to signify one of several possible 'categories within a taxonomy' – a '"species", "sort", or "type" of person' – rather than to demarcate a unified group to whom a clear and well-defined 'social meaning' was attached.[27] For these reasons, Barbara Taylor has suggested that the term 'petty bourgeois' might provide a more accurate reflection of Wollstonecraft's status and politics.[28]

We might with greater confidence describe a number of the popular women novelists examined in Chapter 4 as 'middle-class', given their often more modest backgrounds and occupational status. Yet these women's correspondence and publications also suggest the inability of conventional taxonomies fully to encompass individual lives and, still more crucially, subjectivities. Eliza Parsons, for example, was a wine merchant's daughter, who married the manager of a turpentine factory, biographical details which might seem to justify Copeland's description of her as 'skirt[ing] the lower edges of the middle class'.[29] But Parsons was also connected to the court as a Sempstress in Ordinary to the royal household, and both her letters to the Literary Fund and her many novels attest to her genteel aspirations and profound sense of injustice that a woman who had been raised with every hope that she might become a 'Subscriber' to such a charity as the Literary Fund would become a frequent, and desperate, applicant to it.[30]

Mindful of the many and various pitfalls of imposing a language of social classification that these women writers often interrogated through their discussions of various forms of labour, I have attempted throughout this book to adopt the terms that the individual women writers themselves used to describe the particularity of their own situations and those of their heroines. This means adopting a flexible vocabulary, one which reflects the complexity of these authors' representation of status (whether defined by birth, rank, occupation, character, or a combination of these factors) as they seek to explore, and also to challenge, conventional wisdom about the complex web of social signification generated by the dynamic relationship between gender, station and (manual or intellectual) work.

Domesticity, the novel and the invisibility of women's work

Sustained treatments of work's relationship to gender and writing in the period have, with few exceptions, been confined to studies of the careers and works of labouring-class writers, by far the majority of whom were poets.[31] This growing and important body of work has remapped the eighteenth-century literary landscape, and with it our understanding of the complex ways in which labour, class, gender and writing were mutually constitutive in the period, both in the polite and in the plebeian imagination. One of the effects of this scholarship, however, has been to reinforce the view that cultural assumptions about work in the period can most productively be gleaned from the field of labouring-class poetry alone. Since, as William J. Christmas has written, the eighteenth-century cultural imaginary equated labour and 'rank', then it makes sense to look for illumination into the question of work's relation to writing in the publications of labouring poets, who were 'key commentators' in the debate on 'writing-as-work'.[32] Christmas's important, primary argument that labouring poets were central to the debate on writing-as-work is irrefutable. Yet, his secondary (implied) claim that work was not a particular concern for those authors, including novelists, who were neither plebeians nor patricians, merits further investigation.

The assumption that the subject of labour, manual as well as intellectual, lies beyond the purview of the vast majority of eighteenth-century texts, and especially novels by women, is widely held. According to Edward Copeland, while money was a leading preoccupation of later eighteenth-century fiction, employment was not. Although the harried authors for the circulating libraries, a number of whom are the focus of this book's final chapter, often resorted to 'fictions of employment', the 'genteel' novelists most familiar to us today viewed work as a 'nettling matter' best avoided.[33] For these writers knew, Copeland contends, that the act of seeking employment for a fictional heroine 'turn[ed] the ideology of the genteel novel upside down', 'betray[ing] her class' and placing her virtue in doubt. If the heroine's social and moral standing were compromised by her exposure to work then writers' moral authority could similarly be threatened by their novels' labour plots.[34] By drawing attention to work, and, by association, to the economic imperatives that drove a number of authors to put pen to paper, writers placed their intellectual endeavours in an uncomfortably close proximity to degraded manual labour, such as the making of caps, hats, ribbons and dinners, and thus allowed their professional status as writers and private reputations as women to be called into question. We need only recall Anna Seward's damning assessment of the sonnets of Charlotte Smith as 'everlasting lamentables . . . [and] hackneyed scraps of dismality' – an explicit rejection on Seward's part of Smith's insistent imprinting of her authorial and domestic labours on to her literary works – to see the potentially undesirable effects of presenting writing as work, either explicitly or by analogy.[35] The recognition of such dangers, Copeland concludes, forced female novelists largely to exclude the world of work from their writing, and to jettison the world of writing from their works, for fear of inviting the 'hostility of the very society' to which they and their heroines 'so earnestly aspire[d] to belong'.[36]

Work has thus appeared to be notable in the eighteenth-century novel largely for its absence. In the words of Ann Van Sant, for all its '*formal* inclusiveness', the novel in this period was 'substantively bound by its exclusion of work'.[37] When Sandra Sherman looked for answers to the question of 'what happened' in later eighteenth-century literature to those dependent solely upon their labour for their support, she was forced to turn away from fiction, the original object of her enquiry, to texts that are 'operative outside the conventionally imaginative (literary)', that is to say, to political and economic tracts and treatises, in which, she argues, meaningful imaginative engagement with labour and poverty is exclusively to be found.[38] Where work, or more commonly the threat of work, has been noted in eighteenth-century fiction, it has often been in the form of what Sherman has referred to as the 'sentimental mainstay' of the eighteenth-century novel, the formulaic labour-as-fall plot, in which, as in novels by Burney, Fielding and Charlotte Lennox, the heroine is forced to trade on her domestic accomplishments to earn money as a companion or milliner, but is serendipitously delivered from labour before the novel's close.[39] Even the most radical of women writers have appeared squeamishly genteel in their treatment of work. The fact that Emma Courtney's Wollstonecraftian lament that women were not educated 'for commerce, for a profession, for labour' is tempered by an abject horror at the notion of paid work that causes the 'heart [to] die within me', has, for example, seemed only to underscore both the contemporary association of virtuous femininity and leisure and the need for the woman novelist to distance her heroine from such a devastating course of life at all costs.[40] Where women writers offer a more nuanced and sustained treatment of the experience of work, as Burney does in *The Wanderer*, their novels have been viewed as intriguingly unrepresentative, even precociously ahead of their time in their treatment of themes that more conventionally belong to early Victorian fiction.[41] Yet, as indicated by the many examples discussed in the following chapters, and by those I have not space to enumerate, work – which, for the moment, I am using as a convenient shorthand for various kinds of manual, intellectual and affective labour – is a central preoccupation of the eighteenth-century novel, and not simply as a threat to be avoided or a hurdle to be overcome. Moreover, work is crucial to many female authors' self-construction, their negotiation of the gendered politics of the work of writing forming the cornerstone of their identities as women and as writers.

In order to appreciate the extent to which work is implicated in the fiction and careers of women writers, it is vital that we distinguish those 'fictions of employment' *within* eighteenth-century novels from those fictions of employment that we have created *about* the eighteenth-century novel when we have misread or refused to acknowledge work's central, if much-debated, presence in much of the imaginative literature of the period. If we do not, then we become complicit with the very ideologies that have historically rendered women's work invisible, ideologies which writers, including Scott, Smith, Wollstonecraft and the authors for the popular presses discussed in Chapter 4, strove to challenge. One of the principal contentions of this book is that our critical blindness has, in large part, been caused by the long shadow that the figure of the domestic woman has cast over eighteenth-century studies, and particularly over studies of women's writing of the period. The assumption that work presents a risk to the novel and its female author rests upon the twofold claim that the domestic ideal was widely internalized and disseminated by eighteenth-century women writers, and that this ideal was itself predicated upon middling femininity's location in a private realm that defined itself (morally and economically) in opposition to labour as much as to aristocratic libertinism. If, as Nancy Armstrong has argued, the 'value' of labouring, like aristocratic, women was located in the material body, then the domestic woman's worth lay, by contrast, in her psychic depths.[42] The invention of this 'specifically female form of subjectivity' through such media as the conduct book entailed the creation of a 'new mode of economic thinking', a gendered division of labour which cast politics and business as the preserve of men, while women were expected to perform the cultural work of domesticity itself.

If the domestic woman was a woman of leisure, however, she was certainly not an idle creature. Conduct book morality and Christian thinking about the individual's duty to make good use of his or her time in this life in preparation for the next dovetailed to prescribe a work ethic for the middling, domestic woman.[43] 'Time', wrote Lady Sarah Pennington in *An Unfortunate Mother's Advice to her Absent Daughters* (1761), was an 'invaluable' commodity; 'its loss [was] irretrievable!' and 'one of the sharpest Tortures to those who are on the Brink of Eternity!' '[E]very day' was, therefore, to be looked upon as 'a Blank Sheet of Paper put into [her] Hands to be filled up' with useful employments.[44] Such employments included needlework, domestic management and the nurturing of children. They also included the performance of good or charitable works. If 'time', 'money' and intellect were, to quote *Millenium Hall* (1762), 'talents' bestowed by God, 'of which' must be given 'strict account', then it was a Christian woman's duty to use these talents to 'feed the hungry, to cloath the naked, to relieve the prisoner, to take care of the sick'.[45] Clarissa Harlowe, the eponymous heroine of Samuel Richardson's 1747–48 novel, is as exemplary in her adherence to such prescriptions as she is in all other things, ensuring that her final, 'long days' – she rests for only six hours of each twenty-four – are exhaustingly 'filled up' with 'closet-duties', 'domestic management', 'needle[work]', drawing, music, letter writing, conversation and 'visits to the neighbouring poor'.[46]

While the work ethic of Clarissa and the charitable ladies of Scott's utopia is beyond question – and while the characters themselves view domesticity as work – conduct books frequently glossed their activities as leisure, or, to use Armstrong's phrase, as 'labour that [was] not labour'.[47] By the second half of the eighteenth century, Armstrong contends, such distinctions were thoroughly embedded in the cultural imagination, to the extent that fiction writers could assume that 'virtually everyone knew the ideal of womanhood they proposed'.[48] So 'deeply engraved' was the distinction between 'domestic duty and labour that was performed for money' that 'the figure of the prostitute could freely be invoked to describe any woman who dared to labour for money'.[49] The domestic woman who marketed her accomplishments to support herself, either as a character in, or as a writer of, a novel, was thus unacknowledgeable, a figure who confounded 'a distinction on which the very notion of gender appeared to depend'.[50]

As Harriet Guest cautions, the extension of Armstrong's insights concerning the conduct book to our understanding of the eighteenth-century novel has produced distortions, a number of which Guest's own *Small Change* (2000) brilliantly counters.[51] Among these distortions, I would suggest, and following Judith Frank's lead, is the assumption of labour's antithetical relation to domesticity.[52] If, as Guest indicates, many eighteenth-century women writers eschewed the 'parsimonious domesticity that literary historians of the novel have often represented as the ultimate ideal or inevitable fate of middle-ranking femininity',[53] then it was partly because they were deeply suspicious of a conduct-book ideology that sought to trivialize women not only by insisting that they engage in properly feminine but inconsequential employments, which lacked economic and cultural status as work – needlework being a particular bone of contention – but also by rendering invisible the very real labour daily expended in the tasks of domestic management, childrearing and charitable activities. An 'ordered' home was not conjured by some 'Inchantment', as David Simple discovers before Clarissa Harlowe, but produced by women's 'Sorrow and hard Labour'.[54]

If women writers were highly sceptical of conduct-book representations of domesticity, then they were similarly critical of such literature's insinuation that a woman's motivations to work outside the home were inherently suspicious; few women worked for money solely because they desired to do so, after all. The sleight of hand such writers accomplished when addressing the subject of women's work was to reveal that while motivated by financial and corporeal 'necessity' – a key, yet contentious, term in eighteenth-century labour discourse – the experience of labour not only satisfied bodily wants but stimulated the mind, consoled the heart and enriched the lives of others. Thus when Leonora, the cross-dressing heroine of the first tale in Scott's *A Journey through Every Stage of Life* (1754), takes a position as a teacher in a boys' school she does 'not act like a Person who embraced that way of Life only for a Support, but as if she had chosen it for moral Considerations'.[55] Leonora's story, like that of the many working heroines discussed in this book, is not simply an exemplary tale of how to make virtue of necessity, but a vindication of female labour as a source of personal fulfilment and social betterment. As such, it gives further cause to question the extent to which virtue and leisure were synonymous in the period, and forces us to acknowledge the ways in which the experience of paid labour (manual or intellectual) could be positively constitutive of female identity for women born outside the labouring classes.

The hold that the domestic ideal has had over perceptions of women's experience of, and attitudes towards, labour in the later eighteenth century extends to accounts of women's relationship to the intellectual work of writing, which have traditionally been framed in terms of a fundamental opposition between the needle and the pen, or between private and public spheres. Authorship might have provided the 'literate middle-class' with 'a substitute for the declining home industries which had once enabled the housewife to contribute to the support of the family', as Jane Spencer has observed, but to be a truly respectable writer, as Janet Todd has argued, an author was obliged either to obscure her financial motivations to publish, often by emphasizing her desire to tend to her readers' moral improvement, or to present her economic situation as so grave that her recourse to such an improper and immodest employment was unavoidable.[56] Although Spencer's and Todd's seminal studies are alert to the ways in which many female writers exploited and challenged assumptions about women's unsuitability for authorship, their conclusions have sometimes been used to support the claim that the position of the eighteenth-century female author was at best problematic, at worst untenable.[57] To be a proper lady and a woman writer was a balancing act that a number of literary histories tell us few could achieve without substantial risk.[58] Copeland reinforces such views when he comments that the 'gauge of tension' women felt between their domestic and professional identities 'can be measured by the almost complete impenetrability of the only employment that authors can be guaranteed to know first-hand: novel-writing itself'.[59] And as recently as 1996, Frank Donoghue claimed that writing 'was presumed to be an unfeminine territory'. Although *The Fame Machine* explores 'some of the strategies that women writers employed to try to circumvent the institutional handicaps under which they laboured', it finds that these 'efforts', no matter how 'heroic', were 'destined to fail'. The 'literary career', Donoghue claims starkly, was 'an exclusively male form of social practice' in the eighteenth century.[60]

According to Siskin, during the second half of the long eighteenth century, and as the discourse of labour became ever more central to constructions of authorship, the pressures faced by the woman writer became ever more acute. While residual anxieties about perceiving authorship as work persisted throughout this period, Siskin claims that the predominant trend was towards a new and distinctly modern notion of intellectual labour, which emerged in relation to existing, and interlinked, discourses of labour, professionalism and disciplinarity. Within this period, changes in the division of labour, and their theorization in the works of political economists such as Adam Smith, forced 'complementary shifts in the division of knowledge', with the result that writing was increasingly figured and valued as work, as the intellectual labour of a professional cultural elite.[61] The professionalization of authorship, Siskin and Paul Keen observe, was highly prejudicial to women writers by virtue of their increasing relegation to the reproductive, domestic economy and their virtual invisibility within the division of labour as theorized by political economists.[62] Unfit for the rigorous and implicitly masculine work of (intellectual) labour, women writers were cast as the amateur other against which the professional man of letters was increasingly defined.[63]

Although there is little reason to question Siskin's and Keen's compelling historical accounts of the professionalization of authorship, there is considerable evidence to suggest that we need to reconsider women's experience of, and attitudes towards, this process. As Betty A. Schellenberg has effectively demonstrated in her reappraisal of the careers of mid-century women writers, for too long the 'evidence' of women's experiences of authorship has been 'created by its interpretive frame'. Schellenberg's *The Professionalization of Women Writers in Eighteenth-century Britain* (2005) makes a powerful case for challenging longstanding critical paradigms – among them the presumed antagonism between domesticity and professionalism – that have shaped our understanding of women's textual production.[64] Her claims are amply supported by the wealth of novels, polemics and letters discussed in the following chapters. For while their authors register many of the pressures that recent scholarship has noted – the tensions between propriety and professionalism and between domesticity and labour, for example – they find in these conflicting imperatives not only a subject for their writing but, as demonstrated in Burney's letter to Crisp, a matrix within which to theorize and justify their authorial practice. In the process, they pose fundamental questions about the nature of women's work.

The debate on women's work: now and then

As my interest in literary representations of labour suggests, this book does not offer, nor does it aspire to be, a history of eighteenth-century women's work, indebted though it is to scholarship in this field.[65] None the less, it intersects with such histories, in large part because so many of the questions that have driven and divided scholars of women's work also preoccupied the writers discussed in subsequent chapters. Indeed, one of the secondary concerns of this book is how historians' answers to such questions have been informed by the narratives about women's work constructed by eighteenth-century women writers in response to these same issues. A number of the key issues that historians have addressed since the publication of Alice Clark's and Ivy Pinchbeck's groundbreaking studies of women's working practices during the seventeenth and eighteenth centuries echo those debated by Scott, Smith, Wollstonecraft and female applicants to the Literary Fund.[66] At what point, and for what reasons, did the gendered division of labour emerge? Was there ever a 'golden age' of women's work in which female labour was as valued as its male equivalent? What were the consequences of the separation of work from home? What losses or benefits resulted from changes within the labour market across the eighteenth century? And why was women's work rendered systematically invisible in official discourses about labour, particularly in theories of political economy?

Many historians, following Clark and Pinchbeck, and several 1790s commentators on women's work such as Mary Ann Radcliffe, Priscilla Wakefield and Wollstonecraft, have argued that the picture that emerges from the available evidence of women's working lives is one of an overall decline in employment opportunities. According to Bridget Hill, for example, women's forced withdrawal from productive or *useful* labour, as it was commonly understood in the political economy of the time, arose from a combination of factors including technological innovations and the removal of economic production from the household, both of which combined to restrict women's employment opportunities, to entrench more deeply the sexual division of labour and to devalue the work that women already undertook both in the home and in the labour market.[67] This is not to suggest that the sexual division of labour was an eighteenth-century invention, an offspring of industrial capitalism. Feminist anthropologists have, after all, located the origins of what is sometimes called 'sex-typing' in prehistoric societies, even if they continue to debate whether such indicators constitute a *de facto* sign of sexual inequality.[68] Moreover, it seems clear that the family economic unit, idealized in 'golden age' accounts of the history of women's work, depended upon such gendered distinctions, although, according to Bridget Hill, such divisions were 'strengthened' by 'capitalism', with the effect that women's work was increasingly perceived to be 'inferior', 'unskilled' and undesirable as the eighteenth century progressed.[69]

In recent years, a number of historians, including Maxine Berg, Pamela Sharpe and Amanda Vickery, have convincingly complicated the decline thesis, by demonstrating the need to be more flexible in our understanding of what constituted women's work in the period and by revealing the perils of ignoring regional differences and of taking individual examples as indicative of wider trends.[70] None the less, the perception that, despite some exceptions that prove the rule, women suffered long-term disadvantage with industrialization remains remarkably persistent; as does the view that by the end of the eighteenth century women's role was increasingly perceived in terms of dependence and domesticity rather than in terms of their labouring potential and hence their usefulness as citizens. This broad consensus begins to break down, however, over matters of chronology. Precisely when, if ever, there was 'a golden age' of women's work – a utopian moment that, as we shall see, Radcliffe and Wollstonecraft were particularly instrumental in creating – remains unclear. Equally hard to pin down are the precise origins of the decline that so many historians have documented: might we locate them in the late seventeenth century, as Clark indicated; or the mid- to late eighteenth as Pinchbeck and Hill, among others, have argued? But if the beginnings and causes of this decline have been hard to locate, then its endpoint and effects have been identified with greater certainty and readier agreement. Many historians argue that from around 1750, the year in which Scott's first novel was published, the division of labour, already in existence, became more rigidly gendered, and by the end of the eighteenth century women had 'lost out as far as opportunities for work are concerned'.[71] As a result of these developments, in the words of Katrina Honeyman, 'new perceptions of the relationship between women and work' were formed. Whereas earlier in the century, labour was predominantly 'perceived . . . in non-gendered terms', as something that all working people were 'expected to contribute to family survival and thus to the well-being of the economy as a whole', by 1800 labour was viewed as a masculine preserve and 'dependence and domesticity' were widely understood as women's proper work.[72]

Such accounts dovetail with Leonore Davidoff and Catherine Hall's study of the fortunes of middle-class women from the late eighteenth century onwards. For Davidoff and Hall, the ever more insistent gendering of the division of labour during the latter decades of the century and the coterminous separation of public and private spheres, figure headed by economic man and domestic woman, 'implied that [women] would only become active agents when forced by necessity'.[73] The ideological divorcing of women from labour, they contend, played a vital role in the construction of middle-class identity and consolidation after 1780. The fact that the cultural authority and economic success of this group were, in fact, crucially dependent upon the 'hidden investment' of women's capital and work reveals something of the limitations of the separate spheres model but should not, they argue, lead us to underestimate the potency of the ideology of separate spheres at the beginning of the nineteenth century and its impact upon women's lives.[74]

Yet, as Hannah Barker and Vickery have demonstrated in their studies of female enterprise and business activity among eighteenth-century women of the 'lower middling' and 'genteel' classes, respectively, considerable caution needs to be exercised when interpreting the relationship between so-called official discourses of labour and gender, whether in the form of the law, conduct books or political economy, and the lived experience of women.[75] As Vickery observes in *The Gentleman's Daughter* (1998), the concerted effort made in the period to propagate the domestic ideal and disassociate women from productive labour 'might just as convincingly demonstrate a concern that more women were seen to be active outside the home as provide proof that they were so confined'.[76] But we don't need to rely solely upon what texts insinuate but refuse openly to acknowledge in order to argue that women were active outside the home in the eighteenth century, or, as this book does, that work was considered by many to be an important part of non-labouring class experience throughout the period. If certain kinds of literary evidence, particularly the conduct book, can be used to support accounts of a decline in female employment opportunities and the rise of a restrictive model of domesticity that relegated women to the home, then other texts, particularly imaginative texts, suggest the need for a rather more complex narrative of the kind posited by Barker and Vickery, one that registers the multiple ways in which work and womanhood were mutually and, in many instances, positively constitutive in the period. Certainly, the texts discussed in the following chapters register many of the tensions and trends that have been noted in historical scholarship on women's work, particularly those that subscribe to the decline and domesticity theses. All acknowledge the existence, if not the validity of, the gendered division of labour (indeed, Scott seems to assume that it is already deeply entrenched in her 1750s fiction), and all register the assumed antagonism between domesticity and work (whether that work is manual or intellectual). Yet each of these works, in different ways and with various effects, exposes these seeming social facts as man-made fictions, the debilitating implications of which, they argue, women could and should circumvent. Official discourses do not represent the last word on women and work in the period, these texts indicate, but are simply part of a much broader vocabulary through which female identity could be conceptualized and articulated.

Lexical metaphors seem particularly appropriate in the context of the eighteenth-century debate on women's work not only because this was a debate articulated in print but because it was, in large part, a war of words about language and discourse and their gendered and class implications. Earlier in this introduction, I used the designation 'work', somewhat casually, as a catch-all term to encompass a range of female employments. Such a designation, while convenient, may legitimately be objected to on the grounds that it seems to ignore distinctions between various types of work – for example, between manual, intellectual and domestic employments, paid and unpaid work, and between productive, non-productive and reproductive labour – distinctions which were crucial during a period in which the discourse of the division of labour was to become increasingly instrumental in shaping perceptions, and even the reality, of different working practices.[77] There was, however, a considerable degree of slippage between the key terms that were used to figure labour throughout the eighteenth century, the recognition of which was often used to great effect by women writers who sought to contest the gendered division of labour, the failure to value women's unremunerated domestic labour and the assumed unfitness of gentlewomen for productive, paid work. Broadly, 'labour' was used to describe work that demanded considerable bodily effort, hence its predominant associations both with manual work, particularly with agricultural work, and with childbirth. As Samuel Johnson defined it in *A Dictionary of the English Language* (1755), 'labour' was the 'act of doing what requires a painful exertion of strength; pains; toil'. Yet 'labour' could also be used more generically to signify 'work to be done', a definition which collapsed into the more capacious term 'work', itself given eight possible meanings in the *Dictionary* as opposed to the four given for 'labour'. 'Work' encompassed the physical 'Toil' undertaken by the labouring classes, but was also used commonly to describe the masculine and decidedly more genteel world of 'employment' – that is to say, of 'business' – as well as being a shorthand, hardly worthy of the designation according to Wollstonecraft, for that peculiarly feminine accomplishment, 'embroidery'. Additionally and importantly, 'work' could also conflate the act of labour with its products; it could connote any 'Action; feat; deed' and 'Any thing made', a fact that, as we shall see, Charlotte Smith, exploited to argue for the inalienability of her authorial labour.

With their multiple connotations, the terms 'labour' and 'work' appear to obscure gender and class distinctions: 'labour', like 'work', could be undertaken by both men and women; and 'work', unlike the more class-specific 'labour', could be used to describe the activities of those in business or trade, the labouring classes (those who 'toil') and gentlewomen. None the less, as the writers discussed in this book were all too aware, these terms were hierarchically understood, not only in terms of gender and social station but also in line with assumptions of comparative usefulness and, therefore, worthiness. Thus, on a conceptual level, the value of manual labour, for much of the eighteenth century, derived in large part from its perceived greater utility relative to non-productive work, including intellectual work, and reproductive or domestic work. The fact that the gendered implications of these distinctions were felt by women long before the publication of *The Wealth of Nations*, in which they are famously theorized, is indicated by Mary's Collier's response to Stephen Duck's *The Thresher's Labour* (1736). Duck's poem presented agricultural labour as unequivocally masculine work, the extraordinary physical and psychic demands of which transformed men into 'Hero-like' creatures, whose vital presence within the rural landscape could no longer be ignored. As is well documented, the text's valorization of labour is achieved not only through a satiric rebuttal of pastoral conventions but through an insidious undermining of female work, represented by those 'prattling Females' better equipped to exercise their 'Tongues' than their 'Rakes and Prongs' and the domestic drudges who provide 'Dumplin' and 'Bacon' to sustain their husbands through his daily toil.[78] The price of Duck's heroicization of manual labour, Collier indicated in *The Woman's Labour* (1739), was a high one for women to pay, predicated as it was upon the occlusion of what Donna Landry has described as the 'triple burden' of 'labouring women's oppression': 'wage labour, housework and childcare'.[79]

Women's work, according to *The Thresher's Labour*, is at best what makes men's labour possible; at worst, as in the case of 'prattling' field workers with their loose tongues (and presumably loose morals), it exposes their unsuitability for labour and as women.

Duck's strategy of according labour dignity and heroic potential in part through a devaluing of woman's activities in the home and the labour market was widely echoed in later eighteenth-century political economic discourse. Detailed discussions of the effects of the (non-)representation of women's work in later eighteenth-century political economy are left to the following chapters; suffice it to say here that this body of work, as the women writers I discuss here demonstrate, had significant implications for women of all stations. Particularly deleterious was the shift from what Deborah Valenze characterizes as a 'corporate notion of society', which for much of the first half of the eighteenth century, and in opposition to Duck's poem, viewed female labour as a 'potential source of national prosperity', to a capitalist perspective which 'promoted enterprising individualism as a rationale for economic and social life' and increasingly associated women with the reproductive rather than productive economy.[80] The implications of these trends are amply evident in this book's trajectory, which begins with a consideration of Scott's reliance upon mid-century political economic arguments in favour of female labour to underpin the utopian communities her fiction imagines and her idealized vision of the work of authorship, and which ends with a discussion of the careers and works of popular women writers, who experienced changes in perceptions of female labour in the form of an assault upon their legitimacy as women and as writers. These developments did not, however, prevent female authors from asserting women's viability and hence, according to the logic of political economic thought, their *value* as working subjects. In fact, they made it more incumbent upon them to do so.

Writing about work / writing as work

The debate about women's work in which later eighteenth-century women writers participated was, this book argues, inseparable from contemporary debates about authorship in general, and about the status of woman writers in an increasingly commercialized and professionalized print market in particular. Indeed, the very reason that Copeland cites as the source of female authors' reluctance to write explicitly about work in their fiction – that it would inevitably have an impact on readers' perception of authorial labour – seems to have been precisely the reason why others felt compelled to return to this subject again and again. Through their various representations of women's work and assertions of its social and economic value, the women writers discussed in this book found a means by which they could theorize and defend female authorship as culturally useful and necessary. Such strategic alignments of intellectual labour with other forms of women's work have a history that predates the mid-eighteenth century by at least a century and a half. Laurie Ellinghausen, for example, has recently shown that, as early as the mid-sixteenth century, the poet and former maidservant Isabella Whitney was making creative play out of the discourses surrounding female service to 'explore the issues of gender and ownership that her status as a professional author raised'.[81] More commonly, however, women writers explored these issues via elaborately woven analogies between text and textile production, a trope which, as Kathryn R. King has argued, afforded them a means with which to present writing as a direct 'extension of traditional forms of woman's work'.[82] Most ambitiously developed by Jane Barker in *A Patch-Work Screen for the Ladies* (1723), in which patchwork provides a metaphor for narrative construction and an occasion for the feminist model of female collaboration the text promotes, the text–textile analogy, in King's words, 'collapses the distinction between authorship and domestic activity and, by attaching writing to established conceptions of women's writing, implicitly argues for authorship as a suitable job for a woman'.[83]

Barker's text, ambitious and effective though it undoubtedly is as a manifesto for female authorship and community, gestures inadvertently, however, to a number of the difficulties that attend the project of theorizing writing in relation to other forms of women's work, particularly for writers active later in the century when the model of authorship as intellectual labour became pervasive. Most obviously problematic is the use of the needlework metaphor to figure writing as an appropriate mode of female labour. Barker's text seeks to transform needlework from a source of women's marginalization, something that is symbolic of women's relegation to a domestic economy of which *The Galesia Trilogy* (1713–26) as a whole is highly critical, into something that is empowering and self-authorizing while still acceptably feminine. Yet as labour, and thus as a justification for women's participation in the work of writing, ornamental needlework is profoundly ambiguous, its status derived from its function as a leisured activity, no matter how laborious women may have found the practice of needlework in reality. That this ambiguity is not a problem within the terms in which Barker's text articulates itself is connected to writing's equally ambiguous status as work throughout *A Patch-Work Screen*. The text's heroine, Galesia, views writing poetry not as labour, per se, but as a vocation to satisfy her 'Companions the Muses'.[84] Galesia's identity may be bound up with her poetic work, but she is not economically dependent upon her intellectual labour and openly condemns other women writers who lived by their pen such as Aphra Behn.

In a paradox that would be rehearsed frequently in eighteenth-century accounts of authorship, writing is figured in *A Patch-Work Screen* as a form of labour that stands outside the economic and above the mercenary concerns of the commercial literary marketplace in which it circulates. Needlework and the work of writing are deemed analogous because they are commonly motivated by a sense of duty (to one's sex and one's calling respectively) rather than by pecuniary gain, and because both activities, as King indicates, allow individuals (whether as participants in the creation of a piece of patchwork or as writers and readers of a text) to come together as a community.[85] Crucially, needlework and the work of writing are made possible in Barker's text by their practitioners' leisure, their lack of involvement in other forms of paid and manual labour. Thus, *A Patch-Work Screen* may launch an assault upon the arbitrary opposition of needle and pen, but, problematically for subsequent women writers who wished to challenge the gendered division of labour and accord writing status as work, does so by turning authorship into yet another acceptably female accomplishment, a strategy which seems radically to delimit the possibilities for thinking about women, writing and work the text opens up.

The writers discussed in the following four chapters sought to expand these possibilities for a later literary culture, both by arguing that work could be positively constitutive of female experience and by co-opting the discourse of labour to valorize the practice of authorship in a literary marketplace which increasingly articulated its legitimacy through such language. In focusing upon such a group, my aim is not to silence the voices of those who figured and experienced labour as a form of deracination or 'mental mutilation' as Adam Smith famously put it.[86] Rather, I take it as read that these voices have begun to be heard clearly, more clearly in many instances than those of their social superiors, whose presumed distance from labour has obscured several key aspects of their writing. Many women writers were engaged in exploring the economic, social and moral benefits generated by various kinds of paid and unpaid female labour, the recognition of which fact prompts some justification of the principles of selection this book adopts. In organizing this book, I have been drawn to those authors who had most to contribute to the debate about women's work (that is to say, to those for whom work is a constant point of return rather than an occasional interest) and whose participation in this debate was intimately bound up with changes in the conception of the work of writing across the later eighteenth century. What follows, then, is a series of detailed case studies of a group of women writers who offered a sustained interrogation of questions surrounding gender, labour and authorship across a body of work, over the course of a career and whose treatment of women's work was implicated in key developments in the field of political economy and the literary public sphere's self-theorization. Thus writers such as Frances Brooke, Elizabeth Inchbald and Lennox, who express only an occasional interest in labour in their writing, often in the form of an individual novel's subplot, are discussed only briefly and in the context of other writers' works. This is not to say that the writers whose works are explored in subsequent chapters have the final word on the question of women's work.[87] The relationship between manual, domestic and intellectual labour is, as I have already indicated, a significant preoccupation in the novels and letters of Burney, for example, to whom I return only in the context of Smith's novels. The fact that the small body of scholarship that has addressed the topic of work and the eighteenth-century novel has largely focused upon Burney's (sometimes anxious) meditations on manual, intellectual and affective labour is the principal reason why she is not given more extensive treatment in this book, which attempts to make visible the presence of labour in the works of writers for whom it has not been seen to be a central concern, such as Scott, or whose treatment of the issues surrounding women's work, as in the case of Smith and Wollstonecraft, has been misleadingly overdetermined.[88]

The four chapters that follow address these issues by revealing the connections and tensions that women writers register as they explore the relationship between labour, gender and their own careers as authors. Chapter 1 examines Scott's early fiction and its implication in mid-century political, economic and philanthropic debates about the moral and economic functions of women's work. (One of the arguments of this book as a whole is that the political climate of the 1750s and 1760s, a time when female labour was being foregrounded as essential to national prosperity, made it rather easier for Scott to connect work and writing than it was for a number of her successors.) As an author who has been characterized as a leading proponent of 'gentry capitalism', and whose literary treatment of the poor, commonly mediated through charity, has often been deemed condescending, Scott may seem an unlikely starting point for this book.[89] Yet, I argue, more than any other writer of the mid-century, including her friend Sarah Fielding whose work is also discussed in this chapter, Scott was committed to moving the working woman from the periphery to the centre of the eighteenth-century novel, to exploring the relationship between labour and gentility and to asserting that women's work (if well-executed and properly valued) was individually enfranchising and culturally necessary. Focusing upon four of her 1750s and 1760s novels, and the central role that labour plays within the development of Scott's utopian gender and textual politics, this chapter traces the increasingly sophisticated turn Scott's thinking about labour takes as her career progressed and argues that Scott's treatment of manual, domestic and intellectual labour shows her to be an early theorist of what we now refer to as gift economics. Within the idealized literary economies her fictions construct, I suggest, female labour (whether as teachers, milliners, painters or writers), when given freely, but with appropriate expectation of reward and recognition, leads to the proliferation of material and moral benefits that afford women independence and an opportunity to enrich society as a whole. While Scott's gender politics is more conservative than the feminisms of Smith or Wollstonecraft, and while her commentary on the labour market is more muted and her vindications of novel writing more covert than those of Smith or Wollstonecraft, in her treatment of labour she shows herself to be an articulate voice in the debate on women's work and the politics of authorship.

Work has traditionally been sidelined in studies of Scott's fiction, which have tended to emphasize the ends of labour – the various charitable projects that are funded by her heroines' work – rather than the means. In Smith scholarship, however, labour's presence has seemed unavoidable. Yet Smith's presentation of manual, affective and intellectual labour in her novels is, I argue, overdetermined, and not only by this author's professed antipathy to the hard graft involved in 'writing to live'.[90] Smith's reputation has been indelibly shaped by a particular and, at the time Smith's career was flourishing, much-contested conception of authorship which holds intellectual and manual labour to be at odds with one another and commonly figures that antagonism, in literary terms, as an opposition between poetry and the novel. Thus, Smith's *Elegiac Sonnets* (1784) and *Beachy Head* (1807) have come to represent properly intellectual work, into which the author's creative genius was most effectively channelled, while her novels have often appeared as the rather laboured productions of a writer whose professional aspirations were constantly thwarted by pecuniary necessity. Chapter 2 counters these assumptions by exploring Smith's complex treatment of various kinds of paid, unpaid and intellectual work in her novels, their infamous paratexts, as well as her correspondence. What emerges from this analysis is the very centrality of work to Smith's self-conceptualization and legitimization as a woman and as a writer. Alert to political economic debates on work, and highly critical of the gendered implications of the productive/unproductive/reproductive labour hierarchy suggested by *The Wealth of Nations*, Smith, I suggest, looked back to the Lockean paradigm of labour as self-ownership. As a *femme couverte*, the wife of a debtor and mother to children defrauded of their inheritance, Smith found in the labour theory of value, I suggest, a means to self-possession through authorship that eluded her in life.

If Smith's engagement with questions surrounding female labour and value tells a very personal story, then in Wollstonecraft's case the question of women's work is very much a public concern, the negotiation of which is presented as having important ramifications for the literary public sphere and civil society as a whole. In this, as in the book's final chapter, I turn to the politicization of the debate on women's work during the 1790s. During this decade, so a number of critics have observed, participation in the division of labour came to define middle-class professional identity; at precisely the same time, this identity was being split along gendered lines. Women's subordinate position within the division of the labour and their exclusion from the criteria of literary professionalism that were redefining the literary marketplace at the turn of the century – trends that Wollstonecraft argued were not merely coterminous but mutually reinforcing – threatened doubly to marginalize them. The career of the 1790s woman writer was thus framed by a paradox: to be taken seriously as an author, the woman writer had to articulate her aspirations in the terms of discourses that were apparently unavailable to her. This chapter explores Wollstonecraft's negotiation of this paradox through a two-pronged attack on the gendered division of labour and the literary public sphere which adopted its logic. Central to these twin endeavours, in the novels, non-fictional works and works for children, was Wollstonecraft's construction of the Female Philosopher, an intellectual labourer who, like Adam Smith's professional spectator upon which she is partly modelled, occupies a privileged position within the division of labour, and whose role it is to make visible the work of others and its value known. The female labourer and the Female Philosopher occupy a disquietingly close relationship in a number of Wollstonecraft's fictional and non-fictional works. The nature of this uneasy affiliation and its impact for the future representation of working women in works by women writers are the subjects of this chapter.

If Wollstonecraft's articulation of the relationship between manual, domestic and intellectual labour cast a long shadow over female authors' representation of women's work, then some of its more immediate effects are evidenced by the correspondence and fiction of the group of popular women writers who form the focus of Chapter 4, all of whom were applicants to the writers' charity, the Literary (later Royal Literary) Fund (1790 to present). Marginalized and maligned in their own lifetimes and by literary history, these women were often reviewed (some by Wollstonecraft herself) as uninspired hacks who lacked talent in proportion to their want of money and who wrote novels that were too workmanlike and too laboured. These women's status as amateur drudges rather than legitimate intellectual labourers was reinforced by the very institution that promised to help them. The Literary Fund was founded with the professed intention of challenging the late eighteenth-century political economy's devaluation of authorship as unproductive work, and, according to its published manifesto, *Claims of Literature* (1802), endeavoured to establish intellectual labour as the invisible hand that generated the nation's wealth. As a result, and as part of the wider project to professionalize authorship in the period, a new and hierarchically organized division of literary labour emerged which was to have significant repercussions for women's writing in the coming decades. This chapter explores these developments and women writers' resistance to them through detailed analysis of their correspondence with the Literary Fund. The Fund's archive, which contains many thousands of letters from financially straitened male and female writers and their dependants, contains a vast and largely neglected body of correspondence from women writers defending their talents as authors and their characters as women through a distinctly feminized take on the discourses of labour, productivity and utility that marginalized them. The final sections of this chapter examine the development of these ideas in the form of the professional author as working mother, a model which a number of popular women writers, following Charlotte Smith, presented as a socially valuable alternative to the masculine model of literary professionalism that the Fund and other literary bodies proffered. Such a manoeuvre may seem a retrograde step in the debate on women's work, an attempt to make the woman writer acceptable as a proper (because domestic) lady rather than as an intellectual labourer. To view it as such, however, is to ignore the insistence with which reproductive labour is cast as work by these writers and to be complicit with contemporary economic and gender ideologies that refused to see domesticity as work and which these authors vehemently challenged. Even during the period that, according to Siskin, inaugurated 'The Great Forgetting' of women writers, female authors were none the less actively participating in debates over the future of their profession and insisting that authorship, particularly novel writing, was properly women's work.[91]

1

The 'gift' of work: labour, narrative and community in the novels of Sarah Scott

> What I understand by society is a state of mutual confidence, reciprocal services, and correspondent affections; where numbers are thus united, there will be a free communication of sentiments, and we shall then find speech, that peculiar blessing given to man, a valuable gift indeed; but when we see it restrained by suspicion, or contaminated by detraction, we rather wonder that so dangerous a power was trusted with a race of beings, who seldom make a proper use of it.
>
> Sarah Scott, *A Description of Millenium Hall* (1762)[1]

In this familiar passage, Sarah Scott outlines a socioeconomic vision, and a vision for the novel, that had been many years in the making. Although *Millenium Hall* offers the best-known articulation of Scott's utopian hopes for women, society and fiction, her earlier *The History of Cornelia* (1750) and *A Journey through Every Stage of Life* (1754) had imagined philanthropic schemes and ideal societies which closely foreshadow those elaborated in her more famous work. *Millenium Hall*'s sequel, *The History of Sir George Ellison* (1766), would similarly take up the themes of charitable activism and social reform explored in these earlier texts by tracing its hero's efforts to emulate the community's example in a series of projects of his own, a course of action which proves, through fictional dramatization of authorial intent, the power of exemplary narrative to produce social and political change. While philanthropy has been a principal focus of recent studies of Scott's novels, often figuring as a gauge by which the radicalism (or conservatism) of their sociopolitical outlook can be assessed, the role of labour – invariably a precondition of charity for Scott – has not.[2] In large part because of charity's status as the epitome of domestic virtue, an activity that speaks of and depends upon a benefactor's leisure, but also as a consequence of Scott's identification as a 'bluestocking feminist' – a political stance which, Gary Kelly asserts, upholds 'gentry' values[3] – labour has largely fallen below the radar of Scott studies.[4] Yet, work is central to her fiction, underpinning both her critique of female dependency and her conviction concerning the novel's reformative potential. Labour, whether it takes the form of teaching, painting, millinery, spinning, laundry, carpet making, administering charitable and pedagogical projects or storytelling, is the means by which individuals contribute to the ideal societies Scott's fiction imagines and through which they signal their acceptance of those societies' rules. Within these self-sustaining economies, which position themselves ideologically (and, in the case of *Millenium Hall*, geographically) outside the market economy in which eighteenth-century heroines frequently suffer, work is the currency of everyday life. Carried out not merely for remuneration but for the 'confidence' it inspires and the 'affections' it generates, the labour Scott's heroines perform finds its ultimate reward in the exchange of 'free' and transformative 'speech', bestowed by God, but commonly 'contaminated' by the self-interested desires characteristic of commercial society. The exchange of free 'speech', in turn, links the activities of Scott's heroines – it is the end to which their employments are the means – and the literary work of their author, whose disinterested yet 'valuable' 'sentiments' are offered to her readers in the gift of fiction itself.

The critical conversation about Scott's work, in which *Millenium Hall* remains the most prominent text, has been dominated by a debate about the scope and limits of the utopian models of female community her fiction imagines, a discussion which has been illuminated by considerations of the novels' indebtedness to political economic theory and sentimental discourse, and which has been usefully complicated by accounts of the (antagonistic) relationship between Scott's utopianism and her texts' gender and class politics.[5] This chapter contributes to this ongoing debate by examining the role that women's work plays in Scott's writing and the nature of the moral and textual economies this work supports. The first section focuses on *Cornelia* and 'The History of Leonora and Louisa', the first and longest inset narrative in *A Journey*, novels which moved the working woman from the periphery to the centre of the eighteenth-century novel, and which are thus highly important both in terms of the particular narrative about women and work this book documents and in terms of literary history more broadly. Through their charting of their heroines' successful adaptations to the labour market, these novels reveal the contribution that women's work might make to society's moral and economic well-being if employment opportunities were to be widened and the illegitimacy of the division of labour's gendered logic were to be acknowledged. Moreover, they articulate an implicit critique of domesticity and the structures of dependence it promoted that would be worked through more fully in Scott's later fiction. In making these arguments about labour, gender and domesticity, Scott demonstrates herself to be a writer of her moment, a utopian, mid-century moment in which the political economists upon whose works her fiction draws were, for various reasons discussed below, placing female labour at the very heart of the nation's money and moral economies.

These early novels, while in some ways more radical than their 1760s successors, were also the testing ground for *Millenium Hall* and *Sir George Ellison*. In these later works, Scott's labour plots are not confined to the stories of isolated and exceptional individuals, but are more ambitiously, and in some ways more problematically, conceived as the story of whole communities, the economic and moral principles of which betray the logic of what anthropologists and cultural theorists have identified as gift economics: that is to say, the system of reciprocal exchanges and mutual obligations that has been observed to structure a number of pre- or anti-capitalist societies. An 'economics of beneficence', as Judith Still has suggested, underpins Scott's argument that a community in which women of all ranks work according to principles of disinterested and mutually beneficial exchange, can best serve women's individual needs and those of society as a whole.[6] The logic of the gift, complex and unstable though it proves to be, structures not only the affective communities within the novels analysed here but also, and more successfully, the metatextual community that Scott imagined to exist between author and reader, both of whom, she contended, were obliged to work for the common good through their respective roles in the production and consumption of fiction. As this chapter's final section claims, this framing device enabled Scott to construct the female author as an intellectual labourer whose productions could resist the deracinating effects of the market by dictating the terms of their reception, transmission and circulation, and whose sense of personal worth, moreover, was intimately bound up in the authorial work she gifted to the public.

Writing labour at mid-century

In most early eighteenth-century fiction, female workers are relegated to the textual margins, generally present in the form of the many anonymous or generically named servants and milliners, who come to notice only when they are enjoined to conspire in their superiors' downfall, and who are expeditiously disregarded as soon as they have outlived their usefulness as a plot device. In those few novels, such as Daniel Defoe's *Moll Flanders* (1722) and *Roxana* (1724), in which the labouring woman takes centre stage, the image of the female labourer as corrupt schemer holds fast, and the question of women's work is largely sidelined by virtue of labour's status as a condition from which the heroine must raise herself, by all possible means, in order to realize her genteel aspirations. Samuel Richardson's *Pamela; or, Virtue Rewarded* (1740), despite featuring a famously virtuous labouring-class heroine, did little to challenge these assumptions or to advance the literary representation of women workers. Pamela is rarely seen at work in the novel, and when she is, such as when she embroiders her master's waistcoat, she is engaged in activities that lie beyond the remit of her servant duties, and that prefigure the leisured employments she will undertake as B.'s wife. Richardson's decision not to foreground Pamela's work, when read in the context of the extraordinarily cruel and self-interested behaviour of other labouring women in the novel, most notably that of Mrs Jewkes, and in light of Pamela's eventual removal from a life of labour which the novel presents as beneath her, confirms the heroine's status as an exception to the rule of labouring women's immorality and vanity in the early eighteenth-century novel. The fact that some of the reading public found Henry Fielding's plotting Shamela and Eliza Haywood's amorous and deliciously immoral Syrena Tricksey more credible than Richardson's paragon indicates just how difficult it would be to dislodge such culturally embedded stereotypes. Indeed, they proved remarkably resilient in a literary culture in which women's economic activity was almost invariably deemed suspect.[7]

The downwardly mobile gentlewoman reduced to find work was similarly vulnerable to such prejudice and felt the contempt of society at least as keenly as her lower ranking counterparts. In the words of Camilla, one of the heroines of Sarah Fielding's *The Adventures of David Simple* (1744) – a novel by which Scott's early fiction was much influenced – there is 'no Situation so deplorable, no Condition so much to be pitied, as that of a Gentlewoman in real Poverty', forced to prostitute her accomplishments for wages.[8] In her attempts to find a living for herself and her ailing brother, Camilla experiences the 'World' as the 'Wildest Desart'. Debarred from any kind of 'Community', she is resented by 'the lower sort of People' for taking 'the Bread out of their Mouths', and is exploited by the rich, particularly by those so-called 'Gentleman' who read her readiness to work as a sign of sexual availability, and demand 'a Price . . . for any thing they could do for me' that Camilla deems far 'too dear to pay'.[9] Camilla is rescued from such a desperate course by David's intervention. Emily Markland, the impoverished clergyman's daughter of the anonymous *The Histories of Some of the Penitents in the Magdalen-House* (1760), would not be so lucky. Emily's willingness to accept the most 'laborious work' is read by those from whom she attempts to obtain employment as a sign of 'bad . . . conduct', leaving beggary and prostitution as the only courses of action she can take to feed her son.[10] As Camilla's and Emily's stories demonstrate, the burden faced by the impoverished middle-ranking woman compelled to support herself through her labour was doubly onerous: such figures were the victims not simply of cultural prejudice but of the literary precedent that weighed against them.

In light of the widespread mistrust of working women evident in the early eighteenth-century novel and its readers' responses to such characters, Scott's preoccupation with labouring (if not labouring-class) heroines seems inexplicable, perhaps even naive. It does so, however, only if the immediate historical context out of which Scott's novels emerged is unacknowledged. The mid-eighteenth century marked something of a watershed in the discursive construction of women's work, a period in which a perceived crisis in female labour gave way to a momentary valorization of women's productive labour as vital to the nation's prosperity and moral well-being. The intensification of interest in female labour in political economic theory and philanthropic discourse of the 1750s and 1760s arose from a variety of socioeconomic and political factors, and intensified with the outbreak of the Seven Years War in 1756. The problem of how to deal with unemployed women from the labouring classes may not have been a new one at mid-century, as Deborah Valenze observes, but it was an issue that acquired a particular political urgency at a time when the female labour market was feared to be in decline, when vice and crime were said to be increasing and when political conflict was undeniably exerting pressure upon the male workforce.[11] According to Sir John Fielding, in his *Plan for a Preservatory and Reformatory for the Benefit of Deserted Girls and Penitent Prostitutes* (1758), 'Industry' had plunged into a state of 'Distress', as an unwieldy and undereducated workforce of potentially 'useful Subjects' sank into poverty, vice and idleness.[12]

Harnessing the labouring potential of 'useful Subjects', as Donna T. Andrew has argued, became a leading preoccupation of political economists and the guiding imperative of the charity movement, which flourished at mid-century with the founding of institutions including the Lock Hospital (in 1746), the Marine Society (in 1756), the Magdalen House for the Reception of Penitent Prostitutes (in 1758) and the Lambeth Asylum for orphaned girls (in 1759).[13] In the labour debates occasioned by the establishment of these and like philanthropic institutions, the figure of the prostitute was a recurrent and inevitable point of return. Working outside the productive and reproductive economies, the paid whore was doubly illegitimate; a threat to the nation's wealth and to its martial strength. In the brothel, Fielding observed, the 'Journeyman' and 'Tradesman' were 'decoy'd into a Snare', which jeopardized their 'Property', 'Constitution' and 'Famil[ies]', and which sapped the strength of the nation's 'Manufactures, Fleets [and] Armies'.[14] Such arguments had, of course, long been part of the rhetoric of writings on prostitution. Bernard Mandeville's *A Modest Defence of Publick Stews* (1724), for example, had earlier made a rather similar point to Fielding's *Plan* in its claim that 'Whoring' tempted men 'to live beyond what their Circumstances will admit of . . . [and disposed] the Mind to such a sort of Indolence, as is quite inconsistent with Industry, the main Support of any, especially a trading, Nation'.[15] What distinguished mid-century commentary on prostitution from that of Mandeville and some of his contemporaries was a more widespread understanding of the prostitute as a symptom rather than instigator of socioeconomic problems and a willingness to perceive her body as a site of promise rather than of irreversible degeneration. Street-walkers had not caused a crisis in the labour market, a number of mid-century commentators argued, they were the victims of such a crisis.

Deflecting attention away from the effects that prostitution had upon a male workforce to the question of women's own labour potential and the role it might play in bolstering the nation's money and moral economies, proponents of charities such as the Magdalen House made the case that suitably repentant prostitutes might be 'made of equal Use to their Country' as men, provided that they were offered suitable education and training and that the labour market was itself reformed to allow women access to trades from which they were already or were becoming excluded.[16] Several years before the publication of his 1758 *Plan*, Fielding, in his position as a London magistrate, had 'observed that the Trades for employing Women are too few, that those which Women might execute are engrossed by Men, and that many Women have not the Opportunity of learning even those which Women do follow, on Account of the Premiums paid for learning the said Businesses'.[17]

Although such attacks upon the male usurpation of 'female' trades are more commonly associated with the 1790s feminist polemics of Mary Ann Radcliffe, Priscilla Wakefield and Mary Wollstonecraft: these concerns had played a central role in the debate about women's work for at least sixty years before this time. Many of the arguments and much of the tone of Radcliffe's and Wakefield's attacks on men's supposedly recent usurpation of women's work within the millinery and dress-making professions, for example, can be observed in a 1739 *Gentleman's Magazine* essay, 'By a Lady', which asserted women's right to claim certain employments as their own and thus to be permitted to be 'as useful and as capable as men of maintaining themselves'.[18] Jonas Hanway was one of several mid-century commentators who drew on and developed such arguments both to criticize men who were pushing women out of trades in which the latter 'might do as well' and to condemn a society that prevented women from entering others 'in which their natural ingenuity would enable them to carry on much better'.[19] Although Hanway stopped short of following through the radical implications of his own conclusions, his *Plan* none the less reveals the logic of the gendered division of labour to be not only faulty but profoundly unnatural.

By fitting women for a life of productive work through the education and training that institutions such as the Magdalen House could provide, the charity movement promised to turn the burden that was the unemployed or illegitimately employed labouring woman into 'a great acquisition to the nation'.[20] As 'great' an 'acquisition' as these women's productive labour was their reproductive work in the domestic economy, for which commentators suggested reformed female labourers were invariably destined and in which their skills would ultimately be subsumed. Turning such vicious women into virtuous workers and the '*joyful mothers of children*' would take considerable effort on the part of charitable institutions, but made sound economic sense, Hanway concluded: it would 'only [be] making use of a *few good things* of a *lesser* value, to acquire more *good things* of a much *greater value*'.[21] Through such arguments, the likes of Hanway and his fellow philanthropists made the reformed prostitute an unlikely source of national pride, and, simultaneously, raised the cultural currency of the female labourer. Although, as Valenze has argued, it would be overstating the case to suggest that residual prejudices against working women were eradicated in this period, the discursive association of women's productive work with the language of prosperity and gain in the mid-century, politically and economically expedient though it certainly was, signalled a general acknowledgement of female labour, and a recognition of its value. By the time *The Wealth of Nations* was published in 1776, this value had significantly diminished, and the charity movement that had played such a vital role in the physical and discursive recuperation of the labouring woman was itself in decline. None the less, for this brief time, a time after which, historians document, the actual conditions of the labouring classes significantly worsened, the working woman enjoyed a 'positive image', connected to her 'industriousness and economic potential', which she would not have again for at least the next 150 years.[22] It was against this backdrop that Sarah Scott began her literary career.

That the mid-century charity movement had an impact on Scott's fiction has been noted by several scholars, although exclusively in relation to *Millenium Hall*, a community which, in many ways, resembles the Magdalen House.[23] Such accounts typically read Scott's interest in the Magdalen House and similar philanthropic institutions as evidence of the author's class conservatism and, despite Scott's reservations about marriage, of her commitment to a domestic ideal, which, as we have seen, the charities worked hard to uphold.[24] Yet Scott's relationship to the charity movement and her status as an apologist for domesticity is troubled when her representation of women's work is taken into account. The undoubted debt her novels owe to this movement is not so much to the charitable mission and the domestic ideology they upheld, I would suggest, but to the labour that was the object of that mission. The novels make creative capital out of the valorization of female labour in mid-century economic and philanthropic discourse, while importantly extending the debate on women's work by demonstrating its relevance to the lives of women who are not born to labour. Simultaneously, her fiction works against some of the most deeply entrenched strategies and assumptions of this discourse, particularly the characterization of working women as passive objects of charity, rather than moral and economic agents in their own right, and the conflation of women's productive and reproductive labour. Domesticity (for which, Scott, like Fielding, urged, read: dependence) is almost always presented in the novels as less desirable than a life of labour, guided by 'the spirit of Independency'[25] which alone could prevent women from becoming glorified 'Slaves'.[26] Unlike *Millenium Hall*, in which the radicalism of the novel's vision of labour is (arguably) compromised by the community's sequestration from mainstream society, *Cornelia* and 'The History of Leonora and Louisa' locate their fantasies of female fulfilment and societal remodelling within the labour market itself. Mobilizing, while also subtly redefining, the mid-century equation of female virtue and productive labour, the sentimental labour economies constructed in the early novels bucked the trend of conventional literary representations of women's work, and, in the process, challenged some of the novel's most fundamental assumptions about labour, gentility and femininity.

Cornelia adopts a plot structure which, with various modulations, would become a mainstay of female-authored fiction for much of the later eighteenth century. Its eponymous heroine is a well-educated, orphaned French heiress who is forced to relinquish her fortune and estate to escape sexual threat. Cornelia's exemplary virtue is never in doubt throughout the novel, and is first demonstrated to the reader through her dealings with the labouring poor. Following the death of her father, her sole surviving parent, Cornelia's uncle, a powerful French courtier named Octavio, puts her 'into immediate possession of her whole fortune', though he is not obliged to do so. Rehearsing *David Simple* – in which the hero's acquisition of 'a very easy comfortable fortune' leaves him 'unhappy' rather than 'overjoyed' – and foreshadowing Frances Burney's Cecilia, Cornelia experiences her increase in wealth as an intensification of her sense of obligation to those who rely upon their labour for their support.[27] Fearful of 'defrauding' such individuals by living up to her substantial means, Cornelia 'employ[s] almost all her fortune in assisting' them, 'tho' with such judgement and oeconomy, that she gave no encouragement to idleness'. The heroine takes upon herself the financial care of pregnant women in her community, as well as that of every seventh child of the poor, or all of these couples' children if they have more than seven. Not only that, but she finds work for the 'old' teaching the young to 'read, write, [and] work', so that the latter might 'supply themselves' by their labour in the future (pp. 18–19). In paying her 'debt' to the poor, however, Cornelia inadvertently accrues a more irksome obligation to the man who makes her charitable projects possible. Octavio expects his niece's chastity in return for his generosity in allowing her to inherit all her wealth at once, thus demonstrating, as Scott's later novels would also, that notions of obligation can work to women's advantage only when the terms of such transactions are defined outside a patriarchal economy in which women are invariably expected to give more than they can ever hope to receive.

Forced to flee her family home and her charitable responsibilities, Cornelia travels to Paris content to embrace 'obscurity' and 'poverty' despite having 'been bred up in ease and plenty' (p. 17). Like Charlotte Lennox's Henrietta and Burney's Juliet Granville after her, Cornelia is beset with numerous and peculiarly female difficulties. On her travels she meets and falls in love with a man she cannot marry because of her compromised position, and, like Richardson's Clarissa Harlowe, is unwittingly lured into a brothel where a bawd attempts to prostitute her. Fortunately, Cornelia's would-be client is sympathetic to her plight and secures her work with his cousin, a down-at-heel genteel widow-turned-milliner. Scott's heroine enjoys a successful period of work in the milliner's shop, where she turns around the proprietor's failing business, before becoming a paid companion to one of her customers, being kidnapped by an amorous libertine, living for a brief period in an impoverished, but none the less idyllic, georgic community, and, once her fortune is restored and her uncle banished, marrying Bernardo, with whom she works to populate her 'neighbourhood' with an 'honest, industrious race, happy in themselves, and useful to their country' (p. 270).

'The History of Leonora and Louisa' follows a similar narrative arc to that of *Cornelia*, but adopts a more polemical stance with regard to labour.[28] Narrated by a servant, Sabrina, to her unjustly imprisoned, and narcissistic, royal mistress, Carinthia, Leonora's story emphatically disproves the princess's belief that those who live beyond the scheming world of the court exist in a state of 'Ease and Contentment' that she can only envy from her position of exile (p. 4). Destined to be married off to an ageing miser, Leonora runs away from her family home accompanied by her cousin, Louisa, and a devoted maidservant. Educated, as is Cornelia, in 'female, as well as male, Accomplishments', Leonora determines to support herself and her companions through her labour (p. 80).[29] Knowing, however, that 'Damsels Errant' are liable to find themselves in the kinds of 'perilous Situations' that threaten Cornelia at every turn, the heroine pursues this course of action by masquerading as a man (p. 16). Initially experiencing some difficulty in reconciling this 'Metamorphosis of her Sex to the Delicacy of her Modesty', Leonora first becomes a preacher, a role that 'left her Petticoats tho' it took from her her sex', and in which she dispenses wisdom to her congregation and alms to the poor and distressed (p. 16). The heroine's 'Modesty' is not nearly so intractable as Leonora first apprehends, however, and, without any qualms, she subsequently dons breeches and enjoys successful periods of employment as a private tutor, as a painter (in which role she undertakes to reform her vain clients during their portrait sittings) and as the headmaster of a boys' school, which she transforms by using some of the money paid by wealthier parents to fund the education of the otherwise excluded sons of debtors and the poor. Each of these activities makes the lives of Leonora and her confederates 'easy and comfortable' (p. 77), and allows the heroine to engage in the greater work of relieving the 'pressing Necessities of the Unfortunate' (p. 73), until, that is, Leonora reveals her true identity and marries Calidore, a man she originally befriended while she was performing her pastoral duties as a clergyman.

The parallels between Cornelia's and Leonora's stories are clear; yet, the novels' response to the heroines' respective fates could scarcely be more different. While *Cornelia*'s conclusion celebrates virtue's reward in the form of companionate marriage and the restoration of a community, the closing lines of Leonora's story, in which so 'uncommon' an 'Example' of 'our Sex' does so 'common a Thing as marrying', pointedly deflates the domestic ideal and exposes the insidious economy of dependence it entails. Leonora's marriage is given suitably short shrift by Sabrina, who finds in it proof that 'let our [women's] Talents be equal or superior to them [men], our Spirits above Meanness, and our Situation above Controul, still sooner or later we become their Dependents, perhaps their Slaves' (p. 111). The servant-narrator's unapologetic 'Disgust' at Leonora's betrothal both signals her abhorrence of a (literary) culture in which the virtuous, independent woman worker is seemingly unimaginable and sets out the stakes of Scott's investment in labour in *A Journey* and, retrospectively, in *Cornelia* (p. 111). Like the essays and pamphlets discussed above, Scott's early novels present female labour as a matter of morals as well as economics, a matter that raises fundamental questions about women's role as domestic subjects and, as she puts it in *A Journey*, 'Citizens of the World' (p. 15). Yet unlike the essays and pamphlets, the issue in Scott's early fiction is not how female labour might be used to reform and, ultimately, to domesticate women, but how female labour might reform the nation and afford women alternatives to the sometimes rather less than '*joyful*' institutions of marriage and motherhood.

Underpinning these arguments is the texts' claim that feminine sensibility and economic activity are not merely compatible but ideally linked. *Cornelia* and 'The History of Leonora and Louisa' thus situate themselves within the context of the centuries-old debate about virtue's relationship to commerce, most commonly played out in the mid- to late eighteenth-century novel, as Gillian Skinner demonstrates, in a series of negotiations between the competing interests of Mandevillian mercantilism and the sentimental economics theorized by such figures as David Hume and Adam Smith.[30] Moral sense philosophy, which was at the height of its influence around the mid-century, challenged Mandeville's famous equation of private vice and public benefits. Rather than a mechanism by which mankind gratified selfish interests that, in turn, energized the nation's economy, commerce emerged in sentimental economic theory as a source of cultural refinement, which honed an individual's sensibility, interested him in the cause of others and, thereby, promoted the greater good. Thus in civilized societies, according to Hume's 'Of Refinement in the Arts' (1752), '*industry*, *knowledge*, and *humanity*' were 'linked together, by an indissoluble chain'.[31] In such texts, writers including Scott might have found a compelling philosophical foundation for their claims for the civilizing effects of women's work, were it not for the ambiguous role that women were typically assigned in sentimental accounts of commerce and luxury. If women functioned as barometers of the health of a polite and commercial people, then they were also made scapegoat for the insatiable and implicitly libidinous desires that fuelled the economy, and which represented the unacceptable face of commercialization. Commerce needed 'corrupt femininity', Harriet Guest explains, not only 'to account for the consumption of its commodities' but to 'moralize and masculinize its own self-image'.[32] As the discourses of commercialization and feminization became ever more closely intertwined, apologists for commerce increasingly sought to legitimize commercial enterprise through recourse to the language of manliness, heroism and honour.[33] Commerce, both sociable and economic, might increase man's humanity, Hume wrote, but it would not diminish his 'vigour', 'honour' or enervate his 'martial spirit'.[34]

Scott's 1750s fiction challenged the gendered assumptions underwritten by sentimental theories of commerce by making women agents in the civilizing process of commercialization rather than passive markers of its progress. Moreover, it suggested that women's 'natural ingenuity' might finally prove more of an 'acquisition to the nation' than those masculine virtues praised by Hume. The reformative agency of Scott's heroines is crucially predicated upon their labour. Although Cornelia engages in charitable activities long before she determines to seek 'a maintenance . . . from her own hands' (p. 51), her early projects as her community benefactress are hampered by her dependency and precariously contingent upon the generosity and goodwill of men. Not until the heroine takes a lodging and position in the milliner's shop is she able to act without constraint. Indeed, while labour is a source of endless victimization for other working heroines of the period, including Pamela and Emily Markland, both of whom are subjected to abuse and sexual threat, it is gentility that immobilizes and subjugates Scott's heroines. Cornelia's work as a milliner affords her freedom and a degree of autonomy denied her as an heiress. The 'spirit of Independency' nurtured by the heroine's 'work' is not selfish, however, and consolidates rather than supplants Cornelia's sense of communal responsibility (p. 50). As the assistant to the milliner, Madame du Miteau, a narcissistically sentimental and melancholic woman, whose self-pity and genteel aversion to labour contrast sharply with the heroine's pragmatism, Cornelia works a nineteen-hour day and uses any remaining time she has to undertake the education of the milliner's children.[35] After paying off a debt owed by Miteau, she attempts to reestablish a business that has succumbed to the same 'dejection of spirits' that is ruining its owner's health. By combining the feminine virtues of 'regularity' and 'ingenuity' with her masculine propensity to 'industry', Cornelia is able to 'extend [Miteau's] trade', and soon brings her 'more business than ever' (p. 49).[36] The milliner's health is restored with the business's economic recovery, leaving Cornelia morally at liberty to move on to her next employment as a companion to one of the now self-sufficient milliner's clients.

Cornelia's move from millinery to companionship prefigures that of Mrs Bilson of Sarah Fielding's *The History of the Countess of Dellwyn* (1759), a novel which, in terms of its labour plot, is as indebted to *Cornelia* and 'The History of Leonora and Louisa' as surely as they are influenced by the communitarian impulse and critique of dependency that drive Fielding's *The Adventures of David Simple*.[37] In a subplot of *The Countess of Dellwyn*, the virtuous but impoverished Mrs Bilson looks to paid work as a source of 'Liberty and Self-approbation' when her profligate and adulterous husband is imprisoned for debt.[38] After selling some of her furniture to buy stock, Bilson establishes a 'portable' milliner's shop, which soon provides an ample support for herself, her children and even an illegitimate child of her husband's, whose care she volunteers to undertake (I, p. 180). So successful is her business that she is able to provide work for other 'Prisoners, who had been recommended to her Notice by the Gaoler's Wife', until she receives an offer to become the companion to one of her customers, Lady Dently (I, p. 187). Lady Dently turns out to be a long-lost relative of Mrs Bilson and leaves her companion an inheritance which allows the former milliner and her husband, after the manner of Cornelia and Bernardo, to establish 'Seminaries for young People', in which the children of the poor are 'educated in the strictest Principles of Industry, Virtue, and Religion', to open almshouses for the elderly and to devise schemes to assist young married couples going into trade (I, pp. 205–7). If the Smithian moral of Mrs Bilson's tale, as Skinner asserts, is that 'sentimental virtues . . . *make economic sense*', then the inverse is equally true.[39] For Fielding, as for Scott, economic sense is a guarantor of sentimental virtue, heightening its possessors' sense of individual worth – their 'Self-approbation' – while deepening their understanding of the selfless communitarian responsibilities they are obliged to act upon and which their financial 'Liberty' allows them to fulfil.

A similar dynamic is at work in *A Journey*, in which Leonora moves from one employment to another not as someone who 'embraced that way of Life only for a Support, but as if she had chosen it for moral Considerations' (p. 22), thus reconciling the apparently contrary imperatives towards Mandevillian self-interest and sentimental fellow feeling. Yet 'The History of Leonora and Louisa' goes much further than *Cornelia* had done or *The Countess of Dellwyn* would do in its argument that women could not only contribute to the common wealth through their labour but, by virtue of their feminine attributes, could do so more effectively and more successfully than their male counterparts.[40] As Sabrina is forced to point out to an incredulous Carinthia, the heroine's 'female tenderness' is an asset rather than a liability in her work. While working as a schoolteacher, for example – a disciplinarian role for which Carinthia judges the 'blooming, beardless Pedagogue' utterly unfit – Leonora is 'more submissively obeyed out of love, than other Masters out of fear', thus proving that feminine benevolence is more conducive to the cultivation of 'manly Spirit' than the 'Degrees of Punishment' meted out by her male counterparts (p. 85; p. 84).[41] In this way, Leonora's experience of work not only challenges the gendered logic that was commonly used to legitimize middle-ranking women's relegation to the private sphere but also works to disprove the validity of the gendered division of labour itself.

The heroine's cross-dressing is key to the novel's contention that the gender and class imperatives that limit women's activities to the home, or, if forced by economic necessity to venture out of the private sphere, to such appropriately female employments as millinery and dressmaking, are arbitrary and unjust. Unlike the unambiguously feminine Cornelia, Leonora is 'a Sort of heterogeneous Animal, in whom Art and Dress contradicted Nature', an embodiment of the contradiction in terms that is the genteel labouring woman (p. 84). Yet her 'heterogeneous' appearance unsettles rather than fixes the reader's sense of what is natural, as the following episode makes clear.[42] When working as a painter in breeches, Leonora, 'too humble to be elated with wearing the Appearance of the superior part of the Creation', offers to assist her cousin, Louisa, in the millinery work through which she is attempting to contribute to the group's maintenance. Sabrina compares the potentially comic and incongruous sight of Leonora 'at an Employment so little suited to her Dress' to that of Hercules, forced to substitute 'his Club for a Spinning-wheel' after violating the sanctuary at Delphi (p. 53). The comparison illuminates the strategy of defamiliarization Scott adopts. Hercules may be emasculated by the act of spinning, but Leonora is never masculinized by her work, her success in which, as we have seen, is crucially dependent upon the feminine qualities she brings to it. None the less, her activities interrogate the categories of masculine and feminine and repeatedly expose nature as culture. Leonora's heterogeneity, her skill at combining masculine skills with feminine virtues, renders plain the absurdity of ascribing certain employments, like certain attributes, to men and others to women: such activities are 'of no Sex', the narrator concludes, despite their having been 'chiefly arrogated by one' (p. 84).

Like the non-fictional writings on women's work from the mid-century, the early fiction of Scott and Fielding's *Countess of Dellwyn* argued for the contribution that female labour might make to the nation's moral and money economies. Leonora's story takes such arguments further, however, by considering how the experience of labour might serve women themselves. Leonora's 'humane labours' (p. 67) prove 'how much good a Woman' might do for her 'Sex' by not 'appear[ing] to be of it' (p. 68). That so 'uncommon' a woman will finally be returned to the domestic household, as would the prostitutes and female labourers of mid-century philanthropic discourse and many a sentimental working heroine after them, should be read not as a sign of resignation but as one final attack upon the unnaturalness of the cultural constructions of labour, rank and gender that underpin the logic of the division of labour and underwrite women's psychic and economic subjugation. Leonora's experience of labour works to prove that it is not 'Nature' that 'oblige[s]' women 'to the Industry of Man for [their] support', and 'inflicts . . . Dependence' upon them but literary and social 'Custom' (p. 7).

Millenium Hall, *Sir George Ellison* and labour as gift

Deflecting attention away from the representation of charity in Scott's early novels to the work that makes charitable activity possible urges us to rethink the relationship between gentility and labour as it has commonly been cast in studies of the eighteenth-century novel. That her heroines' labours enable their philanthropic projects does not serve, as it might, to neutralize the implications of Scott's claims for the value of women's paid work by masking that labour beneath a more appropriately feminine and genteel guise. Indeed, the novels argue clearly that it is only when women are possessed of the 'Spirit of Independency' that labour provides, and are thus freed from the obligations that limit their activities within the domestic sphere, that they can be of true benefit to their community. As we have seen, *Cornelia* and 'The History of Leonora and Louisa' make these claims by locating their labour plots within the labour market itself; by forcibly removing their heroines from the domestic household early in their narratives and returning them to it briefly, and in the case of 'The History of Leonora and Louisa', reluctantly, in their closing pages. *Millenium Hall* adopts an altogether different strategy: the construction of a utopian alternative to domesticity in the form of a female community founded upon women's labour, but in which that labour is defined and its value calculated outside the terms of market economics, embodied by the society's 'mercantile' chronicler, Ellison (p. 54).

Qualitative distinctions, of the kind codified in later political economic theory, between productive and unproductive work, between manual labour, intellectual and artistic pursuits and domestic or affective labour do not exist within Scott's ideal community, which understands such activities as equivalents and accords them value in relation to the need of the individual worker, the effort needed to accomplish a particular task and the benefits the work brings to the society as a whole. As such, Ruth Perry contends, the novel sets out 'explicitly to undo market values', and, in the process, it subtly recalibrates the relationship between work and benefit as expressed in the earlier novels.[43] Unlike the 1750s fiction in which work generates benefits for society by financing projects that lead to the material assistance and moral improvement of others, in *Millenium Hall* work and benefit are indistinguishable. Undertaken voluntarily and with an eye to the greater good, labour is a gift to the community in which it is performed; its value lies in its ability to command the respect and 'affections' of others and to oblige them to reciprocate in kind through 'services' of their own. The system of equivalent exchanges that structures the labour economy of the text, and which, as Alessa Johns documents, was to prove attractive to a number of eighteenth-century women utopianists, ensures the community's viability and guarantees the 'freedom' of its members.[44] Moreover, as Still has suggested, it aligns the novel with the work of more recent twentieth-century feminists who have looked to theories of gift exchange for an alternative to patriarchal capitalism.[45] Although deeply critical of commercial society's unacknowledged dependence upon, and exploitation of, notions of gift and service, particularly in relation to women's unremunerated and often unrecognized domestic labour, *Millenium Hall* none the less attempted to recuperate an idealized notion of the gift that might empower those (principally women and the labouring classes) traditionally exploited by the moneyed and powerful's misapplication of its logic and language. The novel's utopian remodelling of female labour as gift renders visible and valuable women's affective work as mothers, homemakers and mentors while also emphasizing the psychic, social and economic gains to be made by allowing women to work outside the domestic economy's oppressive confines.

That the politics of gift economics played an important role in the actual and discursive organization of social relationships in eighteenth-century society has been demonstrated by a number of recent studies.[46] Gift economy suggests, as Mary Douglas explains, that society can be described by 'a catalogue of transfers that map all the obligations between its members'.[47] According to Marcel Mauss's classic work on the subject, *Essai sur le Don* (1923–24), these mutual obligations can be divided into three related categories: the obligation to give; the obligation to receive; and the obligation to reciprocate. The exchange of gifts articulates and encodes these obligations and, in the process, forges relationships between individuals and various kinship and tribal groups that stand outside the logic of the market. Within such societies, gifts are given and reciprocated not for economic gain, although they may generate wealth indirectly; rather, they are exchanged in recognition of the 'contractual morality' that binds the gift economy.[48] If, as Phebe Lowell Bowditch has argued, a market or capitalist economy 'allows for the liquidation of the relationship between the contracting parties', since it can establish relationships only between the *objects* of exchange, then that of the gift '(ideally) serves to create social bonds' between giving *subjects*.[49] Within the gift society, therefore, exchange exists outside the commodity form elucidated by Marx.[50]

Bowditch's parenthetical 'ideally' is significant, gesturing as it does towards the scepticism with which the gift has been viewed by more recent commentators.[51] Particularly difficult to sustain, for these theorists, is the notion of disinterestedness, a crux in more recent accounts of the gift, particularly those in which the gift economy is posited as an alternative to capitalism.[52] For behind the giver's seemingly disinterested benevolence can lie compelling incentives to status and even economic gain, made possible by the act of giving and the simultaneous urging of obligation. The heightened 'symbolic capital', as Bourdieu terms it, generated by the giving of gifts approximates, even while it might appear to define itself in opposition to, economic capital since it too confers authority and status upon the giver. And, as Cynthia Klekar points out, 'a gift already *is* a commodity prior to its recognition as a gift, always. Gift economy can only disguise the calculation and negotiation that informs all economic practices. . . . Rather than enacting a reciprocal and balanced exchange, gift giving provokes an ongoing negotiation of values.'[53]

Millenium Hall signals a complex understanding of the role of the gift and the gendered and class implications of the 'ongoing negotiation of values' it produces. On the one hand, the novel mobilizes the vocabulary of the gift – of reciprocity, mutuality, benefit and obligation – in order to articulate its utopian vision of equitable exchange between individuals. On the other, Scott's work is all too aware that gift discourse was susceptible to corruption by those determined to abuse it in the service of various political and economic ideologies to which it is, in theory, opposed. (That the novel is, in fact, implicated in some of the ideologies it purports to reject will be explored in the following section.) As Linda Zionkowski has argued, and as my earlier discussion of the Magdalen House pamphlets also suggests, the 'ethos of the gift' was most widely apparent in eighteenth-century culture in the form of paternalist and philanthropic discourses, which emphasized both the moral and financial obligations that the propertied owed the propertyless and the cultural obligations the latter owed the former.[54] James Steuart went further to locate this 'ethos' of reciprocal responsibility at the heart of the new science of political economy. In the preface to *An Inquiry into the Principles of Political Economy* (1767), Steuart contended that:

> The principal object of this science is . . . to provide everything necessary for supplying the wants of the society, and to employ the inhabitants (supposing them to be free-men) in such a manner as naturally to create reciprocal relations and dependencies between them, so as to make their several interests lead them to supply one another with their reciprocal wants.[55]

If this passage bears an uncanny resemblance to the quotation from *Millenium Hall* with which this chapter began, then its emphasis upon mutual dependence betrays a telling difference. That 'reciprocal relations' generated 'dependencies' between subjects – a notion fundamental to eighteenth-century theories of contractualism – which naturalized social, gender and material inequality, was a problem with which Scott's fiction was much concerned and for which it sought redress.[56] The discourse of reciprocity, Scott's novels argued, could be only as disinterested and equitable as the ideology it was called upon to uphold. As she would demonstrate in *Sir George Ellison*, the line between her hero's statement that England is a country where 'all live in a state of reciprocal services', where no 'subordination exists . . . but what is for the benefit of the lower as well as the higher ranks', and his cousin's, Sir William's, conviction that 'without subordination and distinctions society must be destroyed' was very fine indeed.[57]

If Scott's novels reveal how concepts of obligation could be exploited to justify social injustice in the name of paternalism, then they point also to the ease with which these notions could be misappropriated by those seeking to naturalize women's subjugation. In 'The History of Miss Mancel, and Mrs. Morgan', the first of *Millenium Hall*'s inset narratives, Scott identifies the difference between such wilful misunderstandings of the gift and those genuine and mutually beneficial acts of giving that will structure the community the women later found. Mr Hintman's 'lavish' showering of gifts of books and money upon Louisa Mancel (p. 90), a young girl whom he 'receive[s] . . . as his child' following her aunt's death, seems, initially, to be motivated only by kindness. Having no child of his own, it seems entirely appropriate that he should make good use of his 'ample fortune' (p. 82) by giving presents to Louisa and anyone who 'shewed any particular civility to her' (p. 90). Mr Hintman's desire to have the 'pleasure of gratifying' his young charge produces the 'wish'd for return of affectation and gratitude' (p. 91). It is clear to the reader, however, as it is, perhaps subconsciously, to Miss Melvyn who 'decline[s] accepting the presents he offered her' (p. 90), that the pleasures Hintman seeks are, like Octavio's, of a much more selfish kind, and that the obligation he forces upon Louisa will lead only to her destruction. Indeed, Scott relies on the fact that her readers will perceive these acts of giving by an older man to a young woman as an inevitable prelude to seduction in order to build up narrative tension until Hintman's timely death (p. 101).[58]

Miss Mancel's near destruction by the gift is mirrored in the story of her childhood friend, Miss Melvyn. Miss Melvyn stands for many of Scott's heroines when she is forced to make a choice between her desire to live an 'eligible' life by 'labour[ing] for a subsistence' and her stepmother's demands that she 'sacrifice her peace to her character' by giving 'the gift of her hand' to a man she does not love. Lacking agency within the economy of exchange, Miss Melvyn determines to fulfil her double 'duty' to 'society' and her 'station' by marrying Mr Morgan despite her scruples (p. 127). But the 'gift' bestowed – not only her body but her peace of mind and potential to contribute to the general good – carries too high a price, its value far exceeding the debt owed to her family and position. In such 'masculine economies', as Julie McDonegal observes, 'women are not only obliged to reciprocate men's gifts with symbolic capital, they *are* symbolic capital'.[59] Mrs Morgan is forbidden by her new husband to see Louisa, to whom the former is connected as the 'soul' is to the 'body' (pp. 130–1). Only when Mr Morgan dies of 'a paralytic disorder' are the women permanently reunited and his wife's 'constitution' restored (pp. 157–8).

If, as Scott demonstrates in Miss Melvyn's story, the cultural construction of women and their labour as gift accords them status only as objects of exchange – or as Luce Irigaray would put it, as 'commodities'[60] – then their role as giving subjects within commercial society traditionally failed to grant them agency also. As feminist critiques of the gift from the eighteenth century to the present day remind us, women – historically associated with gifts and commodities – have been perceived as 'natural' gift givers, whose unwaged services as mothers, daughters, carers or, in two conventional eighteenth-century formulations, as companions ('toadeaters') or agents of charity, have traditionally been undervalued precisely because these acts are understood as gifts given voluntarily and freely rather than as work.[61] Society's exploitation of women's unpaid and unrecognized domestic labour is explored throughout Scott's fiction, but nowhere more vividly than in the story of *Sir George Ellison*'s Mrs Alton, an inhabitant of Millenium Hall whom the hero encounters when revisiting the institution in the 1766 sequel.[62] A victim of a patrilineal inheritance system, which leaves her destitute following her father's death, Mrs Alton is forced to work as a housekeeper, nurse and cook for her brother and his ever-pregnant wife, who exploit Mrs Alton's skills despite the embarrassment their reliance upon her servitude occasions. Deeply invested, like the patriarchal economy as a whole, in rendering women's work invisible, the couple expect Mrs Alton to dine with them despite having prepared their meal herself; and she is forced to 'huddle on [her] cloaths in the little intervals the office of cook would allow' when company is present (p. 103). Although her brother and sister-in-law understand Mrs Alton's repetitive and exhausting work as a gift, undertaken in gratitude for the bed and board they provide, she is all too painfully aware that her situation represents no 'balance between obligations conferred and repaid'. Treated as a 'slave, and yet reproached as a burden', she comes to demand 'payment' for her 'services' (p. 105), but receives only 'presents' from her brother – small sums of money – given without her sister-in-law's knowledge (p. 107). While these gifts silently acknowledge the value of her work, they are worthless in real terms: 'the utmost [she] could save would not have amounted to a sum sufficient to maintain [her], even if [she] lived there to old age' (p. 107). Mrs Alton may live in relative 'affluence' in servitude, but outside this oppressive economy she faces a life of 'poverty', until she is 'enfranchis[ed]' by her admission into Millenium Hall (pp. 107–8).

Scott was not alone in recognizing the ease with which the vocabulary of the gift was prone to exploitation by those who wished to secure women's dependence. That 'Obligations' made individuals 'Slaves', as *David Simple*'s Cynthia puts it, was a recurrent strain in Fielding's fiction, for example, as well as providing a source of inspiration for Jane Collier's satirical *An Essay on the Art of Ingeniously Tormenting* (1753).[63] Like these writers, Scott was committed to analysing the mechanics of such abusive relationships and to suggesting alternative models of human relations that might counter the 'love of *Tyranny*' that Cynthia finds ubiquitous.[64] What distinguishes Scott's fiction from the works of her contemporaries, however, is the central role that labour plays in the utopian gift economy she posits as a solution to the problem of women's 'bondage'. Indeed, the most commonly exchanged gift in the Millienium Hall community is labour itself: Susan, a lame woman, spins for Rachel who, in turn, 'does such things for her as she cannot do for herself' (p. 66); the 'monsters' maintain their garden and cultivate the finest flowers to adorn the Hall in exchange for their mistress's benefactions (p. 75); the 'sisterhood' visit and instruct by example the labourers in the various satellite communities that surround the Hall in return for their liberation from a life of dependency (p. 118). Unlike Mrs Alton's exploited domestic labours, the wide-ranging employments undertaken by the community members are gifts in the purest sense of the word, since they are not 'undertaken on a pure cost-benefit basis', and 'because their products are not commodities, not things we can easily price or willingly alienate'.[65] Unlike commercial society, which exploits women's domestic labours as carers and teachers by maintaining that these employments carry an emotional reward that compensates for no or scant remuneration, Scott's gift economy seeks to recuperate these endeavours as culturally and economically valuable forms of work in their own right.[66]

By laying bare the difference between authentic and exploitative economic systems, *Millenium Hall* reveals that the logic of gift exchange can serve women only when the true cultural and economic value of the diverse work they perform is recognized by the society that is literally and figuratively enriched by it. The Millenium Hall community accords such recognition in various ways, most notably, perhaps, in the community's carpet factory, where the workers are allowed 'great wages' paid in accordance with the individual's need rather than her productivity. All of the factory workers live 'in a condition of proper plenty', but the young and old earn more than their stronger brethren 'as a proper encouragement, and reward for industry in those seasons of life in which it is so uncommon' (pp. 243–4). The moral economy governing the factory's labour practices proves not only just but profitable. However, the novel is clear that the profits generated are incidental to the 'higher' work the factory makes possible: the establishment of 'a fund for the sick and disabled' from which they can draw in 'perpetuity' (p. 247). Thus even at its most commercially minded, the community interrogates, by positing alternatives to, the ethos of capitalism with which the novel has sometimes been aligned.[67] Paradoxically, it is only when the price of labour is understood in direct relation to the value of the work invested, rather than to the volume of work produced, that women can enjoy freedom through communality. By divorcing women from the products of their labour – by refusing to acknowledge qualitative distinctions between housework, gardening, teaching, spinning and charity – Scott accommodates work to the logic of the gift and makes female labour the prerequisite of the novel's moral economy. In *Millenium Hall*, industry – 'necessary to all stations' – is not only 'the basis of . . . almost every virtue' (p. 118); rather, it is the economic and philosophical foundation of the text's utopian project.

This anti-capitalist logic is, initially at least, beyond the grasp of Ellison, who, despite his status as a man of feeling, has 'dedicated all his application to mercantile gain' (p. 54).[68] Throughout his time in the community, Ellison struggles to make sense of the 'georgic utopia', and repeatedly fails in his endeavours because he insists upon reading the community through the lens of the economic ideologies it rejects.[69] Although he understands that the management of the estate by its previous owners – two squires who grew rich while their labourers struggled to 'keep life and soul together' (p. 65) – was both unjust and inefficient, he views the alternative system the founders introduce in its stead with incredulity. Having learned that the community's spinners regularly interrupt their work to teach the children of the local poor to knit and spin, for example, he responds that this must 'lessen their profits' (p. 67). Ellison, who, initially at least, defines profit and loss solely in economic terms (p. 54), must learn to reassess these indicators of value within the context of the moral economy of the gift. The volume of wool the women spin is secondary, the novel suggests, to their teaching the children the means of earning a subsistence; their manual labour is simply a service performed in exchange for the 'meat, drink, and firing' they receive from the community's founders. Should they fail to produce sufficient wool to employ the 'poor old weaver' who works it up to provide the spinners' clothing, then the founders simply 'put more to it', for they recognize that true profit is generated when the gift of benevolence they bestow upon the spinners is passed on, as the logic of the gift dictates it must be, to the children they instruct (p. 67).

In a direct challenge to those philosophers such as Hume, who argued that 'necessity' was the 'great spur to industry', the community ensures that its members are 'set above bodily wants' (p. 110).[70] Enjoying ample food and living in decent accommodation, the women work only for the 'mental enjoyments' their labour provides rather than for any corporeal comfort it might bring (p. 111).[71] As April London has observed, *Millenium Hall* betrays an investment in disembodying the activities of the community's working women, an investment shared by the community's chronicler, who persistently (mis)casts the women's 'georgic enterprise' as 'pastoral leisure'.[72] When Ellison and Lamont first happen upon the community, for example, they witness 'a company of hay-makers'. Determined that the 'pastoral air of the scene' not be 'spolit', Ellison describes the hay-makers' clothes as possessing an extraordinary degree of 'cleanliness and neatness' given the nature of the work in which the women are engaged, and notes his surprise that the women's manners betray no signs of that 'boorish rusticity' he expects of such company (p. 57).[73] Such descriptions, as London suggests, constitute a wilful attempt on Scott's narrator's part to obscure 'the fact of labour that is so central to the women's sense of mission'.[74] However, Ellison's pastoralization of the women's labour, I would suggest, ultimately serves rather than undermines the novel's labour plot. Scott is, albeit for different reasons, as intent upon disembodying the women's labour as the plantation owner. Precisely because she, unlike Ellison, takes the physical reality and intrinsic value of women's work as a given, Scott deflects attention away from the worker's body in order to emphasize the beneficial effects of female labour upon the workers and the community at large. Only if labour is divorced from the fetishized bodies that perform it, and from those bodily wants often seen as a necessary spur to industry in the eyes of contemporary philosophers and political economists, *Millenium Hall* argues, can women be free to enjoy the true fruits of their work: the pleasures of community.

The novel's divorcing of labour from the body not only emphasizes the beneficial effects of woman's work but also makes it possible to argue for the common status of the various manual, affective and intellectual endeavours the women undertake. The potential leveling effect of the novel's situating of happiness, and ultimately selfhood, in the mind is central to Scott's claims for the gift's utopian possibilities. Although the activities in which the community members participate differ according to their 'station', the common status of their services (from spinning and cleaning, to gardening, teaching and philanthropy) as gifts suggests that the community values them as equivalents. Just as the Hall's founders undertake philanthropic activities and administer schemes which allow them to exercise those 'talents' 'for the use of which we must give a strict account', those who lack inheritances or other means find, as do Cornelia and Leonora, a substitute for philanthropy in 'labour', through which they can dispense 'God's . . . bounty' by 'reliev[ing] those who are incapable of gaining the necessaries of life' (p. 244). No matter what the rank of the worker, the community's founders suggest, the gifts she receives in return for the services she performs – the 'free communication of sentiments', 'benevolence', 'friendship', 'communication and improvement' (p. 110) – are the same as those enjoyed by all other members of the community.

That the community believes that the benefits of this utopian sociability can be enjoyed by even by the most deracinated of women is corroborated by the story of the 'monsters' whose 'inclosure' arouses the travellers' curiosity soon after they happen upon the society. Ellison and Lamont learn that, upon first entering Millenium Hall, the group had avoided contact with other community members and had 'confine[d] themselves within so narrow a compass' that they 'enjoyed but precarious health'. Gradually, however, the founders liberated the 'enfranchised company' by encouraging them to think of themselves not as the 'deficien[t]' and 'redundan[t]' 'slaves' they appeared in society but as autonomous subjects who can participate in the building of community through the exchange of the gifts of labour and service (pp. 72–3). The 'monsters' are finally persuaded to visit other members of the community, whom they 'entertain' with 'fruit and wine', and learn to 'assist' their 'neighbours in plain work, thus to endear them, and procure more frequent visits'. Through such interactions, they avoid the objectification they once faced in a society that turned them into 'public spectacles' on the grounds that their 'deformity' rendered them otherwise worthless as domestic or economic subjects. Emancipated by their respective roles in the sharing and exchange of the gift of their labour, the women are gradually socialized until their 'conversation' – the ultimate gift of community – becomes 'much courted' by others (p. 75). Undertaken with an eye to 'mental' rather than to 'corporeal conveniences' (pp. 110–11), the labours of the 'monsters', like those of the spinners and the community's founders, find their reward in a model of utopian sociability – grounded in the giving and receiving of the gift of labour – that makes possible the formation of modes of subjectivity and agency unattainable in a world governed by commercial self-interest.

The fiction of the gift

The question of whether the Millenium Hall community is, in fact, as liberating and egalitarian as its founders believe it to be is one that has preoccupied virtually all commentators on the novel, following the original commentator-in-the-text, Lamont. It is, moreover, one upon which the novel's representation of women's work sheds further light. Far from enfranchising its members, Lamont argues, the community's foundation in the exchange of 'mutual confidences, reciprocal services and correspondent affections' makes individuals 'slaves to one another' (p. 112). This (mis)reading of the community's economic system as one of exploitation rather than equality serves on one level, like Ellison's (mis)understanding of its labour practices, to signal the extent of the society's opposition to the market values he and his fellow-traveller espouse. Confusing gifts and goods, Lamont argues that 'reciprocal communication is impossible', on the grounds that those without means (the 'poor' and presumably the deformed also) are incapable of providing services for men of status such as himself, and are therefore unable 'to return the obligation' owed to their benefactors and betters (p. 112). On another level, Lamont's apparent misunderstanding of the nature of the gift might be interpreted as rather more incisive than the novel will admit, for the rake seems instinctively to realize, as some gift theorists have posited, that truly equitable, disinterested exchange is little more than an attractive fantasy that simply conceals underlying structures of power and dependence. Indeed, Mrs Mancel's account of the benefits conferred by the community's members fails fully to counter the rake's suspicion that the gift is, on one level at least, a convenient fiction created to mask the various cultural and economic ideologies it would ostensibly challenge. In the balance sheet of life, she insists, it is the dependent classes who possess the greater credit (and thus the greater giving potential), since it is they who have it within their power to gift their 'poverty' to those who would relieve them. Pushing the language of gift exchange to its limits, she goes on to argue that, by giving those with means the 'opportunity of relieving' them, the dependent are 'much obliged . . . to that poverty, which enables [them] to obtain so great a gratification' from their ever-indebted superiors (p. 113).

Still reads this passage as evidence that the community does indeed 'lay aside pretensions of superiority' in favour of 'the pleasures of equality and reciprocity'.[75] In order to do so, however, she is forced to omit the lines that immediately follow the quotation cited above and which sit uneasily with the putatively egalitarian ethos of the gift: 'The greatest pleasure this world can give us is that of being beloved . . . . Did you ever see any one that was not fond of a dog that fondled him' (p. 113). Mrs Mancel's comments suggest that Millenium Hall owes more to the logic of contractualism, with its emphasis upon mutual, but inequitable, rights and responsibilities, than to the notion of reciprocal exchange. Moreover, her insistence upon the community members' gratitude conflates moral and economic motives rather too conveniently. The society's founders may argue that the volume of work produced by its members is less important than the fact that they labour, but their workers' gratitude guarantees their productivity none the less. As the Hall's housekeeper explains, it is 'gratitude, and a conviction that this is the only house into which we can be received, makes us exert ourselves to the utmost' (p. 169). But even if gratitude did not ensure that the women worked, it seems that the community's founders would, none the less, be amply repaid. In an argument that seems to run counter to the novel's claims for the necessity and value of women's work, Mrs Mancel implies that community members can return the obligations owed to their deliverers without performing any active service at all: their thankfulness is gift enough. At this key moment in the text, the logic of the gift falters and becomes indistinguishable from the exploitative logic of obligation the novel seeks to overwrite.[76]

The community's apparent replication of structures of dependence is fundamentally at odds with the ethos of equitable and reciprocal exchange that the founders claim underpins the gift economy. Yet it is important to note also that it is at odds with the actual workings of the community itself, which in fact serves, and is served by, its labouring women in more varied and more profound ways than Mrs Mancel and some of the novel's commentators have allowed.[77] *Millenium Hall* is clear that gratitude is only one of many benefits conferred by the community's labouring women and is, in isolation, insufficient to guarantee their place within it. The primary demand placed upon these women by the Hall's founders is not, in fact, that they be grateful – although the women's thankfulness for their deliverance undoubtedly gives pleasure – but that they give service to the community through their labour: 'if [they] are not idle that is all that [the community's founders] desire' (p. 67). Within the utopian society, labouring-class women receive not charity – itself antithetical to the ethos of the gift – but appropriate remuneration for the skills they possess and the services they render.[78] The description of the harsh conditions in which the spinners live before entering the Hall – without 'rags to cover us, or a morsel of bread to eat' (p. 65) – makes clear that the comforts and opportunities they now enjoy are not the result of unwarranted generosity, and therefore deserving of dog-like gratitude, but instead are an appropriate return for the work they undertake. As a result, and in spite of the well-documented strategies the founders deploy to regulate the women's conduct, these formerly deracinated labourers none the less become autonomous subjects – as surrogate 'mothers' to the girls they teach, as 'friends' to their 'relations' and as 'sisters' to their fellow workers – through their participation in the reciprocal economy of gift labour (pp. 66–7).

The position of many of the more genteel members of the community is rather more ambiguous, however. Labouring-class women are more easily accommodated within the utopian society precisely because they already possess the gifts – the capacity to work in diverse and sometimes multiple roles – that the community will call upon, and which will guarantee their future happiness. By contrast, the former dependants housed near the Hall achieve agency of a much more limited and troubling kind.[79] These 'in some measure voluntary slaves', the very antitheses of Cornelia and Leonora, are 'unqualified to gain a maintenance'. Having been 'educated as it is called, genteelly, or in other words idly', they are also unqualified to participate in the 'reciprocal communication of benefits' within the utopia because they have little to offer the community beyond the 'discontent, malignity, [and] ill humour' produced by 'scantiness of fortune', 'pride of family' and an 'idle mind' (pp. 115–16). Although the women are taught in time how 'to be of service to others' (p. 118), they are, in many ways, as much a problem in the moral economy of the Hall as they are in the market economy they leave behind. This is made clear in *Sir George Ellison* when the hero returns to the Hall and 'visits . . . the two societies, composed of the persons those ladies had removed from a state of mortifying dependence'. Here an inmate explains:

> 'We are indeed dependent, but reflexion only can make us sensible of it; here dependence exists without those chains and fetters which render it more galling than the oppressions of the most indigent, but free, poverty. We see our benefactresses feel such true joy in bestowing, it would be ingratitude even to wish not to receive at their hands; in accepting their bounty, we seem to confer an obligation, and do in reality confer a benefit, by being the cause of so much refined pleasure to them.' (p. 101)

The speaker is Mrs Alton, and these comments immediately precede the account she gives of her life as her brother's servant.

Read alongside the subsequent autobiographical account, Mrs Alton's comments map out the scope and bounds of Scott's argument in *Sir George Ellison* and the earlier *Millenium Hall.* Both novels attempt to redefine the terms of women's oppression – of obligation, dependence and gratitude – within the context of a gift economy which would strip these behavioural imperatives of the taint of commercial, patriarchal and paternalist self-interest and reinstate them as pleasurable and reciprocal responsibilities worked towards by all. However, the fiction of the gift, as revealed by Mrs Alton's comments, is that the impoverished gentlewomen she represents – like the grateful dogs they, more nearly than their labouring counterparts, resemble – enjoy any more freedom here than they do in the society they have left behind.[80] In part, this is a problem of language. The proximity of the vocabulary that inscribes the moral economy of the gift to that which characterized the oppressive economy of obligation it seeks to overwrite is a difficulty that the novel ultimately cannot surmount. For individuals such as Mrs Alton, the free 'speech' gifted to them by their participation in the community is at best an ambiguous benefit, polluted as it is by economic and cultural ideologies the novel struggles to supplant. Having internalized notions of gift and obligation as codified by these entrenched ideologies, such characters cannot conceive of themselves as anything other than indebted objects, destined to receive more than they can reciprocate. Mrs Alton may perceive her situation as a dependant within the community to be more equitable than that which she endured as her brother's servant, but this is only because she fails to understand the centrality of labour to the community's conception of individual worth and social cohesion. Recognizing her deliverance from domestic exploitation as a gift, but offering only gratitude in return, Mrs Alton may enjoy 'dependence without . . . chains and fetters', but she fails to enjoy the fruits of reciprocity enjoyed by other community members.[81] Having substituted a life of gratitude for a life of exploited domestic labour, Mrs Alton has merely exchanged one set of 'mortifying' obligations for another. Within the Hall, as in her brother's house, Mrs Alton is destined to perform the cultural work of dependence.

Reading Mrs Alton's story in terms of theories of the gift opens up similar lines of enquiry to those pursued by critics who have read the text within the contexts of other political and economic paradigms: to what extent, for example, does the imagined utopia offer a viable alternative to the problems women face in the labour and marriage markets; and, if it does so, for whom and at what (or whose) cost? An analysis of the novel in terms of the gift labour paradigm to which Scott gestures throughout the text produces some rather different conclusions from those most commonly proffered, however, particularly different from those readings that have identified within the text a defence of class privilege that cannot be reconciled with the novel's utopian and feminist politics. Most significantly, it indicates that, if the novel is a failure in the terms within which it presents itself, then it is not in its treatment of labouring-class women – although much more might be said of the novel's coercive programme of moral and spiritual reform than is possible here – but rather, in its inability to conceive of meaningful roles for a number of impoverished gentlewomen as moral and economic agents within the utopia outside the terms of dependence. To acknowledge such inconsistencies in and problems with *Millenium Hall*'s and *Sir George Ellison*'s arguments about labour is not to diminish the importance of these novels' contributions to the politically charged, and politically sensitive, debate about women's work at mid-century. Neither is it to contradict my argument that one of the unique contributions made by Scott's fiction is its vindication of women's work and attempt to place labour at the heart of female experience and the female-authored novel. That for women such as Mrs Alton the gift remains an enticing fiction rather than a lived reality might suggest that the novels' aspirations are rather higher than its achievements. Yet it is also indicative of, perhaps a self-conscious recognition of, the reach of those ambitions and the difficulty of the project in which Scott engages when she attempts to articulate a utopian vision of female labour as gift that would enable non-labouring-class women to work their way out of the centuries of domestic dependence they had gifted to society without recognition or reward.

The gift of fiction

If *Millenium Hall* and *Sir George Ellison* are not wholly successful in their modelling of female labour as gift, then Scott's conceptualization of authorial labour in terms of the same ethical and economic framework is much more effective.[82] I suggested earlier that Scott's figuring of labour as gift in the 1760s novels marks important developments in, and significant departures from, the earlier works, in which heroines reform the labour market from within, rather than seeking to establish wholly new contexts for women's work. However, in their treatment of the work of authorship, *Millenium Hall* and *Sir George Ellison* occupy common ground with *Cornelia* and *A Journey*, which, like the later novels, argue that the value of intellectual labour lies not only in the intrinsic worth of the sentiments it contains but also in the cultural benefits it generates when readers labour to respond to its example in their own lives. To talk in this way about Scott's novels is to characterize their author, in largely unfamiliar ways, as a literary theorist.[83] Of all of the writers discussed in this book, Scott was certainly the least obviously committed to theorizing her working practices. There are no professional author-characters in her fiction as there are in Charlotte Smith's, although almost all of Scott's heroines are storytellers of one kind or another; nor are the novels accompanied by the kinds of highly self-reflexive prefaces that can be found in the works of Smith and the popular women writers discussed in this book's final chapter.[84] Moreover Scott's correspondence, unlike that of contemporaries and successors such as Burney, Smith and Wollstonecraft, contains comparatively few references to her literary career, her dealings with publishers or her views on other writers, although those that do survive are illuminating. Such evidence underscores Betty A. Schellenberg's recent claim that Scott's authorial career betrays both a reluctance to embrace the identity of the professional writer – she never published under her own name, only anonymously or pseudonymously – and a rejection of increasingly gendered and essentialized models of authorship in favour of a 'notion of intellectual exchange that could to a significant extent transcend barriers of gender, geography, genre and status'.[85] According to Schellenberg, Scott's embracing of the 'disembodiment afforded by print' came at a price, denying her a coherent authorial identity within the republic of letters.[86] While acknowledging Scott's reluctance publicly to embrace the role of author, and the attendant fragility of her position within the republic of letters, I want here to emphasize the extent to which Scott none the less used her fiction as a forum in which to engage in coded meditations upon the novel and authorial labour. Although the strategies she adopted are rather more oblique than those of many of her contemporaries or successors, through paratextual interventions, the use of the frame narrative as structural device and, most particularly, by linking the 'humane labours' of her characters to acts of storytelling, Scott none the less offered a sustained theory of the work of authorship framed in terms of the gift paradigm.[87]

The role that notions of the gift have played in providing a rationale for the function, production and circulation of literary texts has been elucidated by several scholars.[88] Lewis Hyde goes further than most, however, in his assertion that such a rationale not only provides a useful way of theorizing literature from the past but might also model a way of thinking about literature that is necessary for its future survival. For Hyde, the gift paradigm provides an important corrective to accounts which emphasize the market's commodification of literature. Although Hyde recognizes that artworks may exist simultaneously in the market and the gift economies, he contends that only the latter is essential to an artefact's survival: a true work of art can 'survive without the market, but where there is no gift, there is no art'.[89] Hyde's defence of the under-valued cultural work of the imagination is expressed in familiar eighteenth-century terms. In a passage that is as reminiscent of Burney's abandoned introduction to *Cecilia* (1782) – in which the 'Gift' of 'Genius' writes itself upon the novelist's mind[90] – as it is of Percy Bysshe Shelley's description of the poet as Aeolian harp in *A Defence of Poetry* (1821), Hyde suggests that incessant toil cannot make a great artwork, which is 'bestowed upon' a creator whose intellectual labours merely perfect it. Artworks are gifts in two senses, according to Hyde: a gift received from a mysterious creative force and a gift given to the public in the material form.[91] Thus passed on, 'the spirit of [the] artist's gifts' can awaken the recipients' own by encouraging them to emulate the artist's genius and, through emulation, to pass on this gift to others.[92]

Hyde's account of literature as gift may seem idealistic in its divorcing of art from labour and the market, but his arguments would have had a resonance for many early to mid-eighteenth-century writers wary of the expansion and commercialization of the literary marketplace. Frequently, and as discussed in this book's introduction, such anxieties were expressed through the ironic equation of intellectual toil ('commanding inspiration') and manual work ('hard fagging'), of 'Profession' and 'Trade', or 'Genius' and 'Manufacture'. In the first issue of the *Critical Review* (1756), for example – a publication that would play a leading role in the professionalization of literature and authorship – Tobias Smollett wrote: 'the miserable author must perform his daily task . . . otherwise he will lose his character and livelihood, like a taylor who disappoints his customers in a birth-day suit'.[93] In a commonplace manoeuvre, Smollett connects mental and manual toil to signal his disdain for the cultural devaluation of authorship and literature as a result of the literary marketplace's commercialization and to assert intellectual labour's superiority to other forms of work.[94] Even those of Scott's and Smollett's contemporaries who defended authors' right to write with hopes of pecuniary gain were reluctant to recognize authorship as work for fear of degrading it by way of analogy. In *The Case of Authors by Profession* (1758), for example, James Ralph pointed to the absurdity that dictated that a 'Man may plead for Money, prescribe or quack for Money, preach and pray for Money, marry for Money, fight for money', but will be condemned if he 'writes for Money', only subsequently to compare the 'Writer in the Garret, and the Slave in the Mines' to insinuate that authors were above the kind of menial 'drudge[ry]' to which their profession was being reduced by the mercenary interests of the market.[95]

If theorizing authorship as work was problematic for male writers, on the grounds that it transformed their art into a mere trade, then it was doubly so for women writers, whose willingness to engage in such a trade for financial reasons was deemed, at best, suspicious and, at worst, monstrously unfeminine. To quote Oliver Goldsmith's *An Enquiry into the Present State of Polite Learning in Europe* (1759), if tradesmen who published by subscription displayed their 'want [of] skill in conducting their own business' and mechanics, their 'want [of] money', then women displayed only their lack of 'shame'.[96] Scott apparently had some sympathy with Goldsmith's views on 'authors by profession' and the economics of literary production. Writing to Elizabeth Montagu in the year before *Millenium Hall* was published, Scott suggested that only those who were 'rich in purse & parts' could lay claim to literary 'Genius', while those authors who laboured for 'bread, or butter for their bread' were worthy only of the designation 'Writers'.[97] Scott's lack of financial security ensured that disinterestedness remained an ambition rather than a reality for the author, however. That Scott was willing to undertake projects for bread and butter rather than in the disinterested service of 'Genius' is clear from a letter she wrote to Montagu shortly after the publication of *Agreeable Ugliness* (1754), translated from the French *La Laideur Aimable* (1752), by Pierre-Antoine de la Place, in which Scott asked her sibling if she was aware of any other such works that she might 'turn much to [her] profit' by spending a 'little time . . . translating them'.[98] If money played a significant role in shaping Scott's literary career, then it was also important in shaping her perception of the value of her works. Writing to Montagu in the year after *Millenium Hall*'s publication, Scott noted that her now best known work brought her 'very little' money, much less in fact than 'any thing' she had previously published. While personally disappointing, Scott went on to declare that the novel scarcely warranted a higher price than that paid by its publisher: 'a thing like that takes so very little time in writing that I can not say but my time was sufficiently paid for; it was not a month's work, therefore it brought me in about a guinea a day: more than I cou'd gain by a better thing'.[99] By her own definition, Scott was a 'Writer' no matter how much she might have hoped to produce works of 'Genius'.

Such moments in the correspondence outline an economics of textual production, not unlike that mapped out in Burney's letter to Samuel Crisp, that cannot be countenanced in the novels themselves: in which the worth of a text is determined by the time spent in working on it rather than by the sentiments it contains, and in which authors do not always labour to write the best book they can, but the best they can work up in the given circumstances. Indeed, Scott's novels go to great lengths to construct a model of authorial labour that stands outside the economic.[100] The Advertisement to *Cornelia*, for example, opens by presenting the text as a financial risk on the part of both author and publisher, who have 'ventured' its appearance in print in the full knowledge that such 'Works of imagination which have a tendency to inculcate, illustrate, or exemplify morality' will be received warmly by the 'good and judicious part of mankind', but are unlikely to be as 'profitable to the authors, or venders' as those 'compositions of a contrary tendency'. Here, as throughout Scott's novels, pecuniary motives are cast as incidental to the author's higher aim, as declared by Ellison, the supposed 'author' of *Millenium Hall*, of 'benefiting the world' (p. 54). Scott was, of course, neither the first nor the last eighteenth-century writer to assert the novel's reformative potential. Where she departs from many of her predecessors is in her development of these arguments into a sustained theory of the author/reader relationship and of the moral function of the novel, which is manifest not only in the paratextual apparatus that frames her fictions but also in each novel's labour plot and its metafictional role as a reflection on the practice of authorship. To assert, as the Advertisement to *Cornelia* does, that its author wished to educate readers 'in the practice of . . . virtue' was no mere marketing ploy or gesture of conformity to the modesty topos that structures many female-authored prefaces of this period. It was not enough, as she wrote on the preface to *A Journey*, that her readers should 'approve and commend what they observe [to be] virtuous and laudable' in her novels; her authorial labours were designed to encourage others to 'imitate what they thus approve[d]' (p. 1).

In such prefatory statements, Scott imagines the author and reader entering into an unspoken contract, according to which each accepts their obligation to work for the common good through their respective roles in the production and consumption of literary texts. The truly 'useful' author – there is no other kind for Scott – is bound to 'set before us examples which may incite us to virtue, and trace out a path wherein emulation may induce us to walk'. The reader, in turn, has a reciprocal responsibility, to quote from *Sir George Ellison*, to 'endeavour to equal' the virtuous examples gifted to her in print (p. 3). Like the 'humane labours' of Scott's heroines, the work of writing is envisaged as a two-way dynamic here, which, when it operates successfully, confers 'benefits' upon all parties engaged in the production and consumption of the gift-text.

The efficacy of the model of authorial labour outlined in the novels' paratextual material is metaphorically proved on the level of plot on the many occasions in which storytelling is demonstrated to possess reformative agency. In a strategy that, as we shall see in Chapter 4, a number of popular women writers would adopt much later in the century, Scott's novels persistently present their labouring heroines as pseudo-authorial figures. While these characters are not, in any straightforward way, fictional representations of Scott herself, they function none the less as stand-ins for a generic author-figure, and thus become a vehicle for Scott to reflect upon her working practice. To read the novels for the insights they provide into Scott's views on authorship is, of course, problematic. As Schellenberg has cautioned, to extrapolate a 'writer's experience from that of [a] narrative's heroine' rather than from the '"fine-print" of the text's, and writer's, paratext and context, can lead to the misrepresentation of writers' aims and achievements', with potentially significant implications for their place within literary history.[101] Mindful of these pitfalls, it is certainly the case that writers including Scott, Smith and the women writers discussed in the final chapter of this book solicit such readings through their imaginative linking of manual and authorial labour within their novels as well as in the '"fine print"' of their works and lives.[102] Whether it is Cornelia in the brothel offering her story to a rakish would-be client who will be her devoted servant from that moment on, or Sabrina, in an inversion of the Scheherazade myth, attempting to save her mistress through the telling of tales, or Mrs Alton performing the work of gratitude in relating her story to Ellison, the act of narration is presented in Scott's novels as a force for good. While self-justificatory claims for fiction's moral utility were a literary commonplace at mid-century, Scott's fiction reworks from this convention by making storytelling's status as labour clear by presenting it as an analogue to the other modes of manual and affective work explored within the texts.

In *A Journey*, for example, the labours of the storytelling servant, the author for whom she acts as proxy, and the cross-dressing heroine Leonora, are emphatically placed upon a continuum. The equivalence the novel imagines between the women's work is rendered explicit by the metaphors of artistry that pervade the novel. Although, according to its subtitle, the text describes the lives of 'real characters', Sabrina gives the lie to this statement by drawing attention to the 'innocent Art[s]' she must deploy to amuse and arouse Carinthia's 'Curiosity' and thereby serve her 'Moral' project to reform her mistress (p. 105). In fact, these artistic interventions seem more strategic than innocent. When, for example, the princess berates her servant for failing to leave her 'fully satisfied' by a particular day's storytelling, Sabrina responds that such strategies are vital to her project. Without 'Suspence' – 'the Soul of a Story' – her narrative would be 'dead and lifeless', and presumably ineffective (p. 151). The fact that these debates about the ethics of narrative strategy and the competing interests of reforming writer and unreflecting reader occur at the moment when it first appears that Calidore and Leonora might marry is not coincidental, signalling, as I implied earlier, that their betrothal is a concession to reader expectation made by a writer who is much more concerned to expose society's failure to provide women with meaningful and economically viable alternatives to marriage. These allusions to artistry further link Sabrina's storytelling to Leonora's work as a painter – whose 'flattering' pencil works to 'purify [the sitter's] Mind' (p. 76) – and connect both women's work to that of the author herself, who strives to 'paint' 'Vice and Folly . . . in their natural Deformity' (p. 1). All three women are working towards a single reformist purpose: the amelioration of the age through a benign feminine influence achieved through the gifting of their labour.

In *A Journey*, this influence is curtailed by the novel's grudging adherence to novelistic conventions: Leonora must marry and Sabrina's arguments will fall on deaf ears. In *Millenium Hall*, however, the impact of women's labour is greater and extends even beyond the limits of the text itself. *Millenium Hall*'s Advertisement, title-page and opening paragraphs labour even more carefully than do those of the earlier novels to distance the text from the conventional economics of textual production. Written without financial motive, but with an eye to 'general use', the text is presented to its readers as an extended letter written 'BY A GENTLEMAN on his Travels' (title-page) to a publisher-friend, in whose hands the narrative's 'future fate' lies (p. 54). Indeed, Ellison implies that he has no title to any acclaim or profit the text might generate because he cannot take credit for the narratives it contains. Just as property is held in common within the society, the account of the text's generation Ellison provides suggests that it too belongs to everyone and to no one in particular: 'I have no other share [in the story] than that of a spectator and auditor' (p. 54). That this elaborate conceit is an attempt to situate *Millenium Hall* within the moral sphere of the gift rather than the mercenary world of the literary marketplace becomes clearer in the novel's opening paragraphs. Drawing heavily upon the language of the gift, Ellison offers the text, which was apparently 'promised' even before it could have been conceived, in acknowledgement of the obligation 'due' to a man who has endeavoured 'constant[ly] . . . to inculcate the best principles into youthful minds' (p. 53). But the gift of Ellison's narrative is intended to do more than simply consolidate the gentlemen's relationship; rather, it is offered in the hopes that it might serve the 'great end of benefiting the world' by encouraging those receptive readers upon whose minds 'any characters may be engraven' to emulate its example (p. 54).

Ellison's traditional representation of the reader's mind as *tabula rasa*, here, belies a complex dynamic that is central to *Millenium Hall*: the power of narrative to produce readers in its own image. Scott's utopian vision for the novel sees it operating within an economy of textual production that imitates the circular logic of the gift itself. If the work of writing, like the labours undertaken by the members of the Millenium Hall community, is understood as gift, then its value lies in its ability to urge those who receive it to respond in kind by imitating it. This metatextual claim for the novel's power of self-replication is fantastically realized within the text itself by Lamont's and Ellison's reactions to the community. In the novel's closing pages, Lamont is figured as an ideal reader upon whose mind the community's example is now writ large. Won over by the women's 'conduct', he turns to the New Testament to 'study precepts, which could . . . exalt human nature almost to divine' (p. 248), thus fulfilling the author's hopes that her text might 'excite in the READER proper Sentiments of Humanity, and lead the Mind to the Love of VIRTUE' (title-page). Ellison – though much less in need of improvement than his travelling companion – benefits similarly from his visit to the utopian society. Now in possession of the gift of a language that is free from the taint of competition and 'mercantile gain' (p. 54), Ellison finds himself 'fortunate' in being afforded the opportunity of 'communicating' his description to others who may, as he will in the novel's sequel, 'imitate' the community's projects, if on a smaller 'scale' (p. 249). *Sir George Ellison* realizes what *Millenium Hall* intimates in its final vision of Lamont reading the Bible: that the litmus test of the effectiveness of women's work (whether as painters, milliners, benefactors or writers) is their ability to urge others, through the gift of storytelling, to labour to reform the age.[103] If Scott's novels encouraged their readers to labour towards self-improvement and the amelioration of the lives of others, then the author's work would not be in vain.

Both on the level of plot and in its metatextual commentary, Scott's fiction placed women's work at the centre of the novel and the debates about the novel's future. The representation of women's manual, domestic and intellectual work in her novels is, as I have suggested, of its moment, a response to contemporary political economic writing about female labour and to mid-century accounts of writing's relation to work and its gendered implications. Yet for all their embeddedness in contemporary economic, philanthropic and literary debates, the novels are highly innovative and distinctive in their approach to the issue of women's work. Scott was far from the only mid-century woman writer to be concerned with the question of female dependence, the exploitation of women's domestic labour, the consequences of the gendered division of labour, and the economy of obligation that legitimized women's subjugation. Nevertheless the solutions her novels offer to these problems are more ambitious than those envisaged by her contemporaries with the possible exception of Sarah Fielding's *Countess of Dellwyn*, which, as I have suggested, is itself greatly indebted to Scott's 1750s novels. Unlike Charlotte Lennox's Henrietta, who is 'reduced' to going into service rather than accede to her aunt's wishes that she convert to Catholicism, Scott's heroines do not experience labour as a fall.[104] And, unlike *David Simple*'s Cynthia and Camilla, Scott's heroines experience work as a source of personal fulfilment rather than a source of deracination. Moreover, Scott's labour plot serves as an ambitious vehicle for rethinking the intellectual work of the woman writer, a strategy that would, as we shall see, be taken up and elaborated by a number of female authors as the century progressed.

I have opened this book with Scott because her fiction, more than that of any of her contemporaries, sets out the terms of the literary debate on woman's work that would preoccupy and divide female writers for decades to come, despite the relative obscurity of her works, and almost total obscurity of her authorship, by the time that Smith and Wollstonecraft began their careers. The labour and literary marketplaces would undergo significant changes in the years that followed the publication of Scott's mid-century novels, changes which, as we shall see, produced different challenges for women writers, challenges which prompted a range of solutions and diverse compromises. None the less, Scott's complex interweaving of labour, gender and literary politics in these texts had an undoubted resonance for a number of female authors working later in the century. Although not openly, or perhaps even consciously, recognized by her successors, Scott's insistence upon women's dual status as moral beings and as economic agents and her unashamed (if not uncomplicated) defence of the personal, cultural and economic benefits generated by various forms of female labour was none the less a gift to the women writers who succeeded her.

2

Somebody's story: Charlotte Smith and the work of writing

> Nothing saddens the heart so much as that sort of literary labour which depends on the imagination, when it is undertaken unwillingly, and from a sense of compulsion. The galley-slave may sing when he is unchained, but it would be uncommon equanimity which could induce him to do so when he is actually bound to his oar. If there is a mental drudgery which lowers the spirits and lacerates the nerves, like the toil of the slave, it is that which is exacted by literary composition when the heart is not in unison with the work upon which the head is employed. Add to the unhappy author's task, sickness, sorrow, or the pressure of unfavourable circumstances, and the labour of the bondsman becomes light in comparison.
>
> Sir Walter Scott, 'Charlotte Smith', in *The Lives of the Novelists* (1821)[1]

> [E]very Man has a *property* in his own *person*. This no body has any Right to but himself. The *labour* of his Body, and the *work* of his Hands, we may say are properly his. Whatsoever then he removes out of the State that Nature hath provided, and left it in, he hath mixed his *labour* with, and joyned to it something that is his own, and thereby makes it his *property*.
>
> John Locke, *Two Treatises of Government* (1690)[2]

Charlotte Smith, poet, novelist, playwright, writer of books for children and mother of nine, wrestled with questions surrounding the nature and cultural status of women's work more than any other woman writer of her generation. Manual, intellectual and domestic labour are central preoccupations of the poetry and novels, as they are of Smith's correspondence. Throughout her career, the subject of work lay at the heart of Smith's liberal gender and social politics, while the discourse and vocabulary of labour formed the cornerstone of her provocative interventions into contemporary debates on the politics of authorship itself. Financially dependent upon her literary career, as she repeatedly reminded her readers, Smith unequivocally presented writing as work in her letters, novels and their paratexts, and often of such a menial and debased kind that many judged her views on authorship to be distasteful, unladylike and unprofessional. The privileging of labour in Smith's works and authorial self-presentation has cast a long shadow. Indeed, it is difficult to think of another writer whose reputation has been more wholly and more detrimentally determined by readers' understanding of the (non-)relation of work to writing than that of Charlotte Smith. The critical narrative that has traditionally been related about the author's career, and epitomized by Sir Walter Scott's famous account, closely resembles the sentimental labour plots described in this book's introduction: of a genteel woman who falls into (literary) labour through no fault of her own and, by making a virtue of necessity, faces the prospect of an irrevocable loss of status. Smith's works played an important part in fabricating this story and also, this chapter argues, in undermining it; for woven into these texts are intriguing counternarratives that present various forms of work as a source of self-realization and pride, and that expose the stable domestic life, which the author claimed to crave as an alternative to living by her pen, as a source of intellectual and psychic impoverishment. For all these reasons, an exploration of the publications and reception of this most troubled of female authors offers perhaps the fullest account of the tangled web of contradictions and possibilities conjured for the professional woman writer by the question of women's work.

The scholarly recuperation of Charlotte Smith has gathered significant momentum in the years following the publication of Stuart Curran's pioneering work on Smith's poetry, which first asserted the writer's status as arguably the first, and undoubtedly one of the most important, of the Romantic poets.[3] Meanwhile, Smith's reputation as an innovative and influential Romantic novelist is slowly but emphatically being established in a series of articles and essays that will no doubt multiply in the coming years as a result of the recent publication of the complete works.[4] Historically, however, readers have been unwilling to acknowledge Smith's novels in the same breath as her poetry, unless to insinuate the former's inferiority to the latter. In her review of *Emmeline* (1788) for the *Analytical Review*, for example, Mary Wollstonecraft noted that, while Smith's debut work of fiction possessed some characteristics that 'distinguish[ed]' it from the 'numerous productions termed novels', it none the less had the 'same tendency as the generality, whose preposterous sentiments our young females imbibe with such avidity'.

Only in the descriptions of 'romantic views' and in those 'sonnets' in which 'the poetical talents of the author appear[ed]', did Wollstonecraft find those 'touches of nature in the delineation of the passions' of which she could approve.[5]

Between the 1760s, when Sarah Scott's career was at its height, and the 1780s, when Smith's first collection of poetry and first novel were published, conceptions of authorship underwent subtle yet significant changes, epitomized in law by the debates over intellectual property, in which the case of Donaldson *v.* Becket (1774) marks an important turning point, and in discourse by the publication of Adam Smith's *The Wealth of Nations* (1776), which famously cast authorship as unproductive labour, but which paradoxically provided a vocabulary for theorizing writing as work. During this period, as we shall see, literary commentators demonstrated an increasing willingness to perceive writing as labour, coupled with a more sure-footed insistence that writing had to be viewed as such if its cultural value was to be recognized. As Wollstonecraft's review of *Emmeline* indicates, however, this emergent model of authorship was hierarchically organized by genre, by gender and by economic considerations, none of which worked in Smith's favour. Thus, to simplify the rather more complicated set of arguments traced below and in the following chapters, novel writing was increasingly viewed as a degradingly femininized, financially expedient and inferior mode of textual work, while poetry was supposed to be the offspring of disinterested genius and thus a higher art form. The effects of this emergent (gendered) division of literary labour were keenly felt by Smith, and their influence upon the literary scholarship devoted to her works is hard to overestimate. According to many of her readers from the eighteenth century to the present, Smith channelled her most valuable creative energies into the properly intellectual work of poetry; her novel writing, on the other hand, was merely a rather laborious, if unchallenging, means to feed her children. Sir Walter Scott's description of the writer as a 'galley-slave' – a description of which the ever-strategic, canny self-marketer Smith would have approved – driven by financial necessity to produce work in which 'heart' and 'head' were fatally divided has loomed large over Smith's career; so too has her relentless parading of her private woes in print, a strategy that has often been read as a sign of gendered and authorial impropriety. In the words of Edward Copeland, 'Contemporaries knew to expect nothing but gloom from Charlotte Smith, who made no attempt to hide the autobiographical nature of her work, turning her life into public property through a string of deeply personal novels.'[6] Failing both to take the cultural work of domestic propriety and her novelistic labour seriously, Smith emerges in such accounts as a writer who found the work of penning fiction too much to bear. Copeland speaks for many of Smith's contemporaries and modern-day readers when he argues that 'Plots for her novels often seem little more than a laborious necessity . . . . Characters tire her as well.'[7]

Smith, of course, professed to share her audience's presumed disdain for her fiction. As she famously wrote to Joseph Cooper Walker in October 1793, she 'love[d] Novels "no more than a Grocer [did] figs"'.[8] The words may be borrowed from Henry Fielding, but the sentiment has come to seem uniquely Smith's own; and, indeed, her fiction often echoes the letter to Walker in its elevation of poetry and pejorative depictions of novel writing as a form of drudgery that exhausts mind and body, and leaves the author subject to the underhand dealings of booksellers and the self-serving, ungentlemanly jibes of reviewers. There are several reasons to view such pronouncements of distaste with suspicion, however, not least the recognition that Smith was an astute manipulator of literary and cultural conventions, who presented her life and views in print in far from transparent ways. As several scholars have observed, to appreciate Smith's skills as a writer it is necessary to read her sceptically, against rather than on the terms she herself offers in her texts and their paratexts. Jacqueline Labbe's work on Smith's poetry is particularly convincing in its claims that we need to recognize the centrality of performance to Smith's poetics of literary self-display. In this light, Smith's posturing as the needy woman of the prefaces to *Elegiac Sonnets* (1784), the educated author of the footnotes to *Beachy Head* (1807) or the multiple, cross-gendered subjectivities explored in *The Emigrants* (1792–93) emerges as an elaborate authorial masquerade, the effect of which, Labbe claims, is to question, rather than to consolidate, prevailing conceptions of 'the nature of the gendered self' and of gendered authorship.[9] Similar performative gestures have been detected in Smith's correspondence. Sarah Zimmerman, for example, has argued that Smith's letters betray a resolute determination to 'confuse conventional distinctions between autobiography and fiction' in order to win over correspondents who might have helped her financially and legally.[10] Like the poems, Smith's letters were, in part at least, a means to the end of securing financial stability. The creation of 'Mrs Charlotte Smith', the genteel but impoverished wife of a feckless man, forced to write to support the children to whom she was devoted, was vital to the success of this project.

Curiously, such insights have failed to have an impact on studies of the novels, which have often taken Smith's prefatorial assertions of authorial embarrassment and indignation at their word.[11] That labour – one of the signatures of Smith's writing – has been read not as the enabling thematic I will argue it to be here but as a trope that signalled Smith's scorn for trafficking in print for money arises from a reluctance to read her treatment of work, unlike other aspects of her writing, as strategic. It stems also from a failure to read the novels in the context of wider debates about the economics of authorship in the eighteenth century's final decades, debates in which Smith actively participated. Ironically, it seems that the very persistence with which Smith identified writing as work has allowed readers to discount her contribution to the contemporary thinking about authorship as intellectual labour. The more Smith emphasized the incessant toil involved in establishing and maintaining a literary career, the easier it became to dismiss her as a reluctant literary practitioner – a mere '*Author by profession*' – rather than the ambitious literary theorist she undoubtedly was.[12] By contrast, I argue here for the rewards of reading Smith's novels and their complex representation of work as Labbe reads the poetry, against the grain of Smith's own posturing and outside the terms of the artificially organized division of literary labour that Smith's fiction challenged.

This chapter examines Smith's treatment of labour, primarily in the fiction, in order to tease out its implications for the novels' arguments about gender, domesticity and authorship.[13] I begin with an examination of Smith's figuring of manual, affective and intellectual labour in *Marchmont* (1796), arguably her fullest contribution to contemporary debates on woman's work, to reveal how the novel retriangulates its author's rhetoric about the relation between women's work, domesticity and abjection, thus paving the way for a reassessment of Smith's (Lockean) self-conceptualization of her authorial labour as a form of inalienable property. Smith's figuring of writing as work was not simply a strategy to gain her readers' sympathy; rather, I contend, it was an attempt to break down the barriers that prevented women writers from laying claim to the new models of literary professionalism that were being cemented in this period. Only when we, like Smith, grapple with the complex question that is women's work can we recuperate her distinctive and ambitious construction of professional authorship as an embodied activity that was simultaneously a labour of mind, body and heart – and, unequivocally, women's work.[14]

'[W]hich was her work': reading labour in *Marchmont*

In the eight-year period between the publication of *Emmeline* and *Marchmont*, the topic of work became ever more central to Smith's fiction. In her first novel, women's work almost exclusively takes the reassuringly domestic and benign form of philanthropy (itself ambiguous as work), although the threat of having to seek a maintenance through paid labour hovers menacingly over the genteel, but debt-ridden, Mrs Stafford for much of the text. While Smith's subsequent novels would remain preoccupied with the cultural work of domestic femininity, they would increasingly urge readers to understand this work (usually unfavourably) in relation to other forms of labour, such as the manual work of the rural and urban labouring classes – in *Desmond* (1792) and *The Wanderings of Warwick* (1794), for example – and the intellectual labour of the professional author – most memorably portrayed in *The Banished Man* (1794). Of all Smith's early novels, however, it is *The Old Manor House* (1793) that is most overtly preoccupied with the question of work. Something of a rarity even among the working fictions this book focuses upon, *The Old Manor House* features a heroine who is born, rather than falls, into labour. Despite the fact that rumour has it that the orphaned Monimia's parents were what 'many would call genteel', the novel strikingly refuses to validate these claims.[15] Equally striking is the persistence with which the novel's opening chapters present Monimia – unlike her spiritual mother, Pamela Andrews – at work as the seamstress and servant to the belligerent matriarch, Mrs Rayland. Yet, the overall effect of *The Old Manor House* is to occlude the labour the heroine is apparently born to perform. The novel's chivalrous and typically disappointing hero, Orlando, from whose perspective the narrative is ostensibly written, repeatedly seeks to recast the working girl as a wronged romance heroine, whose character and demeanour he believes to be superior to her rank, and whose deliverance from labour he intends to secure.

In his Pygmalion-like efforts to mould Monimia as his future wife, Orlando manages the orphan's education scrupulously, 'direct[ing]' her in her reading in a bid to 'render her mind as lovely as her form' (p. 23). Kathryn R. King has read the heroine's initiation by Orlando into the world of words as a critique of the drudgery of domestic service and a celebration of the life of the mind, arguing that the young woman's will to achieve 'mastery over language and entry into culture', even before her lover takes her instruction upon himself, implies a quiet but determined opposition to manual, waged labour.[16] Yet King's reading of Monimia's attempt to exchange the needle for the pen that might write her out of labour and dependence overstates the heroine's resistance to her work at Rayland Hall. One of the most unusual, and most radical, aspects of the treatment of work in *The Old Manor House* is the fact that Monimia, unlike the community's gossipmongers, never questions her status as a labouring woman. Significantly, the discomfort she experiences during her period of service arises not from an objection to the nature of the work itself, nor from the fact that she has to work; rather, she objects to the conditions in which that work is undertaken, before the prying eyes of her abusive mistress and her aunt, Mrs Rayland's housekeeper-companion. Thus, and in an unusual turn of logic, the novel is able to suggest that Monimia is much less of a dependant than her socially superior lover, Orlando, because she is born to, and eminently capable of, work. As Monimia protests when the hero determines to 'appeal against the tyranny' of her mistress: 'I can work in the fields, or can go through any hardship; but Mrs Rayland will be very angry with you, and will not suffer you to come to the Hall again, and I shall – never – never see you any more!' (p. 16).[17] Any genteel disdain for labour expressed in *The Old Manor House* is Orlando's rather than Monimia's. Although being forced to seek 'work in the fields', a declining and increasingly precarious industry for women by the 1790s, would represent a loss of relative status and greater physical and financial 'hardship' for Monimia, she does not lament the prospect of taking such a course, merely that Orlando's rank makes it unthinkable that he might escape the dependence that fetters his own existence and support himself, and his future wife, by his own labour.[18]

Although Monimia's work is foregrounded in the opening chapters of *The Old Manor House*, raising questions about the treatment of female labourers and their exploitation in the service of misplaced political ideologies – in this case, the nostalgic feudalism symbolized by Rayland Hall – the overall effect of the novel is to displace the subject of work and the questions its presence initially provokes. The heroine's later experiences of labour as a milliner and governess are related briefly and retrospectively after Orlando's return from the American Revolution. When Monimia once again is forced to seek out paid employment, this time after becoming Orlando's wife, she is compelled to do so without her husband's knowledge or consent, for fear of 'shocking his tenderness and pride' (p. 424). From the beginning of the novel to its conclusion, when Orlando finally inherits Rayland Hall and Monimia is rescued from labour once and for all, the romantic hero refuses to admit the fact of women's work: he 'sees' Monimia 'always busy' yet makes 'no remarks upon what occupies her' (p. 424). Yet, in these instances of wilful blindness, Smith's true labour plot comes into focus. As Scott's novels had before it, *The Old Manor House* pointedly demonstrates the failure of literary forms to accommodate the reality, and to acknowledge the legitimacy, of women's work. Smith's novel reveals that there is simply no place for women's work in the world of the romance, which, as Mary Anne Schofield has argued, disguises the 'awfulness of life' beneath the mask of fictional form.[19] The romance plot into which Orlando attempts to write himself as a young knight, fighting for his inheritance and the woman he loves, cannot admit the rather unromantic truth that Monimia is born to work, unafraid of it and much better able to provide a 'subsistence' for herself and her loved ones than the man she marries (p. 424).[20]

Marchmont, although less explicitly concerned with labour than *The Old Manor House*, returns to, and elaborates further, the implications of the opposition between the world of romance and the world of work in two plots that offer competing accounts of labour and its transformative potential. Smith's ninth novel, as Kate Davies and Harriet Guest have recently suggested, 'marks an important turning point' in her fiction. Articulating a loss of faith in the revolutionary idealism articulated in *Desmond*, and an abandonment of all hopes of achieving the 'enlightened cosmopolitanism' imagined in *The Banished Man*, *Marchmont* moves 'away from the possibilities of political reform and towards local and limited forms of social improvement' through individual acts of benevolence.[21] The story of Althea Dacres, a woman whose political consciousness develops only to have her sphere of influence contract, dramatizes this scaling down of ambition on the level of plot, and mourns its necessity. The novel's resistance to the political logic that structures the narrative becomes apparent in its final paragraph, in which the heroine and eponymous hero are finally united in marriage after having endured a series of psychological, economic and legal trials that would threaten to overwhelm even the most resilient of Smith's characters:

> The virtues that Althea so early possessed, and which adversity had served to improve and strengthen, were far from failing under the influence of prosperity; and the happiness of her husband, and of his family, *which was her work* (for without her they must have been lost); the blessings she diffused around her, as well by her example to the rich, as by her benevolence to the poor, were her earthly reward. – Marchmont indeed

> sometimes trembled as he considered his felicity; and believing it too great to fall to the share of any human being, he, with awe and gratitude, endeavoured to deserve its continuance. [emphasis added][22]

Marchmont's conclusion, facilitated by the improbably serendipitous appearance of the novel's *deus ex machina*, Mr Desborough, is doubly conventional: it fulfils the expectations of the romance plot by restoring estates and inheritances to their rightful heirs, and seems to endorse prevailing constructions of gender by positioning its heroine within the domestic household as a benevolent matriarch and putative mother, 'which was her work', should we be in any doubt about the matter. Yet *Marchmont* is neither so neatly, nor so completely, bound by the structure of the romance plot as it may appear to be. Rather, like the closing lines of 'The History of Leonora and Louisa' in Scott's *A Journey through Every Stage of Life* (1754), *Marchmont*'s conclusion is a site of tension rather than of resolution. As Angela Keane has observed, the formulaic nature of the endings of Smith's novels is commonly belied by the complexity of the plots that precede them. The romance imperative that structures her works is persistently undermined, Keane demonstrates, by those characters, including *Desmond*'s Josephine de Boisbelle and the injured soldier of *The Old Manor House*, who must fall in order that the hero and heroine can triumph.[23] *Marchmont* similarly has its casualties, most notably the former servant, Phoebe Prior, who endures similar hardships to those faced by her heroine-double, Althea, but who loses her husband, her mind and her life by the end of the novel. Phoebe Prior, like Josephine and the maimed soldier, vividly demonstrates the unjust and disquietingly violent economy of romance.

If the concluding paragraph of *Marchmont* registers an opposition between novelistic convention and Smith's commitment to those individuals marginalized by rank or gender, then it also underscores another site of tension within the novel and, indeed, in Smith's fiction more widely: the vexed question that is the nature of women's work. Read in isolation from the rest of the novel, the model posited in its conclusion might seem anything but vexed. This is, after all, women's work of the most familiar kind, the 'labour that is not labour', to borrow to Nancy Armstrong's phrase, which was supposed to fill the days of the exemplary domestic woman.[24] Despite the apparent conservatism of its conclusion, however, the novel as a whole questions the reification of conduct-book domesticity as women's work. Volumes two and three of this four-volume novel, in particular, reveal the private consolations and public utility of a variety of female employments – including teaching, needlework and philanthropy – undertaken by a woman cast from her home and forced to live in a devastated community in which familial and social ties have been severed as a consequence of the failures of paternity and paternalism. That these employments will become secondary to the domestic work of the model wife and benefactress by the novel's closing lines is as disappointing to readers as it evidently is, I will argue, to Smith herself (p. 416). The lasting impression created by the final page of *Marchmont* is not of the heroine's good fortune and domestic 'happiness', but rather of the psychic cost paid by a woman forced to give up work and give in to romance.

Marchmont is structured around two converging stories of misplaced loyalty, dispossession and exile. The first focuses on Althea Dacres, who, at the age of only ten months, is abandoned by her recently bereaved father, Sir Audley, in order to facilitate a second marriage to a wealthy heiress. For much of her childhood, the heroine is raised by her maternal aunt, Mrs Trevyllian, but is reluctantly readmitted to the Dacres' family home at the age of sixteen, shortly before her guardian's death. There, and in a thinly veiled reference to Samuel Richardson's *Clarissa* (1747–48), Althea refuses to accept her father's demand that she marry a thoroughly objectionable lawyer, Mr Mohun, and is sent to Eastwoodleigh House, a run-down Devonshire estate newly acquired by Sir Audley and once belonging to the Jacobite Marchmonts. Now inhabited by the impoverished Mr and Mrs Wansford, a couple who once worked as servants to Althea's mother, this formerly grand estate has been reduced to a 'heap of ruins' (p. 64). Eastwoodleigh is, in the words of Davies and Guest, 'a site of historic desolation', which 'documents the Marchmonts' private wounds as well as their political consistency'.[25] Each room in the house and every square yard of land that surrounds it bears witness to the 'unfeeling rapacity of the creditors' of the once prosperous Marchmonts, the neglect of its absentee landlord, Sir Audley, and 'the excessive pride and misguided loyalty of its Royalist owners' (pp. 89–90). It is here that Althea reads the Marchmont family history, and, despite her opposition to the family's Tory politics, falls in love with the eponymous hero.

Both exiled from the familial home and both thwarted by the law, Althea and Marchmont are united by a common suffering that cuts across their political differences. However, a succession of financial problems prevents the couple's union. Althea has been defrauded of her mother's inheritance and, we later learn, of the Trevyllian estate, to which she is next in line. Marchmont, too, has been defrauded of his rightful legacy by the extravagance and complacency of his dissolute father, and spends much of the novel leading a peripatetic life in England and France, relentlessly hounded by the appropriately named Vampyre, and unsuccessfully trying to support his financially straitened mother and sisters. When Althea and Marchmont eventually marry, they are forced into debtors' prison and released only after the intervention of the 'reformer', Desborough (p. 414). Althea's fortune is restored to her and much of the Eastwoodleigh estate is reclaimed, but Marchmont declines to live in his ancestral home for fear that he too might yield to that 'fatal pride that had ruined his father' and so nearly his family (p. 416). Unlike Rayland Hall, which, as Davies and Guest argue, emerges in the final pages of *The Old Manor House* as a symbol of 'national restoration through private rapprochement', Eastwoodleigh 'serves only as an occasion for meditation, sentiment, or mourning'.[26] Overburdened by the weight of history and ravages of the time, the devastated landscape at Eastwoodleigh offers few of the consolations that nature provides elsewhere in Smith's novels and poetry. The grounds of this once prosperous estate have been laid waste by a greed that has deprived the Marchmont family and its tenants of its 'ancient woods, and even of the trees in the hedge-rows that were fit for sale' (p. 89). Althea's exile in this ravaged community fails to have the effect anticipated by Sir Audley, however. Far from reconciling her to a marriage that would serve only the mercenary interests of her father, the physical discomfort she experiences at Eastwoodleigh urges her to look to labour as a means both of supporting herself and of forging connections with other exiled and dispossessed persons, which prove more enduring and fulfilling than familial relationships.

It is at Eastwoodleigh, then, that the first of *Marchmont*'s two labour plots gathers momentum. The second, to which I will return, focuses upon the hero's unsuccessful efforts to secure paid work in England and France. Like Smith's Emmeline, Althea resolves not to sacrifice her 'integrity' by 'selling her person and her happiness for a subsistence';[27] like Rosalie, the heroine of *Montalbert* (1795), she would '"rather dedicate [her] whole life to the most humiliating poverty, . . . not only go into service, but submit to the most laborious offices, even to work in the fields, than condemn [her]self to become the wife"' of a man she does not love.[28] In common with the majority of Smith's heroines – Monimia being an exception to the rule – Althea avoids both 'service' and 'work in the fields' by making the most of her scant fortune. Indeed, even when she does undertake paid work in the haberdasher's shop she establishes with the Marchmont sisters in Margate, the novel is at pains to emphasize, as Scott's *The History of Cornelia* (1750) and *A Journey* had done, that her work is motivated as much by her affection for the Marchmont women as it is by financial necessity. None the less, Althea immerses herself in various forms of labour throughout the novel, from which she and those for whom she works derive pleasures and consolations that are placed in jeopardy as the heroine moves inexorably towards marriage and the fulfillment of the expectations of romance.[29]

At Eastwoodleigh, for example, Althea acts as an unpaid 'school-mistress' to the Wansfords' daughters (p. 82), and, despite her own financial distress, performs 'a thousand kind offices' in the local community, using any money she does not need for herself to 'clothe the half-naked infants of one poor cottager, relieve by a trifling weekly allowance the helpless superannuated father of another, pay a nurse for attending the wife of a third, and purchase flax or wool for the industrious family of a fourth'. She instructs the poor 'how to work' and even undertakes needlework herself for those families unable to provide for their own support (p. 115). The heroine's remaining energies are channelled into intellectual pursuits. In addition to devouring the Marchmont family history, she immerses herself in 'works of political philosophy' by Jean-Jacques Rousseau and Thomas Paine – 'not usually . . . part of the studies of young women' (p. 209), Smith comments archly. As in Scott's fiction, these various types of unpaid work – manual, affective and intellectual – are imagined to be complementary rather than antagonistic – as so much labour and conduct-book discourse declared them to be. When affective response and charitable acts prove insufficient to help those in distress – as they do for those families for whom the heroine offers to 'work herself' (p. 115) – Althea turns to her own labour as a substitute for sentiment and pecuniary generosity. Similarly, when manual work and charitable gifts prove incommensurate with the reality of rural poverty – when poverty is so acute that it is 'not in her power greatly to alleviate the distresses she witnesses' – the heroine responds with '(what the poor do not always find) compassion and attention' (p. 115).

Affect, in other words, exceeds the bounds of the heroine's labouring potential, just as labour can make up for the inadequacies of affective response to redress the wrongs identified by the woman of feeling. By the time that Althea goes to work with the Marchmont women in their shop, affect and labour have become almost indistinguishable. Like the spirited Lucy Marchmont, who rejects her aunt's warnings against going into business by retorting that '"we shall be happier if we have something to employ us" than if we were to exist in a "vegetative sort of life"' (p. 241), Althea looks forward to the prospect of 'respectable industry' (p. 246). Moreover, the realization that she will be able to draw on her 'by no means inconsiderable' 'skill as a milliner', and make use of her artistic talents to 'create for her unfortunate friends another branch of their little trade', causes her to reflect 'with pleasure'. The fact that Althea's pleasure derives from 'the power she possessed of assisting . . . Mrs Marchmont and her daughters', rather than from any pecuniary advantage she might hope to enjoy as a result of her industry, masks, of course, the heroine's financial distress and seems to transform manual work into an exercise in disinterested benevolence (p. 246). None the less, there is no attempt to deny, here, that the heroine will work, or to deny that the work she will undertake will be menial, repetitive and difficult. Indeed, as Smith assures the reader, the heroine's solitary upbringing has left her uniquely disposed to a life of hard work. Like Lucy, she enters the business aware of, but not in the least intimidated by, the 'confinement', 'constant occupation' and 'unpleasant circumstances' in which she knows she must labour (p. 246).

If the line between manual work and the work of philanthropy is blurred in *Marchmont* as it is in Scott's 1750s fiction, then so too is that between physical and intellectual toil. Unlike *The Old Manor House*, *Marchmont* does not present learning as a possible substitute for, or way out of, labour, but presents these endeavours as analogous: both forms of activity provide a comforting diversion from the realities of everyday life, and both tend towards the amelioration of the poverty, injustice and distress faced by others. In a return to the labour plots of the 1750s novels of Scott, Althea's efforts to feed and clothe the 'little humble circle' at Eastwoodleigh with her money and the labour of her own hands enable the heroine to 'look forward with cheerfulness to the few and simple duties that in such a situation, and with so small a fortune, she had to fulfil' (p. 114). If such work helps her to avoid sinking into 'the dejection which most young persons would have yielded to' (p. 116), then so too does her reading, which gives the heroine's thoughts a 'philosoph[ical]' turn that 'in the common intercourse of the world they would perhaps never have taken' (p. 210). The heroine's various labours alleviate the pain of solitude and the grief she experiences as a result of her banishment, at the same time that they make collective reparation for the devastation wrought by the Marchmont family's demise and the consequent failure of paternalism.

As Davies and Guest argue, *Marchmont* is a novel in which 'history is so internalized and privatized that the cruelties it exacts become obsessively intimate and abject'; as the dispossession of the Marchmont women makes clear, 'history makes its victims in the private sphere'.[30] But it is not only the Marchmont family that has suffered as a result of their ancestors' political allegiances; rather, it is the local poor who truly represent the extent of the 'evil[s] the ruin of such a house brings with it!' (p. 210). Althea's philanthropic acts, together with her work for the poor, her period of paid employment and her self-education in political philosophy manifest her desire to alleviate the pain that history inflicts upon its unwitting victims. Yet, it is important to recognize that it is not the desire to help that spurs the labour that seeks to alleviate this pain, but rather the labour that produces the desire for reparation. What begins as an almost involuntary compulsion on Althea's part to carry out 'the few and simple duties that in such a situation, and with so small a fortune, she had to fulfil', soon develops into a deep-seated commitment to the plight of the labouring poor as a direct result of the labours she undertakes at Eastwoodleigh. Her reading of works of political philosophy, for example, informs her interactions with the four 'half-naked, half-starved children' of a day-labourer who had '*gone for a soldier*', to whom she gives money, just as her acquaintance with their plight informs her reading, allowing her to discriminate between the competing arguments of political thinkers such as Paine and those other 'sage persons' who express an unfathomable 'desire to conquer other countries when there is so much waste in our own' (p. 209).

If Althea views her various labours as continuous with, and supplementing, one another, then Marchmont's efforts to find employment, by contrast, confirm his sense of the inviolability of the hierarchical distinctions between different modes of work and his own unfitness, as a gentleman, for labour. For the novel's hero, labour is primarily productive of mental degradation, a belief that is painfully reinforced by his efforts to follow 'the unhappy Chatterton' and become a professional writer (p. 177). Marchmont's intellectual aspirations all too quickly give way to a reluctant acceptance that authoring poems and novels is no longer an art but a business, governed by the self-interest of publishers and the all-too-predictable demands of readers. After yielding to the necessity of 'avail[ing himself] of literary patronage', Marchmont gradually learns to sacrifice his own opinion to the judgement and experience' of an adviser, who persuades him to rework a short poem into a longer and more substantial work. The task not only 'cost[s]'

Marchmont 'a good deal of labour' but also leaves him out of pocket when he finds himself liable for printing costs following the poem's publication (p. 178). For those writers who take their work seriously, Marchmont learns, literary labour is as likely to generate debt as profit. Thus the hero learns what his creator already knew: that, within the commercially driven and inequitable economy of textual production, novel writing makes more financial sense than writing poetry. Since novels do not excessively 'trouble' the minds of readers, they 'demand much less care in the composition' than poetical works' (p. 178). Unlike Smith, however, Marchmont is incapable of launching a successful career as a writer of fiction because he is paralysed by his belief that novel writing, in the sense of writing something truly innovative, has become an impossible task, the bowing shelves of the 'circulating libraries' proof that 'almost every possible event [is] already in print'. Too proud to 'borrow' from other writers' plots and incapable of inventing one of his own, Marchmont abandons his literary career before it has properly begun (p. 179).

The gendered division of labour *Marchmont* constructs in its account of Althea's and Marchmont's divergent experiences of work is reminiscent of that established in Frances Burney's *Cecilia* (1782), a novel that greatly influenced Smith.[31] Smith's hero appears to follow in the footsteps of Burney's linen-draper and would-be gentleman, Belfield, who, finding himself unable to salvage his deceased father's business, is forced to seek 'Labour with Independence', first as a farm worker and, subsequently, as a writer.[32] Althea, similarly, seems to mimic Burney's heroine as she turns to philanthropy to ameliorate the condition of the labouring poor, although it is important to note that Cecilia, even in her utmost desperation, is not forced to undertake paid employment. Moreover, as in the earlier novel, *Marchmont*'s labour plots serve to interrogate the cultural construction of domesticity as woman's work. As Judith Frank has persuasively argued, *Cecilia* is a 'meditation upon, and critique of, the creation of the domestic woman'.[33] In her analysis of Cecilia's interactions with the poor, Frank interrogates Armstrong's claim that the eighteenth-century domestic woman was constructed in opposition to 'an aristocratic model' of display and superfluity, to focus on the leisured woman's construction in relation to the poor.[34] Understood in terms of this latter relation, Cecilia's charitable activity emerges as a manifestation of an overwhelming 'grief' prompted by her awareness of the changes in the division of labour that were making the labouring class's position increasingly untenable. At a time when 'actual labour' was increasingly 'stigmatized for middle-class as well as already leisured women', Frank suggests, it became the genteel woman's 'job' 'to absorb the poor's plight' as a form of melancholic affect that was imagined to be the domestic woman's equivalent of labour, but naturalized, through the discourse of philanthropy, as a form of leisure.[35] The domestic woman could not have been asked 'to manage a more difficult and damaging range of social contradictions', as Frank remarks, an argument which Burney's novel pointedly makes in its vivid portrayal of Cecilia's mental disintegration.[36]

Marchmont revisits *Cecilia*'s concerns with the contradictions surrounding notions of affect, leisure and labour for gentlemen and women in the later eighteenth century, but reworks, partially through regendering, its labour plots, in order to exert further pressure upon the domestic ideal. Indeed, *Marchmont*'s contribution to the debate on women's work can best be understood in terms of its dialogic relationship to Burney's novel. Smith's heroine takes on the characteristics of both Cecilia *and* Belfield, sharing Burney's heroine's acute sense of indebtedness to the poor and the dispossessed, and, through her paid work, pursuing 'Labour with Independence'. And yet, Althea resembles neither character wholly: she imagines labour not as 'total seclusion from the world', as Belfield does, but, rather as Scott's heroines had done, as a social and collaborative enterprise; her encounters with the poor do not push her, as they had pushed Cecilia, to the edge of sanity, but arouse her political consciousness.[37] It is, in fact, Marchmont, not Smith's characteristically pragmatic heroine, who is immobilized by affect and a sense of alienation of which his thwarted labours are both cause and symptom. In this way, Smith rewrites Cecilia's story as Marchmont's, a strategy that serves to denature affect and the domestic ideal with which it is synonymous to render both objects of critique. Marchmont's comically cross-gendered performance of the cultural work of domesticity diverts attention away from the damage the domestic ideal inflicts upon those who internalize its logic – a central preoccupation of Burney's novel, as Frank suggests – to the damage it inflicts upon society as a whole by unfitting its disciples for more meaningful and socially useful forms of work.

Marchmont experiences labour, as Charlotte Lennox's Henrietta and Sarah Fielding's Camilla had before him, as a fall. Smith's innovation in her reworking and regendering of the fall-into-labour plot device lies in her implicit condemnation of the complacency that the experience of private misfortune produces in those individuals who, like Marchmont, but unlike Althea (and Smith herself), are unable to transform their private grief into political consciousness. That Smith intends Marchmont's experience of labour to be viewed in the spirit of satire rather than pathos is made clear when the hero journeys to the Continent. Marchmont's account of his travels through the war-torn landscape of Revolutionary France recalls Althea's experience of exile at Eastwoodleigh – another landscape that bears the indelible imprint of political bad faith. Recollecting one of Laurence Sterne's letters, in which the writer 'talk[ed] of a house he inhabited on the banks on the Sorgue', the hero imagines that he might be standing in the very same spot as the erstwhile traveller. The scene before Marchmont is entirely different, however: 'Alas! how changed, since this animated pen described it, are all but the local charms of this country' (p. 300). As it does for Althea, exile from polite society forces Marchmont to confront the realities of rural life and labour, and yet the hero's response to these uncomfortable truths could scarcely be more different from that of his future wife. Rather than provide common ground between the hero and the poor, Marchmont's work makes sympathetic identification with the rural labourers he encounters impossible. The heightened sense of melancholy and dislocation he experiences as a result of his fall into labour is thrown into stark relief by the blissful emotional and intellectual numbness of the labourers he encounters while travelling through France.

When, for example, the hero encounters a vine grower, who, in a reversal of charitable logic, supplies the hero with food, he finds occasion to envy the man's humble existence:

> He, said I, meditates nothing about Revolutions – he hardly understands the term. Under the old government he worked hard; – the new one has made to him (fortunate man!) no sensible change: he still works hard for the daily bread he eats. . . . Is it good then to be such a being? When I reflect on the vice, the folly of cultivated, of polished life, I am ready to answer, that it is; but Rosalind's remark recurs to me. – 'It were then good to be a post!' – I hesitate, and consider whether a human being, no more enlightened, rises as many degrees as he ought to do in the scale of intelligent creatures designed to be
>
> '– only lower than the angels;'
>
> and finally, whether I would exchange my sensibility, (I hate the word, it is so prostituted) . . . for the calm stupor of ignorance, for the stagnating content of an animal who in the human form is, in intellectual rank, hardly superior to the cattle he drives a-field. (p. 295)

The vine grower, like so many of the rural labourers the hero encounters, is curiously detached from the political conflict that is destroying the very landscape of his homeland, not only because of his geographical distance from France's capital but also because of the 'mental mutilation', as Adam Smith had famously described it in Book V of *The Wealth of Nations*, he has experienced as a result of his participation in the division of labour.[38] Marchmont's account of the labourer's intellectual degradation does not, however, lead him to question contemporary working practices, or, as Adam Smith had done, to consider how their effects might be mitigated by social or educational reform. The 'mutilation' endured by the manual labourer is instead considered to be a blessing, since it blunts his mental faculties and thus blinds him to the degradation that repetitive, mechanical work produces. By contrast, for the man of feeling, Marchmont insists, labour is a debilitating curse since it yields a surfeit of affect that manifests itself only in solipsistic grief and debilitating shame.

Marchmont's dehumanization of the workers he encounters might seem to endorse Sandra Sherman's recent claim that late eighteenth-century fiction was characterized by a failure to imagine 'the poor's gritty reality' and 'complex subjectivity', were it not for Althea's passionate, yet pragmatic, response to the deprivation and exploitation she observes at Eastwoodleigh.[39] *Marchmont*'s heroine, unlike her future husband, steadfastly refuses to sentimentalize or to gloss poverty and labour. Echoing Mary Wollstonecraft's condemnation of the 'Arcadia of fiction' in *A Vindication of the Rights of Men* (1790) – a passage to which I will return in Chapter 3 – Althea criticizes those who 'have been strangely mislead by romantic description' to believe 'that at a distance from London there reigns Arcadian simplicity, and that envy detraction and malice, only inhabit great cities' (p. 93). Unlike Marchmont's idealized, anaesthetized workers, the labourers she supports and works for are all too acutely aware of their predicament. Rural life, Althea insists, is brutal and brutalizing, producing degrees of 'hatred' and 'calumny' among the poor for which even their 'abject poverty is no defence' (p. 93). Despite her unflinching views on the labouring poor's degradation, however, Althea puts forward powerful arguments for workers' rights, which recall, even if they do not precisely ventriloquize, the radical sentiments of earlier novels such as *Desmond*. In the post-revolutionary Europe of *Marchmont*, 'ideas of equality' might be 'visionary', but the rights of man, his entitlements to 'the necessaries of life', no matter how lowly his station, remain incontrovertible, the heroine believes (p. 210).[40] Her work, at least until the novel's final volume, is to do all that she can to ensure that these needs are met. Through her reading of history and political economy, her charity and her work for the poor, Althea is able to respond to the reality of poverty in a manner to which Marchmont is utterly unequal.

The novel's critique of Marchmont's need to create comforting fictions about labour and poverty to alleviate his guilt over his family's failure to fulfil its paternalist responsibilities at Eastwoodleigh is reinforced when the novel's two labour plots converge, and the hero and heroine are united. Following their marriage, Althea abandons her former labours and devotes herself solely to her duties as a wife. Yet at precisely the moment that she gives up her labour, Althea is forced to stand in for the labouring-class worker, whose sensibility the hero cannot acknowledge for fear that the grief this recognition would produce would consume him entirely. The work of domesticity, Althea learns, is the work of self-denial. Despite the fact that she, like all women, possesses 'more fortitude than men', Althea will find that emotional restraint is hard work that 'cost[s] her some effort', much more, it seems, than any of her former employments. During their period in the King's Bench Prison, surrounded by the '[d]irt and famine' (p. 384) that Smith had herself witnessed during her own time there in 1783, the heroine is forced to 'tranquillize her spirits', so that Marchmont is not 'oppressed with a degree of despondence, which he would never have felt had he had only his own troubles to contend with' (p. 361).[41]

This double manoeuvre, whereby the heroine learns to manage her passions while the hero gives in to the consolations and distractions of a heightened and excessive sensibility, rehearses a familiar pattern in Smith's writing, and one which Diane Long Hoeveler has explored in relation to *Emmeline*. Hoeveler reads *Emmeline* as emblematic of a wider, covert assault by women writers upon 'the new bourgeois order' that emerged in the later eighteenth century. *Emmeline* is characteristic of this critique, Hoeveler contends, both in its championing of a new breed of 'sentimentally feminized' man of feeling (Godolphin) and in its 'masculinization' of the eponymous heroine, who develops reason and suppresses her passions under the guise of feminine passivity. Emmeline's self-victimization is hailed, in these terms, as a cause for feminist celebration on the grounds that her performance enables her to negotiate the patriarchal world successfully without transgressing the bounds of propriety.[42] Hoeveler's account of *Emmeline*, while compelling, overstates the opportunities such 'self-victimization' affords Smith's heroine. Indeed, the tragic costs of such exercises in self-mastery are writ large across Smith's fiction, particularly in *The Old*

Manor House. In one of the most disturbing scenes in this novel, the young Monimia expresses self-control through the violent mutilation of her own body. No sooner has the young woman come to acknowledge her feelings for Orlando than she is forced to understand that, as a servant, she cannot articulate these desires. Facing the prospect of being forced to witness an impending confrontation between Orlando and Mrs Rayland, Monimia finds herself 'quite unequal to the misery of being present at an interview'. Fearful that she might unwittingly betray emotions that would reveal to Mrs Rayland her relationship with the hero, the servant intentionally trips over a roll of linen and 'falls with violence against an old heavy gilt leather screen . . . [running] the sharp-pointed scissors, with which she was cutting the linen, into her arm a little above the wrist' (p. 59). Monimia's actions, which prefigure similar scenes of self-mutilation in Wollstonecraft's fiction, reveal the psychic damage that she has suffered both as a labouring woman, mentally and physically abused by her mistress and aunt, and as Orlando's love-object and project, cruelly awakened to feelings that, because of her status, she is unable to express. Although less obviously violent, Althea's efforts to suppress her emotions and 'shew that [the] presence of mind, that reasonable fortitude, and [that] truly feminine courage' that Marchmont so admires, carry a similarly hefty price: the heroine's self-effacement (p. 357). Domesticity, Smith thus insists, *is* work for women, not simply because it represents the genteel woman's equivalent of labour but because it demands that women work constantly, and in spite of themselves, to suppress those passions, emotions and aspirations, which in other situations (and in other novels) they might have channelled into more personally, politically and economically meaningful forms of activity.

Here, at the point at which the argument of *Marchmont*'s labour plot comes into sharp focus, Smith's novel takes a final, and intriguing, turn. The reader whose eyes stray beyond the final lines of *Marchmont* proper will find in the original 1796 edition of the novel Smith's advertisement for a new, and overdue, edition of *Elegiac Sonnets*. The text informs subscribers that Smith's

> domestic Misfortunes, and personal ill Health, together with Difficulties that arose in procuring a Likeness, have unavoidably delayed the Publication of the Work greatly beyond the Time it was intended to appear; but it is now in such Forwardness, and the Ornamental Parts are in such Hands, that she hopes in a very short Time to fulfil her Engagements with the Public.[43]

With these words, the novel goes full circle, forcing the reader to recall *Marchmont*'s heart-breaking preface in which Smith familiarly presents herself as a long-suffering mother, who turned author 'from necessity' rather than 'choice' in order to support her unjustly defrauded children. Here, Smith reminds her readers that, for the past twelve years, she has been 'labouring under the heaviest (and now the most irremediable) oppression that was perhaps ever practised or suffered in a country boasting of its laws'. Entirely dependent upon her 'labour' for her subsistence, she has been forced to spend day after day in the 'unremitting' drudgery of producing some thirty-two volumes in just eight years (p. 3). The only recompense for her incessant 'toil', Smith claims, was to be found in her children, particularly in her beloved daughter Anna Augusta ('that lovely Being'), whose premature death following the complications of childbirth produced a degree of 'anguish' in her mother 'as only they who have felt it can imagine'. The death of Anna Augusta – 'who alone had power to sooth [*sic*] my wearied spirit' – denied Smith not only the companionship of a much-cherished daughter but also the consolations of motherhood that drove and justified her literary labours (p. 3). Smith was bereft, and able to finish *Marchmont*, she recollected, only because she had already 'received money from my present publisher, who would have been injured if I had not forced myself to fullfil my engagement' (p. 4). Smith's publishers and readers expected her to work through a period of grief that would have paralysed even the most determined and professional of authors, but she would not allow herself to become another Althea. Smith refused to be the emotionally numb automaton others demanded that she be, using her novels as a means of working through, in the double sense of occupying herself as a diversion from and of coming to terms with, her grief by offering the novel as a memorial to her deceased daughter. As a professional, Smith would complete her work, but only by making the physical and emotional cost of that work clear.[44]

These book ended authorial intrusions do more than simply remind the reader of the 'hard fagging', to borrow Burney's term, involved in producing texts. More importantly, they put the notion of woman's 'work' as described in *Marchmont*'s concluding paragraph under stress by reminding us that Althea's domestic labours are not simply unsatisfactory; they are, in fact, a fiction, made possible by the very real and sometimes painful, sometimes comforting, labour of her author. The true casualty of *Marchmont*'s plot is not, then, Phoebe Prior, but Smith herself, who paid a hefty price for the intellectual, manual and affective work she invested in writing fiction in which her heroines earn the right to enjoy the financial stability and leisure to which Smith aspired in life, but of which her novels were deeply sceptical. The novel's advertisement exposes the very real work that underwrites the domestic ideal.

'[T]o live only to write & write only to live'[45]

Marchmont's preface and the advertisement that appears on the final leaf of the first edition are just two of many examples in the novels, poems and letters where Smith positions herself explicitly in relation to both the domestic realm and the professional, literary public sphere. Throughout her career, Smith notoriously argued that her domestic labours as a mother and her professional activities as a writer were inescapably linked.[46] This is not to say that the relationship between domesticity and professionalism (between women's cultural work and their paid labour) is ever clear-cut in Smith's writing. If 'domestic misfortunes' provided the rationale for her career as a writer, then they also compromised that career by preventing her from achieving her true potential, and by threatening (as in the case of Anna Augusta's death) to render her utterly incapable of picking up her pen again. And yet, as the preface to *Desmond* makes clear, Smith's personal situation was much more than a justification for her decision to become a writer; on the contrary, she argued that her experience of hardship made that career choice politically, as well as financially, necessary. The circumstances that led to her 'involuntary appearance' in the 'character' of author – her disastrous marriage to Benjamin Smith, the couple's debt and her legal battles over her father-in-law's estate – forced Smith to confront inequities so antithetical to the 'cause of truth, reason, and humanity' that she was obliged to expose them before the reading public (pp. 4–5). Through such exposure – what she referred to in the preface to *Desmond* as the 'slight skirmishing of a novel writer' – 'learning and genius' would 'finally triumph', as they '*must*', over the 'phalanx of prejudice' (p. 5).

Smith anticipated that many of her readers would doubt her capabilities, as a woman, to rise to the ambitious authorial task she had set herself, but none the less asserted that her sex made it more, rather than less, incumbent upon her to embark upon this project. Although society held that the '[k]nowledge, which qualifies women to speak or to write on any other than the most common and trivial subjects . . . cannot be acquired but by the sacrifice of the domestic virtues, or the neglect of domestic duties', Smith argued forcefully 'that it was in the *observance*, not in the breach of duty, [that] *I* became an Author; and it has happened, that the circumstances which have compelled me to write, have introduced me to those scenes of life, and those varieties of character which I should otherwise never have seen' (pp. 3–4). Her insistence that a woman could be a mother by vocation and an '*Author by profession*', without compromising her proficiency in either role, set out not only to undermine an increasingly entrenched equivalence that was supposed to exist between femininity, domesticity and leisure – that, to quote the preface to the sixth edition of *Elegiac Sonnets*, 'The Post of Honour is a Private Station' – but also to challenge the new political economy of authorship that was emerging in the eighteenth century's latter decades.[47] Like Smith's treatment of labour, her mobilization of the gendered discourses of privacy and publicity gave the lie to the author's rhetoric, in that it set up an opposition between the domestic (the feminine, the private) and the professional (the masculine and the public) in order to insinuate the illegitimacy of a distinction that was beginning to have marked and unwelcome implications for women writers in the eighteenth century's final years.

The period between the 1760s and the mid-1780s, when Smith published *Elegiac Sonnets*, witnessed significant changes in the practice and conception of professional authorship, which were intimately related to wider shifts in the nation's economy. As Clifford Siskin has argued, the reorganization of the division of labour in the second half of the century 'toward a specialized professionalism that altered the occupational fates of women and men' of all classes produced complementary shifts in the 'organization of knowledge'. A new model of 'disciplinarity' began to emerge, which 'fostered narrow but deep subjects such as Literature', and recast the 'work of knowing' as an occupation in its own right.[48] Adam Smith's *The Wealth of Nations* played a vital, if complex and controversial, role in setting out the terms of this newly professionalized identity and in establishing the relation of intellectual to manual labour. On the one hand, *The Wealth of Nations*'s differentiation of unproductive from productive work (a particular flash point, as we shall see, in the debates over authorship prompted by the founding of the Literary Fund) seemed to question the legitimacy of authorship, on the grounds that intellectual labour, unlike its manual counterpart, was powerless to 'shape social and economic relations'.[49] On the other hand, as Siskin demonstrates, the distinction Smith's treatise drew between those who laboured and those 'few who could "examine" them and thus transform them into objects of knowledge' laid down the foundation for a new kind of literary authority. The modern author was a disinterested professional, whose privileged position within the division of labour was founded upon his ability to engage in intellectual work – the characteristics of which were drawn from the vocabulary of the division of labour (industriousness, rigour, specialization, and so on) – without being adversely implicated in the trucking and bartering practices to which commercial man was supposed to be naturally inclined. This new model of intellectual labour was prejudicial to women writers.[50] Excluded from Adam Smith's homosocial model of the division of labour, which, as I elaborate in Chapter 3, rendered all but invisible their paid and domestic labour, women were also excluded from the criteria of expertise, intellectual rigour and professionalism that came to define the modern author. If the literary was increasingly associated with the 'masculine' in the century's final decades, with those traditionally 'male' subjects such as economics and politics that were held to be superior to such inferior, ubiquitous and feminine productions as the novel, then the woman writer, so Siskin has argued, was the 'amateur' other against which the professional intellectual labourer was defined.[51]

A principal mechanism through which the (gendered) distinctions between the professional and the amateur, the disinterested intellectual labourer and the financially motivated drudge were maintained and policed was the critical review.[52] Laura Runge has recently identified three key 'pressure points' in the 'emerging discourse of literary professionalism' articulated in the contemporary reviews that had a marked effect upon the careers of women writers: the male critic's need to treat the female writer with due chivalry while maintaining a position of intellectual authority; an insistence that women were not equipped to deal with masculine subjects such as politics and economics; and, finally, a widely held conviction that women writers should confine their works to the subject of private life, as long as that private life was not their own.[53] All three of these 'pressure points' feature prominently in reviews of Smith's fiction. In the wake of her eloquent, yet vigorous, defence of women's right to engage in the 'business' of 'politics' in the preface to *Desmond*, for example, a number of critics pointed to Smith's unfitness as a political commentator (p. 3). Such was to be the essence of the *Anti-Jacobin Review*'s unsurprisingly hostile response to *The Young Philosopher* (1798), which decried the novel as 'unconstitutional'. With typically chivalric condescension, the reviewer commented that the author's political views in this, her bleakest, novel 'would be dangerous were they not so trite and frivolous', and added gallantly that he would be delighted to 'whisper in [the author's] ear that she ha[d] not any depth in political philosophy'.[54] Turning to matters closer to home also proved ineffective as a means of winning round Smith's detractors. As she acknowledged in the preface to the sixth edition of *Elegiac Sonnets*, hers was not an age 'when the complaints of individuals against private wrong [were] likely to be listened to'.[55]

Accusations of 'egotism', against which she tried to defend herself in the prefaces to *Desmond*, *Marchmont* and *Elegiac Sonnets*, would plague Smith throughout her career. *The Young Philosopher*, by no means the most obviously autobiographical of the novels, was further criticised by the *Anti-Jacobin* on the grounds that Smith 'so frequently introduced allusions to her own affairs' in her writing.[56] Damned when she forayed into politics, and condemned when she failed to venture beyond her own doorstep, Smith was caught in a familiar double bind. The criticisms she faced were not unknown to many female novelists in the last decades of the eighteenth century, and not only when reviewed by the conservative press. None the less, there is something particular and exceptional about early Smith criticism, a particularity which signals the exceptionality of the author's conceptualization of the work of writing. The terms in which Smith's most vehement critics derided her novels insinuate an opposition not simply to female authorship but to a model of authorship that was very much Charlotte Smith's own.

Smith's career-long endeavour to render visible the work of writing through her allusions to her domestic life – the properly feminine work that both occasioned and impeded her literary career – and her insistent imprinting of her authorial labour on to the pages of her novels' prefaces and footnotes and their semi-autobiographical plots, was crucially at odds with the notion of literary professionalism the reviews set out to promote. According to the *Critical Review*, Smith's novels fell far short of the standard of 'genius'. Its crushing eleven-page assault upon *The Old Manor House*, which appeared in May 1793, began with an extended meditation upon the status and function of the novel, intended to demonstrate how spectacularly the celebrated 'Mrs. Smith' failed to fulfil the genre's promise. The reviewer allowed that, of all literary productions, a 'well written novel' had a 'more legitimate claim to an ascendancy over the human mind' than any other, but cautioned that few possessed the 'happy combination of parts and acquirements' necessary to achieve this end. The 'creative powers of inventions' or the reflections of a distinctly feminine sounding 'tender and susceptible mind' might 'produce occasionally circumstances to interest and affect the heart', but the critic concluded that 'he who aspires to pre-eminence as a novelist' requires 'superior qualifications, both mental and acquired'.

The reviewer's gendering of the author as male, here, is far from unintentional. The only writers deemed to have 'arrived to that degree of fame which will entitle their labours to the admiration of posterity' are Cervantes, Le Sage, Rousseau and Voltaire. Read in the context of the great tradition of European writing, the essay continued, *The Old Manor House* was noticeable only because its plot contained so 'much' of which to 'disapprove'. The novel's length – some '*thirteen hundred pages*' (italics in original) – proved to be a particular bone of contention for a reviewer who had been obliged to 'read *all*' of the work, prompting him to ask if it 'can be wondered at if we *sometimes* yawn, and exclaim in the words of Hotspur, "Oh! it is as tedious as a tired horse or a scolding wife"'.[57] In a critical manoeuvre that is as typical as it is misogynist, the reviewer conflates the authorial and textual body in order to deny Smith authority as a woman and as a writer. Unable to labour efficiently either as a dutiful wife or as an author, Smith is grotesquely presented as an old nag, whose exhausted body can produce only tired plots and tedious characters. The review's recourse to the language of exhaustion in its critique of *The Old Manor House* has much the same effect as Sir Walter Scott's formulation of writing as work in his biography of Smith in *The Lives of the Novelists*, despite his evident admiration for his subject. Understanding the novels as the products of an inefficient slave economy, in which the labourer's productivity was impaired and her mind degraded by relentless toil, allowed Scott to recuperate Smith, the woman reluctantly fallen into labour, but not her novels, which seem too tired to be attributed with true literary merit.[58] For Sir Walter Scott, as for the reviewer for the *Critical*, Smith's novels were, quite simply, too laboured.

That Smith's critics (and some of her champions) seized upon the vocabulary of work to denigrate her novels is unsurprising; her persistent figuring of writing as 'unremitting labour' was a gift to reviewers (*Marchmont*, p. 3). Drawing on such tropes not only allowed the reviews to condemn her fiction, and the political insights it contained, as the work of a mere hack but also enabled them to chastise the novels while appearing gallantly sympathetic to Smith's claims that she was an 'involuntary' author who disliked the business of writing fiction as much as they disliked the fact that their business obliged them to read it. The deployment of the language of labour in Smith's early reviews is not merely opportunistic; neither does it reflect Smith's own views on literary labour. In rejecting the novels in these terms, Smith's early reviewers sought to reject the model of authorship she forwarded, a model which presented a radical challenge to the criteria of literary merit the reviews articulated and defended. Not only did Smith's argument that women had as much right as men to write about politics contest the 'gendered logic', which, as Paul Keen has argued, was mobilized to police the literary public sphere in the 1790s,[59] but her insistence that writing was labour, as physically demanding as that of 'the Danaids or of Sisyphus', unsettled longstanding constructions of the author as a disinterested professional, whose mental exertions were commonly troped in the language of work, toil, labour and industry, but whose activities were understood to be fundamentally different in kind from those of the manual labourer.[60]

The model of authorship Smith cultivated offered a pointed critique of the manual/intellectual labour dyad as it was commonly articulated in late eighteenth-century political economy, particularly in *The Wealth of Nations*. Here, Adam Smith argued that the work of writers, like that of 'churchmen, lawyers, physicians, . . . players, buffoons, musicians, opera-singers, opera-dancers', the king, his officers and even 'menial servants', was unproductive in the sense that the labour invested in such endeavours 'does not fix or realize itself in any permanent subject, or vendible commodity, which endures after that labour is past, and for which an equal quantity of labour could afterwards be procured'.[61] This was not to say that such work was devoid of value in Adam Smith's terms, although a number of the economist's critics suggested that this was the undeniable implication of his claims.[62] On the contrary, it was to argue that the value and authority of the man of letters was predicated upon his lack of productivity, his non-participation in the making of the nation's wealth. Only those who were possessed of the 'leisure and inclination' enjoyed by men who were 'attached to no particular occupation' could engage in the properly intellectual work of writing.[63] That the denial of authorship's status as productive labour and material practice evident in political economic theory and contemporary theorizations of literary genius persisted even as the discourse of authorship was increasingly characterized by the vocabulary of labour (mental labour, toil, exertion and endeavour) may seem paradoxical, but it was, perhaps, inevitable at a time when the literary public sphere sought strenuously to avoid some of the more negative associations (with mental degradation, for example) that the vocabulary of labour carried. According to Charlotte Smith, however, inevitability did not legitimize the arbitrariness of the distinctions (between professional and amateur, between intellectual, manual and domestic labour, and between disinterestedness and partiality) to which this particular construction of authorial labour gave rise and which would prove so unaccommodating for financially dependent and often thus highly productive writers such as she. Smith's troping of writing as work stands as a bitterly ironic reflection on accounts of professional authorship that figured writing as a form of specialist labour, even while they positioned these unproductive labourers, as *The Wealth of Nations* had done, outside or above the concerns of the market.

At least one of Smith's contemporaries understood the radical implications of her representation of the work of writing. Mary Hays, an author who was as interested in, and troubled by, the gendered division of labour as the author of *Marchmont*, used Smith's deployment of the language of labour in the novels and poems to praise both the writer and her work.[64] Hays's biography of 'Mrs Charlotte Smith' appeared in Richard Phillips's *Public Characters of 1800–1801*.[65] Originally, Phillips had approached the author to write her own autobiography for the publication, but Smith declined, disingenuously claiming that 'It is very difficult to speak of oneself, & I find it would be difficult to speak of the very unhappy Man whose name I bear without injuring myself by withholding too much truth or my children by telling it.' (Given Smith's customary frankness about her personal affairs, it seems that her reluctance to undertake this project was more likely a consequence of a 'heavy domestic affliction' of which she complained in a letter to Hays dated 26 July 1800.)[66] It is difficult to imagine that Smith would have been anything but pleased with Hays's account, which mined the correspondence between the two writers, as well as Smith's novels and poetic works, to offer a sympathetic reading of the distinctive model of authorship she constructed. Although Hays did not shy away from describing the exhausting physical effects of Smith's efforts to support her family by her pen, she refused to present her, as Sir Walter Scott would later do, as a tragic drudge. Hays refuted claims that writing for profit blunted Smith's 'genius' (p. 44) and vigorously contested the reviewers' accusations that her subject's career conflicted with her spousal and maternal responsibilities.

One of Hays's principal source texts appears to have been the preface to the second volume of *Elegiac Sonnets* (1797), a work that, alongside

The Old Manor House, is singled out for particular recommendation in the biography. In the preface to the *Sonnets*, Smith wrote that she was 'compelled to complain of those who have crushed the poor abilities of the *author*, and by the most unheard of acts of injustice (*for twice seven years*) have added the painful sensations of *indignation* to the inconveniences and deprivations of indigence'. The 'inconveniences and deprivations' to which she alludes here are not those of authorship but of the 'disadvantages [Smith] laboured under' as a debtor's wife and *femme couverte*, disadvantages that 'pals[ied] the hand and distract[ed] the head' and thus 'doubled' the burden of literary 'toil'.[67] Hays rehearsed and developed Smith's own claims, arguing that it was not the case that the labour of writing compromised Smith as a mother, nor that Smith's maternal labours constrained her literary achievements. It was the unnecessarily hard work of being 'Mrs Charlotte Smith' that threatened to render the author incapable of fulfilling her personal and professional obligations and proved so 'little favourable to the muse' (p. 55).

Closely following the language and argument of the prefaces to *Desmond*, *The Banished Man* and *Marchmont*, as well as *Elegiac Sonnets*, Hays's biography strenuously attempts to refute the hierarchical relationship of intellectual to manual labour, and literary excellence (or genius) to domesticity, drawn in contemporary accounts of authorship and endorsed by reviewers of Smith's work. Instead, she presents Smith's achievements as a unique combination of innate talent and indefatigable 'application to the desk' (p. 63), ironically the very 'mental and acquired' qualifications that the *Critical* found lacking in its review of *The Old Manor House*. In the first instance, Hays presents Smith's turn to writing as a natural and instinctive response to 'the accidents and calamities' that beset her throughout her life:

> When wearied with the futility of society, or disgusted with its vices, it is the privilege of genius to retire within itself, to call up, with creative power, new worlds, and people solitude with ideal beings. It is to the improved taste, and feeling heart, that Nature, unveiling her charms, gives a zest to simple pleasures, and sheds over ordinary objects a touching grace. (p. 44)

In the manner of *Celestina* (1791) – in which Smith's poet-heroine '[i]nsensibly' writes as 'idea[s]' take 'possession of her fancy' – Hays's biography seems to endorse, here, those theories of genius that presented the writer as a kind of medium, capable of channelling the Muses, rather than as a wholly autonomous agent in her own right.[68] Where Hays departs from such accounts, however, is in her conviction that domestic life was not only hospitable to but actively helped to fashion Smith's 'genius'. Such arguments posed a direct challenge to theorists of genius such as Isaac D'Israeli, who, in *An Essay on the Manners and Genius of Literary Character* (1795), argued that 'domestic life' was 'rarely', if ever, 'congenial' to intellectual 'pursuits'.[69] Smith's genius, by contrast, Hays argued, was nurtured and refined by her close relationships with her children. Motherhood proved eminently congenial to Smith's literary pursuits. When her children were young, Smith 'rocked the cradle' with one hand while holding a book in the other and allowing another child to sleep 'on her lap'; as they grew older, the children would accompany her on 'walks' during which she would compose 'those little pieces of poetry' that would become *Elegiac Sonnets*. While her children were 'healthy and happy', Smith's dedication to her profession was beyond question (p. 63).

In these early sections of Hays's account, writing is cast as an involuntary and natural act, provoked by, and capable of allaying, the author's sorrow and weariness with the world. Unlike Marchmont, who finds neither emotional nor financial relief in labour, only a heightened awareness of his own abjection and failure, Smith finds consolation in writing. And unlike the hero's retreat into the imagination, which signalled his cowardly retreat from political responsibility, Smith's indulgence of her 'feeling heart' made 'politics', as she would claim in the preface to *Desmond*, her 'business' (p. 3). Instinctive affect and mental toil thus combine, here, to effect social and political transformation. The imaginary communities that Smith's 'genius' conjured to 'people her solitude' were worked up into novels that looked constantly to 'new worlds' – and, in the case of *The Young Philosopher*, to *the* New World – where exiled individuals would live free from the tyranny, inequality and prejudice.[70] Although, initially, Hays seems to downplay the work involved in writing, by describing Smith's literary productions as the effusions of natural genius and maternal sensibility, as the biography progresses, it is subsequently clear that the imaginative and physical work that facilitates the kinds of political transformation Smith projected in her poems and novels was both real and exhausting. Hays dwells, particularly, upon the toll authorship took on Smith's 'health', which 'suffered considerably', she wrote, as a consequence of her career. Crucially, though, Hays maintains that it was not the labour of writing that produced Smith's emotional and physical distress, but the failure of the literary market to value that work in accordance with the labour invested in its creation.

Writing was a source of 'delight rather than . . . complaint' for Smith (p. 63). As Marchmont had discovered, however, negotiating fees with ruthless publishers and unfeeling patrons, unwilling adequately to remunerate the author for the work she had undertaken, evoked feelings of 'repugnan[ce]' and 'humiliat[ion]' (p. 62). This is not to say that Smith wished to divorce her intellectual endeavours from the commodified realm of the market. By drawing attention to the fact that she 'was compelled to provide the necessities of a numerous family, almost entirely by [her] own labour', and by reminding her readers just how prolific and productive a labourer she was, Smith revealed that she was happier to exploit rather than endorse what Zeynep Tenger and Paul Trolander have identified as a fundamental 'antagonism between the discourses of genius and political economy' in the latter decades of the eighteenth century.[71] It was *as* work – as physical, emotional and intellectual hard graft – rather than as a disinterested, involuntary or recreational mental activity that writing was valuable, as Smith provocatively argued and as Hays recognized, even if the literary marketplace was reluctant fully to acknowledge it as such.

In making this latter point, Hays's argument takes its steering hand not from the prefaces to Smith's work but from the content of the novels, and particularly from their damning indictments of the modern literary marketplace's failure to live up the standards of professionalism it claimed to uphold. Almost every player in contemporary literary life is subject to criticism in Smith's fiction, from publishers who harass their authors for texts as tradesmen hound debtors for payment – a 'precious recipe to animate the imagination and exalt the fancy!', as she wrote in *The Banished Man*[72] – to the corrupt reviewer who is all too willing to dismiss the works of women writers unless their authors happen to be 'connected with some bookseller whose interest he had at heart'.[73] The novels' objection to such old-boy-networks – a modern, and degrading, form of literary patronage – was matched only by the contempt they display towards literary coteries and, particularly, towards the exclusive world of the bluestockings.[74] Much of the little attention that has been paid to the author-characters that feature in Smith's fiction has focused upon those such as Mrs Denzil, who seem to resemble and speak for their creator. Yet, the novels' unflattering depiction of self-styled women of letters, in novels including *Montalbert* and *The Wanderings of Warwick*, are at least as interesting for the insights they provide into Smith's views on authorship and her aspirations to a model of literary professionalism – professional in the sense of being a skilled practitioner of her art, rather than of someone who simply writes for a living – that her critics denied her.

Although a number of prominent women of letters supported Smith by subscribing to the fifth edition of *Elegiac Sonnets*, she evidently felt out of place in bluestocking circles, recalling in a letter to Hays that one of Elizabeth Montagu's famous gatherings provoked in her 'a violent inclination to yawn' with boredom, even 'tho I suppose every body talk'd their very best'.[75] Smith's disdain for the world of the literary salon recurs in her novels in the form of a series of searing condemnations of literary affectation and a female amateurism from which the author vehemently dissociates herself. *Montalbert*'s 'Amazonian' Lady Llancarrick and her companion, Miss Gillman (also known as '*The Muse*'), are typical of Smith's bluestocking characters; they are 'absurd', hungry for celebrity – 'never did a female breast pant so vehemently for fame as that of Lady Llancarrick' – and widely, though inexplicably, celebrated by 'some retainers of *The Tuneful Nine*' for their 'genius' (p. 235). The scene in which Lady Llancarrick and Miss Gillman are first introduced to the reader, a scene in which they happen upon the novel's would-be hero, Walsingham, reciting a poem of his own composition, provides an occasion for reflection upon questions of literary worth.[76] The ensuing discussion between these malevolent muses and Walsingham juxtaposes two distinct models of authorship that are inflected by the class and gendered positions of the speakers. Walsingham's poetry is presented, as *Elegiac Sonnets* is in Hays's biography, as a means of memorializing and coming to terms with private sorrow. Lady Llancarrick and Miss Gillman, however, are literary predators, feeding on the pain of others in order to compensate for their lack of inspiration and insight. Walsingham is 'disgusted at the folly' of Miss Gillman, who interrupts his reverie and enquires into his character and the meaning of his verse, so too is the reader when, later in the novel, Lady Llancarrick and Miss Gillman view the heroine's distress following her daughter's kidnapping, 'with the sang froid' of 'amateur[s]', hoping to find a source of inspiration for the play and novel they are working on (p. 250).

These women are amateurs in more than one sense of the word. Fundamentally, they lack talent: had Lady Llancarrick's reverie not been interrupted by the sound of Walsingham reciting his verse, the reader suspects that her period of 'waiting' for Miss Gillman's 'fine fancy' to realize itself in some 'happy' poetic effusion would have been long indeed (p. 238). Furthermore, their aspirations are bogus: both crave transitory 'fame' rather than posthumous reputation, although the fashionable Lady Llancarrick will find, to her cost, that 'she could not drive into the temple of Fame in a Phaeton, four in hand, without being commoded by equal or superior skill' (p. 239). Finally, both women are emotionally and intellectually disengaged from the subjects of their writing; although they perform their 'sensibility' they ultimately reveal themselves to be incapable of feeling 'true sympathy' for any individual (p. 250). As a consequence, their work is derivative and lacks the application discernible in the works of whose, who, like Smith, lived to write and wrote to live.

Smith would elaborate this critique of literary amateurism in *The Wanderings of Warwick*, the sequel to *The Old Manor House*, in which the eponymous hero embarks upon a career as a writer after leaving the army. Warwick's experiences, under the guidance of the 'redoubtable' author and critic, Mac Gowan, occasion some of Smith's most bitter condemnations of the literary marketplace, which no doubt reflect the fact that Smith wrote the novel reluctantly, and only because she was contractually obliged to do so (p. 95). Having benefited from the patronage of Mac Gowan, who 'puff[s] up' a pamphlet written by Warwick, despite the fact that 'there was not much solidity in [the author's] arguments', the hero is appalled to witness the lengths to which critics will go to decry the work of authors, so much more worthy of the title than he (p. 97). He is shocked, for example, when Mac Gowan urges him, in order that he might advance his own career,

> to crush the hopes of industrious indigence – of a mother, perhaps, who had recourse to her pen to supply bread to a family for whom she had no other resource – of a daughter endeavouring to assist in the support of a helpless superannuated parent, whom she could not leave to engage in any of the few occupations for which women are qualified (pp. 275–6).

Warwick's comments imitate, and, through imitation, constitute a critique of, the mock-chivalric sentiments of those reviewers who, in the specious name of literary (but hardly poetic) 'justice', pity the woman writer while 'dismiss[ing] to oblivion the pathetic tale and laboured description which had cost the fair author many a pensive hour' (p. 98).

Although Warwick makes no grand claims for the writing produced by these 'fair' and industrious women, the admiration that is their due becomes apparent when the model of textual production they practise is read alongside that followed by the bluestocking Mrs Manby – a figure who has been read variously as a caricature of Hannah More or Hannah Cowley.[77] Manby is a 'great favourite' of Mac Gowan, who 'saw, or fancied he saw, some traits of original genius in the effusions which he called poetry', and whose support transforms her into a literary celebrity and unwarranted 'success'. As her confidence increases, Manby resolves to find out whether she can achieve recognition for her merit without relying upon 'the partiality of her friends', and determines to publish her next volume of poetry anonymously (p. 98). A copy of the work is reviewed by Mac Gowan, who, unaware of its author's identity, deems the 'wild and incomprehensible jumble of images' he had 'once praised when it was the avowed production of Mrs Manby . . . intolerable nonsense' when published by an unknown (p. 99). Smith's delicious dismissal of Manby functions as an attack both upon the supposed disinterestedness of reviewers and upon literary amateurism. Warwick finds that there is much more to respect in the undervalued productions of the indigent but professional woman writer who takes her work seriously, than in the effusions of a celebrated literary woman who exploits public favour, but is unwilling and unable to work to produce anything of worth in return.

The hostility towards bluestocking women evident in *The Wanderings of Warwick* and *Montalbert* is informed by Smith's conviction that amateurism and merit were incompatible. Only truly professional writers could lay claim to literary excellence, and only those who subscribed to authorship's demanding work ethic could count themselves as one of this group. In making these arguments, Smith made a significant, but unjustly neglected, contribution to the debates on the professionalization of literature. Indeed, the attempt to diminish bluestocking cultural capital in these novels is entirely consistent with the emergent discourse of professionalism, which sought to render literature a more exclusive, because specialized, field. However, Smith bucks the prevailing trend of literary professionalization in a number of important ways, not least by eloquently defending the right of women writers labouring for bread to call themselves professionals at a time when the words 'woman writer' and 'professional' would have been understood to be antonyms.[78] Smith's unapologetic insistence that writing was 'work', work which she undertook 'in the *observance*, not in the breach of duty' to her children, put pressure on culturally constructed notions of gender and challenged the arbitrary distinctions between intellectual and manual (and mental and domestic labour), which defined the new literary professionalism. Moreover, this figuring of writing as work allowed Smith to make powerful claims to property in her own person. For Smith, as for Althea Dacres, work was more than a matter of necessity; it was a matter of self-possession.

Smith, Locke and the labour theory of property

Property was a leading preoccupation of Smith's life. For some thirty years, she was embroiled in a legal battle over her father-in-law's West Indian estate which would ruin her financially and destroy her health. Property also looms large in the novels, in which heroes and heroines are frequently forced to prove their entitlement to inheritances of which they are defrauded, or to assert their right to claim possession of their own bodies and minds. Work is never far away from the question of property in Smith's fiction. In *Emmeline*, for example, and in a scene that Smith would reinvent for a number of her female characters, the young heroine refuses her guardian's dictates that she marry a man she does not love with the following defiant riposte: '"Neither as the wife of Maloney, nor as Emmeline Mowbray, will I stay my Lord, another day", answered she, . . . "I must determine to hazard going to Mrs. Watkins's, who will probably give me an asylum at least 'till [*sic*] I can find some one who will receive me, or some means of providing for myself the necessaries of life"' (pp. 25–6). Strikingly, but characteristically for a Smith heroine, Emmeline's assertion of her right to self-ownership is grounded in her awareness of her labouring potential and, thus, in her ability to exist outside the domestic and reproductive economies. Smith would similarly make labour the foundation for her claims to self-possession, but, unlike Emmeline, expressed concern that the nature of her (literary) work might lead to precisely the kind of self-effacement that she sought so vigorously to fend off.

These anxieties come to the fore in Smith's epistolary negotiations with Thomas Cadell and William Davies over the illustrated edition of *Elegiac Sonnets*, in which she expressed her fears that the production process, by which her writings were transformed into commodities, might also turn her into public property. The inclusion of a portrait of Smith proved to be a particular sticking point for the writer and her publishers. She was dissatisfied with the likeness that had been commissioned and, desperate to manage her authorial Self before the reading public, Smith requested in a letter dated 5 March 1797 that Cadell and Davies reproduce the following lines from *The Comedy of Errors* beneath the engraving in order to guide readers' interpretation of the image:

> Oh! grief has changed me since you saw me last
> And sorrowing hours with times deforming hand
> Have written strange defeatures in my ~~fate~~ face.[79]

Smith's initial penning of 'fate' rather than 'face', coupled with her vivid description of sorrow writing itself upon the authorial body, is telling, betraying as it does her understanding of the potent, and potentially unstable, combination of personality, grief and labour which defined her authorial self-presentation and shaped her literary reputation. The more sorrow Smith experienced, and the more she wrote to alleviate and articulate that sorrow, the more that work wrote itself on to her body and personality. Thus writing, the activity through which she sought to support and market the image of 'Mrs Charlotte Smith', threatened to 'defeature' her very identity.

Smith's anxieties that the act of writing might lead to a fatal loss of self-possession demand to be read in relation to more widespread concerns about the nature of authorial property in the period. As Susan Eilenberg and Mark Rose have demonstrated, late eighteenth-century defences of authors' proprietary ownership of their works rested upon a presumed analogy between the corporeal and the incorporeal; between things (i.e. books) and thoughts.[80] As Eilenberg demonstrates, one of the (many) philosophical and legal problems generated by such analogies was the insinuation that the act of publication could lead to an 'alienation or forfeiture of identity'.[81] Although contributors to the later eighteenth-century debates on copyright and intellectual property disagreed about the point at which a text ceased to be the property of the authorial body that produced it, there was broad consensus that if a writer's thoughts were an extension of their person – that is to say, their property – then to publish was to risk becoming the possession of another, to allow oneself to be 'defeatured', defaced and defamed. For women writers, these dangers were particularly keenly felt, for, as Hays acknowledged in her biography of Smith, women were already commodified as the property of their fathers, guardians or husbands, before their entry into print. Thus the 'penalties and discouragements attending the profession of an author' fell, Hays wrote, 'with a double weight' upon women. Frequently 'arraigned' by critics, 'not merely as writers, but as *women*', female authors' temerity to publish left their 'their characters, their conduct, even their personal endowments' open to 'severe inquisition' and to potential annihilation (p. 63).

In making such claims, Hays, like Smith in the letter to Cadell and Davies, seems to foreshadow Catherine Gallagher's influential account of the relationship between gender, authorship and ownership in *Nobody's Story* (1994). Pointing out that the terms 'woman', 'author' and 'marketplace' shared 'connotations of nothingness' throughout the long eighteenth century, Gallagher argues that a host of women writers from Aphra Behn to Maria Edgeworth persistently conceptualized their authorial selves as 'dispossessed, in debt, and on the brink of disembodiment'. Thus, for the eighteenth-century woman writer, authorship signalled 'the writer's inability to *own* the text', an inability that is 'explicitly linked' to the 'author's gender'.[82] Smith, of course, had more reason than most to present authorship in these terms. Literally as well as figuratively indebted to friends, publishers and the reading public, she suffused her letters with the same language of credit, debt and disembodiment that Gallagher identifies in the work of Smith's contemporaries, particularly that of Burney and Edgeworth. Take, for example, a letter to William Davies in which Smith wrote of her difficulty in completing *A History of England* (1806), the third and final volume of which would be authored by Hays. Smith thought the work so far completed was 'well done', and intimated that she had 'labour[ed]' sufficiently hard on the project to 'preserve [her] credit with the public'. Yet, she resented the 'price' her publisher, Richard Phillips, had offered her for the work, arguing that the payment was not 'by any means adequate to the labour' it had 'cost' her. Like Burney and Edgeworth, Smith associates her rising authorial capital with a heightened sense of indebtedness. To complete the work for an inadequate fee, she might still do credit to her reputation, but she would lose out financially; to stand up for her right to have her work properly remunerated, she might be forced to renege upon her obligation to Phillips, and thus stood to 'lose that part of [her] good name' that she had worked most of her adult life to achieve.[83]

While Smith's letter signals the untenability of her position as author in a textual economy in which her currency was always liable to debasement, her recourse to the language of credit and debt in her discussions of authorship, here as elsewhere, is not, however, a sign that she could not conceive of the act of writing as 'the production of property'.[84] It was precisely *because* Smith conceived of writing as work – as bodily, material practice – that she could write herself out of the economy of dispossession that Gallagher claims frames the work of many of her contemporaries and assert her right to what Smith persistently referred to as her 'property' in her texts and her person.[85] If writing brought with it the risk of disembodiment – of one's property falling into the hands of another – then Smith recognized that the imprinting of authorial labour on to the pages of novels and poems could ward off such a threat. By exploiting the terrifying prospect of her imminent erasure – by making this 'defeaturing' and the labour of resisting it the subject of her novels and poems – Smith earned the right to claim her productions as her work and thus, as her 'property'. The vocabulary of labour thus emerges in the letter to Davies, as it would throughout Smith's works, not as that of drudgery and slavery but as the language of self-ownership.

Nowhere in the fiction is this more apparent, perhaps, than in *The Banished Man*. The lengthy monologue in which the author-character Mrs Denzil introduces her melancholy tale invites the reader to interpret the narrative 'I' as having two referents simultaneously. The quotation marks which open the narrative are soon forgotten as the reader encounters the difficulties faced by two women (one fictional, one real) both 'overwhelmed with present troubles, and future dread for the fate of my children' (p. 273). The fact that there are no closing quotation marks separating Mrs Denzil's first-person account from the narrator's subsequent commentary (a suggestive typographical error which means that Denzil's first-person narrative bleeds into Smith's third-person narrative some nine pages after the monologue begins) only adds to the sense of confusion, leaving many readers in little doubt that Mrs Denzil is 'overtly Charlotte herself'.[86] Whether deliberately or not, Smith blurs the line between fact and fiction, here; simultaneously, however, she goes to great lengths to distance her own character and situation from the woman she presents as her textual alter-ego. Those readers who identify Mrs Denzil with her author are informed in a pointedly worded footnote that the women's situations are 'totally different'. Indeed, Smith claims that the situation in which she and her children have found themselves is infinitely worse than that into which the Denzils have been plunged: 'Not one of my children's relations ever lent them an house', Smith remarks, 'though some of them have contributed all in their power to take from them the house we possest of our own' (p. 271). Smith is characteristically disingenuous, her comments serving only to emphasize that the women's grave situations differ in kind, but not in degree. Where fact and fiction undeniably cohere is in the women's shared recognition that labour is their sole form of property. Mrs Denzil claims to have lost 'every thing *but my head*'; 'learning' is the only 'marketable' 'commodity' she can claim to 'possess', and is her family's sole source of financial support (p. 273). Echoing her character's sentiments in a letter written by an ailing Smith to James Upton Tripp in the year in which *The Banished Man* was published, Smith commented: 'I have no resource but my own labour which this cruel disorder . . . sadly impedes.'[87] Labour reveals all that the women have lost; but it also demonstrates the sum of all they have. In a letter to Joseph Cooper Walker dated 25 March 1795, Smith wrote that *The Banished Man* 'was the best [novel] I have yet done', not least because it 'cost' her 'more time and trouble than I have yet given to any thing'.[88] Fragile though her dependence on her labour was, the work of Smith, like that of Mrs Denzil, was a source of pride, and offered a vestige of autonomy in a society which persistently sought to deny her agency as a woman, a wife and a worker.

Such moments in the letters and novels reveal that Smith's conception of authorial labour owed much more to Lockean natural rights theories of possessive individualism than it did to the discourse of the division of labour outlined in *The Wealth of Nations*. Locke's *Two Treatises of Government*, which famously argued that property was created when the individual 'mixed his *Labour*' with '[w]hatsoever he removes out of the State of Nature', was at least as influential in shaping the construction of authorship in the century's last quarter as *The Wealth of Nations* would prove to be. This was especially so in the context of the copyright debates that were staged in the courts and the press in the period, and particularly in the wake of the landmark case of Donaldson *v*. Becket in 1774, which upheld the principle of limited copyright, while doing much to cement the argument for authors' proprietary relationship to their works. Smith's understanding of literary professionalism as a combination of industry and personality is clearly indebted to the Lockean paradigm as it was interpreted and mobilized by defenders of proprietary authorship and perpetual copyright. Locke's work was, as Rose documents, frequently used by authors and booksellers to argue that '[a] work of literature belonged to an individual because it was, finally, an embodiment of that individual' whose personality and labour were imprinted 'on the common stock of the world as a "work of original authorship"'.[89] Just as physical property was produced when man drew from the land and mixed the common stock of nature with his labour, so the author drew from the common stock of language and transformed it into intellectual property by mixing it with the labour of his mind.[90]

As a woman, a *femme couverte* and the wife of a debtor, forced to sell the copyright to all but one of her works, the Lockean paradigm might seem an unlikely precedent for Smith's claims for property in her person and productions.[91] Yet, it was for precisely these reasons that Locke's theory of proprietary ownership was so seductive to the author. One of the tragic ironies of Smith's career was that, for her works to remain her own property in philosophical terms, she had to relinquish her legal title to them. As she explained to Cadell, if she retained the copyrights to her works, any profits they made could be claimed by her husband's creditors in lieu of his debts. The only way to translate the novels and poems into property and profit was 'to sell intirely [*sic*] *all* my literary property – Which, once bought and paid for, no claimant against him can, as I am well informed affect'.[92] But Smith's conviction in the labour theory of property was such that it could withstand even the pressure of having to sell the title to her works. Her vigorous defences of her right to understand her works as her own property brought her into conflict with publishers on more than one occasion. When, for example, Cadell and Davies objected to Smith's proposal to compose a new volume of poetry a matter of 'months' after the second volume of *Elegiac Sonnets* was published, accusing the author of deliberately withholding poems to which they were legally entitled in order to fill another, potentially lucrative, volume of verse, Smith penned an angry response. In a letter that marked the beginning of the end of her relationship with her publishers, Smith argued that anything she had composed or rewritten since the second volume of *Elegiac Sonnets* had appeared belonged 'neither [to] the Subscribers nor [to] the holders of the Copy right of the former volume'. Rehearsing, as Catharine Macaulay had done in her *Modest Plea for the Property of Copyright* (1774), the familiar troping of writing as farming or harvesting, Smith contended that such an argument was as ludicrous as the actions of a 'farmer who buys a crop of wheat of another complain[ing] that he the Seller look'd out for the sale of a crop of oats a year after'.[93] To sell the copyrights to her works may have been distasteful to Smith, but as a gesture of pragmatism rather than 'will'[94] it did not dispel her faith in the inalienability of her authorial labour.

For Smith, writing always brought with it the threat of dispossession; once in print, her story (her labour) might cease to belong to her and become the possession of others. Fully aware of these dangers, however, Smith resisted the commodification she feared. Her novels' reliance upon autobiographical plotlines and their emphasis upon the labour invested in the act of writing were crucial to this resistance. Her fiction's nuanced self-referentiality was not a sign of egotism, as Smith explained to readers in the prefaces to *Elegiac Sonnets*, *Desmond* and *Marchmont*; neither her seeming identifications with her characters nor her self-portraits as a reluctant, ceaselessly toiling writer were that transparent. The footnote differentiating Smith's experiences from Mrs Denzil's, the pointed dissociation of Althea's domestic 'work' from her own, less than blissful, labours as a writer and mother in the advertisement for *Elegiac Sonnets*, and *Marchmont*'s damning critique of its author-hero's fall into labour, are just three moments in the novels where the author puts herself at one remove from those characters with whom her readers might identify her in order to make more wide-ranging arguments about the nature and status of labour, gender and authorship at the time. Adopting such approaches allowed Smith to challenge, while seeming to endorse, critical assumptions that a woman's body and work were interchangeable. More importantly, they enabled her to resist, even while she exploited, the emergent model of literary professionalism and the debates it engendered about writing's relation (or non-relation) to work. Thus, the connection between author and work was not severed when Smith seemed to make herself one of the subjects of her fiction; rather, it allowed her to call that work her own. As Smith subconsciously acknowledged in the letter to Cadell and Davies, her 'face' and her 'fate' were intimately bound up with one another. By insistently imprinting her life and labour on to the published page, Smith ensured that her works were too much her own ever to become the property of another.

To divide Smith's work, as it has sometimes been divided, according to a binary model which sets her properly intellectual (poetic) labour apart from her (lesser) work as a novelist is to be unsympathetic to the complexity of the labour plots that structure her works and to obscure her contribution to contemporary debates about work, gender and domesticity. Moreover, it is to misrepresent the complexity and the ambition of the model of authorship she proffered and which was deeply implicated in her treatment of work in the novels. Drawing upon Locke's labour theory of property and its reimagining in late eighteenth-century debates on copyright and intellectual property, Smith argued that professional authorship and domestic femininity were entirely compatible with one another. In a manoeuvre that was to prove enabling for a number of women writers, particularly – if somewhat ironically given her contempt for the 'trumpery Novels' of the Minerva Press – for the commonly derided women who wrote for the circulating libraries, Smith broke down the rigid and, as she saw them, arbitrary divisions between manual, intellectual and affective labour articulated in political economic theory and challenged the gendered division of literary labour that emerged from it.[95] Smith's role in these public debates about the nature of women's work had a very personal dimension, however. For her, as for so many of her heroines, the question of labour was ultimately a question of self-ownership, and for this reason, above all, Charlotte Smith's readers were left in no doubt that they were reading somebody's story.

3

The 'business' of a woman's life and the making of the Female Philosopher: the works of Mary Wollstonecraft

> [T]he men who, by their writings, have most earnestly laboured to domesticate women, have endeavoured, by arguments dictated by a gross appetite, which satiety has rendered fastidious, to weaken their body and cramp their minds. But, if even by these sinister methods they really *persuaded* women, by working on their feelings, to stay at home, and fulfil the duties of a mother and mistress of a family, I should cautiously oppose opinions that led women to right conduct, by prevailing on them to make the discharge of such important duties the main business of life, though reason were insulted. Yet, and I appeal to experience, if by neglecting the understanding they be as much, nay, more detached from these domestic employments, than they could be by the most serious intellectual pursuit . . . .
>
> Mary Wollstonecraft, *A Vindication of the Rights of Woman* (1792)[1]

> Life is but a labour of patience: it is always rolling a great stone up a hill; for, before a person can find a resting-place, imagining it is lodged, down it comes again, and all the work is to be done over anew.
>
> Letter from Mary Wollstonecraft to Gilbert Imlay 1 January 1794[2]

The previous chapters of this book have explored the imaginative connections drawn between manual, affective and intellectual toil in the novels of two writers who, for different ends, capitalized on the valorization of labour in various branches of pre-Smithian political economy both to condemn female dependency and to legitimize their authorial practice. Here, I address the complex turns that the debate on women's work took in the specific context of the 1790s and, more specifically still, in the non-fictional and imaginative publications of one of the most vocal and eloquent commentators on this issue, Mary

Wollstonecraft.[3] Her extensive, but by no means internally consistent, reflections upon the labour and literary marketplaces signal crucial, and in many ways decisive, developments in the narratives about work and authorship this book examines. Most particularly, an investigation of her polemical writings, philosophical works, travel literature and novels suggests that the more labour was prized in late eighteenth-century writings on political economy, and the more centrally its language figured in the republic of letters' self-presentation at the century's close, the more vital and the more difficult it became for women writers to press the discourse of labour into the service of their gender and textual politics.

Wollstonecraft's efforts to negotiate this paradox in her writings on various kinds of women's work, from 'domestic employments' to the 'serious intellectual pursuit[s]' of the Female Philosopher, had significant implications for the future of women's writing about work. Her determination to appropriate, especially for women 'in the middle class' (*VRW*, p. 75), a vocabulary and ideology of labour that became more deeply entrenched at a moment when the logic that underpinned this vocabulary and ideology became more exclusionary, produced a number of tensions in her writing with which twentieth- and twenty-first-century feminists have struggled. If, as this chapter suggests, Wollstonecraft's career sheds further light on the gains and losses made by eighteenth-century women writers who participated in the debate on women's work, then an investigation of her writings in the context of these exchanges also offers new insights into the work of this controversial writer. Some of the most vexed and contested aspects of Wollstonecraft's work, particularly those concerning the relationship between her class and gender politics, appear rather differently, if no less comfortably, if they are viewed as inevitable repercussions of a career-long attempt to valorize the intellectual work of the Female Philosopher through a sustained attack upon the division of labour itself.[4]

The language of work in the labour and literary marketplaces of the 1790s

Wollstonecraft's liberal use of the terms 'labour', 'employment', 'business', 'occupation' and 'work' in this chapter's epigraphs is characteristic of her Sisyphean endeavour to contest the gendered division of labour in her published writings and to decry the extraordinary depths to which men of letters sank when they attempted to pass off meaningless female accomplishments as valuable 'employments', a convenient fiction fabricated to reinforce the emergent discourse of separate spheres and to naturalize women's subjugation as the only cultural work for which the female sex was fit. The persistence with which Wollstonecraft returned to this language throughout her literary career is notable, and gives further cause to qualify scholarly accounts that have presented such vocabulary as inaccessible to, and unwanted by, the middle-ranking or genteel woman writer, to whom the world of work was supposedly anathema. Ever more central, as we shall see, both to the professional classes' self-presentation and to the republic of letters' rhetoric about its public function and utility, the language of labour was an indispensible weapon in the hands of the 1790s feminist whose attacks upon the gendered division of labour would earn her a place within the literary public sphere. Content not merely to reveal how this language had been falsely deployed to dupe the female sex into slavish submission, the self-styled Female Philosopher sought to co-opt its vocabulary in order to redefine the 'business' of women's lives in moral, economic and intellectual terms.

Wollstonecraft's efforts to renegotiate women's role in the nation's political and moral economies through the language of labour must be understood both as a response to the 'cultural revolution' that led to the consolidation and professionalization of the middling ranks at the turn of the century and as a critique of this process's ramifications for women, whose claims to professionalism were commonly deemed tenuous at best.[5] As a number of historians and literary scholars have demonstrated, the cultural authority of the emergent professional middle class was primarily predicated upon its members' participation in the labour market, an ideological shift, which, as Clifford Siskin observes, necessitated that the very 'concept of work' be 'rewritten' so as to become 'the primary activity in forming adult identity', regardless of social position.[6] For 'adult', Wollstonecraft would no doubt have argued, read 'male'. The 1790s middle-class professional, as she famously wrote in *A Vindication of the Rights of Woman*, was characterized by industry and rigour. A specialist whose 'eye' was 'steadily fixed on some future advantage', and whose 'mind' was 'strengthen[ed] by having all its efforts directed to one point', he was also, and unequivocally, a 'man' (p. 129). Women, by virtue of their association with leisure, their increasing exclusion from the division of labour and, thus, from the markers of status and prestige associated with participation in the making of the nation's wealth, were debarred from the forms of 'active citizen[ship]' in which the modern male professional was engaged (p. 216).

There was simply, as Harriet Guest observes, 'no moral or professional language available to articulate feminine virtue' in the new political economy of the later eighteenth century. It had 'no place and no value'.[7] If Adam Smith was right to insist that 'every individual [was] a burthen upon the society to which he belongs, who [did] not contribute his share of productive labour for the good of the whole', then women of leisure were little more than parasites.[8] While men '[i]n the middle rank of life' were 'prepared for professions', women of the same station were denied any 'scheme to sharpen their faculties'. Rather than 'business, extensive plans, or any excursive flights of ambition', their attention was engrossed by trivial and romantic flights of fancy (p. 129). Destined only for marriage, women were denied the right to participate in the economy except in their 'morally ambiguous' roles as 'consumers or commodities', which meant, as Guest suggests, that the terms in which they could be represented were 'restricted almost completely to those of corrupt feminine desire'.[9] A number of 1790s feminist writers, including Priscilla Wakefield, sought to counter the damaging effects of women's association with idleness and, thus, lasciviousness by suggesting that political economy's reluctance to represent women as active and productive citizens was simply an oversight. As she wrote in *Reflections on the Present Condition of the Female Sex* (1798), *The Wealth of Nations* (1776) might 'not absolutely [have] specif[ied], that both sexes' had to engage in productive labour 'in order to render themselves beneficial members of society, . . . but since the female sex is included in the idea of the species, and as women possess the same qualities as men, though perhaps in a different degree, their sex [could not] free them from the claim of the public for their proportion of usefulness'.[10] Wollstonecraft's twofold solution to the problem of women's cultural and economic marginalization was even more provocative than Wakefield's: to make the recuperation of the language of professionalism and the discourse of the division of labour the cornerstones of her projected 'revolution in female manners', while at the same time criticizing political economy's failure to see the inestimable contribution that many women were already making to national prosperity as wives, as workers and as writers.[11]

If appropriating the language of the division of labour was integral to Wollstonecraft's gender politics, then it was vital also, as we shall see, to her endeavours to establish the Female Philosopher's role within the republic of letters. When, in this chapter's opening epigraph, Wollstonecraft puns on the word 'employment' to reveal female accomplishments as undeserving of the designation, she does so both to argue for the personal and cultural benefits that might be generated if women were to be afforded the opportunity to pursue more meaningful forms of work and to condemn the role that literature had played in re-enforcing fictions of gender designed to naturalize the separation of public and private spheres. If women were 'allowed to have an immortal soul', she argued, they had to be allowed an 'employment' on earth (*VRW*, p. 132). But unless women were educated to see through society's efforts to confine their 'business' to those 'employments' that 'insult[ed]' their 'reason', they would never be led to 'right conduct' (*VRW*, p. 133). Such women's amateurish complacency – their failure to recognize that domestic life was a more serious 'business' than they were capable of imagining, but only one of many meaningful 'employments' they might usefully pursue – was matched only by that of those male writers whose literary 'labour' to 'domesticate women' was, in Wollstonecraft's eyes, scarcely worthy of the name.

That Wollstonecraft's attack on the language of the division of labour, here, is yoked to a critique of men of letters is characteristic of her work more widely, and crucial to an understanding of the inextricability of her gender and literary politics. Wollstonecraft's contribution to the debate on women's work was shaped, more explicitly than that of any of her predecessors or contemporaries, by her recognition of an insidious collusion between the market and print economies. Recent scholarship would suggest that this collusion, while far from new, became much more deeply entrenched amid the political and literary conflicts of the 1790s. According to Paul Keen, the intensification of political 'turmoil' in the revolutionary decade provoked a 'crisis' in the republic of letters, to which 'the broader hegemonic shift towards the meritocratic bias of the professional classes' offered a putative, although not unproblematic, solution.[12] As outlined in this book's introduction, and elaborated more fully below, early to mid-century understandings of the man of letters, derived from the tradition of civic humanism, had come to seem untenable by the 1790s. Members of the new republic of letters increasingly modelled themselves as a cultural 'elite', whose credentials lay not in landed wealth or leisure – the traditional qualifications for disinterestedness – but in an 'intellectual industriousness' that allowed for the production of new forms of proper and '(symbolic) capital' that existed 'outside the unstable fluctuations of commerce'. The cultural authority of this generation of self-styled 'intellectual labourers' rested not upon their refusal to participate in the division of labour; its members 'worked', Keen observes, '*because* they were disinterested'.[13]

With ever more conviction, authorship was constructed and valued in the 1790s as mental toil, a form of labour superior to, yet demanding the same qualities as, manual work. The language of labour (of specialization and industry, in particular) took on what Gruffudd Aled Ganobcsik-Williams terms 'a new ideological force' in 'writers' self-representations' in this period, 'becoming both a declaration of political loyalties and a stance on the role of proper intellectuals'.[14] The substitution of mental industry for landed wealth as the foundation of intellectual authority might appear to signal, as it seemed to signal to a number of 1790s reactionaries, a will to democratize the republic of letters, to encourage wider participation in, and further expansion of, print culture. However, the centrality of labour – an ever more rigidly class- and gender-bound concept as the century progressed – to 1790s constructions of authorship proved highly effective in shoring up the literary public sphere's defences against such unregulated expansion. To figure writing as work was, in Siskin's words, to 'masculinize the literary', to gender textual production in ways that were to have damaging and longstanding consequences for women writers.[15]

Wollstonecraft herself deemed it far from coincidental that the changes in the republic of letters' self-presentation at the century's close were coterminous with what she and other 1790s feminist commentators understood to be a fatal decline in women's employment opportunities. As she would remind readers, the language of industry, toil and specialization through which the republic of letters sought to establish its legitimacy during this period of crisis replicated that used to justify women's exclusion from the division of labour in society at large, an exclusion which, moreover, a number of the literary public sphere's members sought to naturalize through their contributions to the 'science' of political economy. Similarly, women's increasingly marginalized position within the labour market, a subject to which I turn in more detail in the following section, was used to deny their suitability for the less physical, though no less strenuous, work of writing. To effect reforms in the labour market, therefore, Wollstonecraft insisted that it was necessary to urge simultaneous reforms in the republic of letters that sanctioned and adopted its practices. By the same token, she argued forcefully that the exclusive, increasingly male-dominated republic of letters could be reformed only once a successful reevaluation of gendered roles outside its exclusive sphere had been achieved. This double reformist strategy – a strategy that inflects Wollstonecraft's treatment of manual and intellectual labour in the works for children as well her more famous prose and fictional works – is the subject of this chapter.

Wollstonecraft's attempts to professionalize gender through her interventions into debates on women's domestic, manual and intellectual labour have been read, most insightfully by Harriet Guest, as an attempt to appropriate for women the discourse of the division of labour that legitimized the cultural authority of the professional middle-class male in this period. This chapter argues that such endeavours must additionally be recognized as part of a specifically literary agenda: a project to condemn the gendered discourse of labour, according to whose terms the literary public sphere was remodelled in the 1790s, in order that the Female Philosopher's place within that sphere might be secured. Such a reassessment asks us to confront anew the intricate web of coalitions and divisions between women that Wollstonecraft's works weave and, further, forces us to acknowledge the woman writer's increasing dependence, not only upon the language of labour but upon the figure of the female labourer herself, as sources of authority. The making of the Female Philosopher, Wollstonecraft's writing reveals, was dependent upon a wholesale, and determinedly strategic, reassessment of the 'business' of *all* women's lives.

Writing about work in the 1790s: Wollstonecraft in context

For the most part, this book has investigated representations of women's work in fictional texts in which neither manual nor intellectual labour, for reasons already elucidated, has traditionally been considered to be a leading preoccupation. This chapter marks something of a departure from this strategy. Although Wollstonecraft's novels, *Mary: A Fiction* (1788) and *The Wrongs of Woman; or Maria* (1798), are examined in this chapter's conclusion, my primary focus here is upon the figuring of the manual/intellectual labour axis in a group of non-fictional texts that promised to address the reality of women's work – 'misery' devoid of 'its caps and bells' rather than the 'Arcadia of fiction', as Wollstonecraft put it[16] – more explicitly than their predecessors had done or their more conservative counterparts were prepared to do. (That these texts, paradoxically, bear the hallmarks of precisely those fictional representational strategies – sentimentalization and idealization – that Wollstonecraft condemned will be explored in more detail below.) Wollstonecraft and her contemporaries Mary Hays, Mary Ann Radcliffe and Priscilla Wakefield built on the arguments put forward by previous commentators on women's work at the same time that they promised to inaugurate a new era of writing about female labour. And although the substance of their arguments was often less original than it has sometimes appeared to be – many, for example, replicating observations made by Sarah Scott, Sarah Fielding and other mid-century commentators on female labour – these writers' contributions to this ongoing discussion were, none the less, distinctive for a number of reasons. Some of these distinctions are generic. When read alongside the novels discussed in Chapters 1 and 2, for example, these non-fictional texts are notable for the directness and scope of their critiques, which point towards structural inequalities in the division of labour as a whole, rather than providing anecdotal examples of injustice through the isolated experiences of fictional characters. The polemics further differ from earlier fictional works in the explicitness of their calls for women to be allowed more meaningful – that is to say, more economically viable and more socially useful – roles within the division of labour, an explicitness matched only in mid-century fiction by Scott's *A Journey through Every Stage of Life* (1754). Among the principal injustices that 1790s discussions of women's work expose are men's encroachment upon traditionally female trades, the inadequacies of education, the prejudices that greeted genteel women seeking legitimate work and the threat of sexual intimidation faced by women workers of all ranks. The picture that emerges from such texts is unremittingly bleak. As Radcliffe argued in *The Female Advocate* (1799), powerless to battle against the 'prohibition against [them] having an employment', and tormented by 'the shrill voice of censure', those women forced to support themselves by their labour were 'irremediably doomed to sink, never more to rise'.[17] If man was punished by a life of labour following his expulsion from Eden, then it was woman's peculiar fate to be denied the right to earn her subsistence, and thus either '"to starve for want of employment"' (p. 108)[18] or to be forced to accede to the 'absolute necessity of bartering [her] virtue for bread' (p. 26).

The Female Advocate notes a steady decline in women's employment opportunities from the beginning of the eighteenth century and nostalgically laments the passing of a golden age of economic self-sufficiency for women. According to Radcliffe, women did not have to look back many decades to locate the origins of the 'destructive precedent, wherein men ha[d] been made substitutes in women's occupations', a trend that *The Female Advocate* presented as a direct consequence of the demise of cottage industry. When 'manufactures and commerce were not so extensive', Radcliffe argued, 'and while the father and mother were employed in trade, the mother and daughters were employed in the domestic concerns of the household'. In this 'refined age' of 'contracted' wants, the tradesman gained 'credit' for 'employ[ing] his wife or daughters' and women 'were never at a loss for employment; they found enough to do in spinning, knitting, and preparing necessaries' (p. 64). Like Radcliffe, Wollstonecraft similarly regretted the loss, and longed for the return, of a golden age of labour in which economic production was located in the home and was thus untainted by the corrupting influence of nascent capitalism. In this 'garden more inviting than Eden', she wrote in *A Vindication of the Rights of Men*, 'springs of joy murmur[ed] on every side. . . . Domestic comfort, the civilizing relations of husband, brother, and father, would soften labour, and render life contented' (p. 56).[19]

Radcliffe's and Wollstonecraft's accounts foreshadow, and may well have directly informed, the pioneering early twentieth-century histories of women's work by Alice Clark and Ivy Pinchbeck, which document a decline in women's employment opportunities across the long eighteenth century as Britain moved from agrarianism and the home as the locus of economic production to industrialization and wage labour.[20] As discussed in this book's introduction, the golden age and decline theories of women's work that Radcliffe and Wollstonecraft posit have been convincingly challenged by a number of historians who have pointed to regional and national variations in the eighteenth-century labour market and illuminated women's successful adaptations to the burgeoning consumer revolution as manufacturers, businesswomen and entrepreneurs.[21] Despite these important interventions, however, the argument that the later eighteenth century witnessed the contraction of the female labour market has proved remarkably resilient in both historical and literary scholarship, in which 1790s polemics are still commonly cited as corroborative evidence.[22] Closer investigation of these texts, however, casts doubt upon their historical usefulness.

Indeed, the nearer we approach 'evidence' in these works, the further we seem to seem to enter the 'Arcadia of fiction' against which Wollstonecraft railed. When Radcliffe, for example, recalled in her *Memoirs* (1810) the horror she experienced twenty years earlier when looking at 'columns of female wants in the public papers', she both is and is not presenting the reality of women's work in the period.[23] Publications such as *The Times*, *The Daily Advertiser* and *The Morning Chronicle* did include 'wanted' advertisements placed by women seeking positions as servants, cooks, milliners, companions, governesses and teachers; however, as a legitimate means of finding employment for members of the middling ranks, they also contained column upon column of advertisements placed by men.[24] Radcliffe's suggestion that there were disproportionately high numbers of advertisements placed by women is not borne out by the sources to which she alludes, and, thus, betrays more disconcerting anxieties. At stake for Radcliffe, it seems, is not the fact that women were seeking positions in their droves, but that women of her station were being forced to advertise for work, perhaps even that they were being forced to work at all. Radcliffe's genteel horror – the refrain of *Memoirs* – bespeaks an all too familiar investment in class privilege that is at odds with the egalitarian promise of *The Female Advocate*'s title: the recovery of 'The Rights of Women'. My point, here, is not to suggest that 1790s polemicists' assessments of the labour market are discreditable – a matter that lies beyond this book's interest in representation and its relation to prevailing ideologies. Rather, my intention is to close the gap that has been found to exist between fictional representations of labour and the purportedly more realistic accounts offered by 1790s feminist polemicists. The fact that a number of scholarly accounts of women's work have recapitulated the claims made in contemporary commentaries upon the division of labour should not obscure the numerous investments that colour their authors' representation of women's work, and which reflect an intensification of female authors' commitment to this recuperation in response to changes in the division of labour and the literary marketplace at the century's close.

Wollstonecraft scholarship has been particularly attentive to many of these multiple and sometimes conflicting investments and their relationship to the tangled web of cultural ideologies, which, as Barbara Taylor points out, have 'marked organized feminist politics from their inception'.[25] A central focus of this body of work, and a source of much debate, has been the relationship between Wollstonecraft's progressive gender politics, her regressive attitudes towards female sexuality and her unapologetically 'middle-class' construction of class difference.[26] In a series of essays provoked by this question, Cora Kaplan has influentially argued that Wollstonecraft constructed 'working-class women' 'through the confusing alterity of a double discourse'.[27] On 'one page' of the *Vindication*, Kaplan observes, labouring-class women appear 'as oppressed workers', as much victims of culturally constructed notions of gender as their middle-ranking counterparts. Elsewhere, however, they appear as 'lascivious servants who initiate and infect their bourgeois female charges'. Wollstonecraft presents the 'ghettoization' of these women, Kaplan argues, as essential for the protection of their superiors' moral health, and, in the process, inaugurates a literary tradition, which 'with important differences and significant elaborations, would become familiar in women's fiction in the century to come': the mapping of 'female excess and transgression' on to the body of the working woman in order that 'their middle-class creators could disavow these dangerous elements of their own subjectivity'.[28]

The 'brief, though not unsympathetic passage on the horrors of prostitution' and 'references to the dirty backstairs habits that female servants pass on to ladies' that Kaplan elucidates are not, however, wholly representative of the intricate argument about women's work made in *A Vindication of the Rights of Woman*, which as frequently challenges common prejudices against working women as it endorses them.[29] Despite its attacks upon the 'nasty' and 'immodest habits' of servants and the abject morals of prostitutes, the second *Vindication* argued that virtue was at least as likely to be found among the labouring classes as it was among their social superiors (p. 197). Indeed, it can be surprising to the modern reader that so much of the *Vindication* is, in fact, devoted to valorizing working women as modern-day heroes, as in the following account of the unenviable, yet dignified, lives of 'poor women'. These women, Wollstonecraft argued, were doubly cursed: not only were they doomed to suffer the lot of their sex and 'keep together families the vices of the fathers have scattered abroad' but they were additionally burdened with the lot of Adam and bound to labour to 'maintain their children by the sweat of their brow'. Greater adversity only heightens these women's capacity for virtue, however. Although lacking educational and financial 'advantage', they prove more 'actively virtuous' than their leisured superiors, whose lives are as 'abject' as their vacuous 'employments' are 'trifling' (p. 145).

Wollstonecraft's figuring of female labour as a form of modern-day heroism, here, hinges upon a crucial separating out of valuable work from mere drudgery, which, in turn, rests upon a differentiation between activities that require reflection and promote the greater good, and those that dull the mental capacities and serve only a misguided sense of the worker's self-interest. Such qualitative distinctions were offered by Wollstonecraft as a more just alternative to the arbitrary and gendered criteria by which various forms of work were traditionally accorded status within the division of labour, and, as we shall see, provided the foundation for her valorization of the Female Philosopher's intellectual toil. Yet no matter how politically necessary and personally expedient this latter strategy was, Wollstonecraft's articulation of a new division of labour, which conferred value upon certain kinds of work at the expense of others, was not without cost. Rather than overturning hierarchies, Wollstonecraft simply reimagined them from a different vantage point.

Heroic labourers and patient drudges: *A Vindication of the Rights of Woman* and *An Historical and Moral View*

The embattled female hero who works to support herself and her children appears in several incarnations in *A Vindication of the Rights of Woman*. Prior to the description of the 'actively virtuous' poor woman described above, she appears, in more genteel guise, as a respectable widow, 'left . . . without a sufficient provision', but '[r]aised to heroism by misfortune' (p. 119). Offered as a counter to Rousseau's Sophie, the 'unnatural' heroine of *Emile* (1762), Wollstonecraft's widow labours to achieve a series of triumphs over psychic and economic adversity. In 'the bloom of life', she 'subdues every wayward passion to fulfil the double duty of being the father as well as the mother of her children'. Her exertions give 'a sacred heroic cast' to the exercise of her 'maternal duties' and reap national 'reward[s]' by producing a generation of virtuous citizens whose 'habits' and 'character' are equal to their 'mother's example'. Having completed this, the great 'task of life', the widow 'calmly waits for the sleep of death' (p. 119). At the portrait's close, the female hero is heard speaking from beyond the grave to reflect upon her achievements on earth: 'Behold, thou gavest me a talent – and here are five talents' (p. 165). The biblical allusion confirms Wollstonecraft's faith in the indissoluble link between financial self-sufficiency and 'active' virtue. This is not to say that Wollstonecraft's argument for women's work is principally an economic one. Although, like Scott, she urged that female labour should be properly remunerated, Wollstonecraft cast the benefits that women might personally experience as a result of expanded employment opportunities as subordinate to the *social* benefits their work would generate. Like Scott and Smith, the ability to ensure an individual's financial stability was indicative of valuable work for Wollstonecraft only in so far as its realization allowed the worker to turn her 'intelligent eye' away from the immediate necessity of alleviating present wants and look to futurity and the greater good.

Here, as throughout the *Vindication*, valuable work is distinguished from menial or degrading employments on the grounds that it calls upon and, in turn, refines the powers of the mind. Domesticity was no better than such degraded employments as service and prostitution, Wollstonecraft suggested, when carried out by 'notable' women whose servile minds could not comprehend that work's value. Such women might run their husbands' households like 'good managers', but since their only 'wages' were 'the caresses of a husband' whose respect they failed to command, they did so 'discontentedly', and thus proved 'very unfit to manage a family' (p. 135). The unfitness of Wollstonecraft's domestic manager lies, on the one hand, in her economic and emotional dependence upon her husband: as a 'trusty servant' rather than a true partner, she lacks the capacity to exercise the judgement necessary to her work's success, and drives her husband to seek comfort in more '*picquant* society' (p. 136). On the other, her failure derives from her confusion of remuneration and value: since the 'rewards' she gains from her work are slight, she cannot perceive its importance. Unlike the male professional, who, 'when he undertakes a journey, has, in general, an end in view' (p. 129), the 'notable' woman is locked in the present, fixated upon the emotional and bodily satisfactions that her husband, ironically, seeks elsewhere. An agent in her own dehumanization, she executes the great 'task of life' with the unreflective complacency of a 'patient drudge' and the unthinking loyalty of 'a blind horse in a mill' (p. 136). In this passage, as in the quotation with which this chapter began, Wollstonecraft deploys the language of labour – in this instance, the debased language of drudgery and service – to counter those writers whose historical abuse of such language had led to the systematic degradation of the women's bodies and minds, and to substitute in its place a recuperated notion of valuable work. Only the latter, she maintained, could provide the economic, corporeal and intellectual freedom that constituted 'active citizenship': 'for how can a being be generous who has nothing of its own? or, virtuous, who is not free?' (p. 217).

Wollstonecraft elaborated this argument further in a final incarnation of the female labourer-hero in the *Vindication*, the woman of fashion fallen into labour who appears in chapter IX on 'Unnatural Distinctions'. Here, Wollstonecraft declared that she had 'often wished, with Dr Johnson' that some of those 'pale-faced creatures' who 'drive helter-skelter about this metropolis' because they are too 'wanton' to 'exert themselves' in any other capacity could be placed 'in a little shop with half a dozen children looking up to their languid countenances for support' (p. 217). The allusion is to *Rambler* 85, otherwise known as 'The Mischiefs of Total Idleness', an essay which expressed characteristically Johnsonian anxiety about the debilitating effects of leisure on gentlemen and women, and praised those writers on education who 'contrived, that every woman of whatever condition should be taught some arts of manufacture, by which the vacuities of recluse and domestick leisure may always be filled up'.[30] If female education continued to exclude such practical 'arts', Johnson warned, and idle women were to be 'turned loose at once upon mankind, with no other business than to sparkle and intrigue', 'confusion and slaughter' would surely follow.[31] Shades of Johnson's influence are evident throughout the *Vindication*, as indeed they are throughout Wollstonecraft's work more widely.[32] Yet, while she endorsed the *Rambler* essay's contention that idleness debased the female sex, Wollstonecraft's declaration of her indebtedness to Johnson is not wholly sincere, as her account of shopkeeping as a source of aristocratic redemption suggests. Nowhere in *Rambler* 85 is such work imagined as a viable female employment. For Johnson, as Wollstonecraft reveals in a sleight of hand that rivals Wakefield's brilliantly wilful misreading of Adam Smith in *Reflections*, 'business' and 'employment' were unequivocally gendered and culturally determined activities. Like men of leisure 'whose rank or wealth exempt[ed] . . . them from the necessity of lucrative labour', women are 'debar[red]' from 'many employments' in Johnson's essay on the grounds that the 'weakness of their sex' and prevailing social conventions – 'the general system of life', as he puts it – render them unsuitable for such work.[33] In fact, women's business is strictly confined to the drawing room throughout *Rambler* 85 and its approving description of the sight of 'a knot of misses busy at their needles'[34] – the only female 'employment', in fact, listed in Johnson's essay – provoked a number of vicious attacks in the *Vindication* upon a pursuit that 'contract[ed women's] faculties more than any other that could have been chosen for them' (p. 144).

Johnson's contention that women were creatures of leisure, but that their leisure time had to be regulated and filled with appropriately feminine 'employments', is indicative of what Judith Frank has described as the 'dizzying contradictions surrounding women and work' in the eighteenth century, contradictions which Wollstonecraft's *Vindication* sought to tease out and dispel.[35] Central to this effort was her determination to contest the construction of female industry as merely a passive virtue, virtuous only to the extent that it prevented women from falling into vice by keeping idle hands busy. Only through labour, the *Vindication* argued, could women cultivate those principles which were necessary to their full participation in 'civil life' (p. 216). Reimagining the 'garden more inviting than Eden' passage from the first *Vindication*,

Wollstonecraft looked to a future in which society would 'be so constituted, that man must necessarily fulfil the duties of a citizen, or be despised' and his 'wife, also an active citizen', be 'really virtuous and useful' by refusing to be 'dependent on her husband's bounty' (p. 216). In this utopian economy, the rehabilitated woman of fashion reduced to labour emerges as an exemplary citizen. If it was Johnson's 'wild wish' that gentlemen should forgo a life of 'ease' for one of industry,[36] then it was Wollstonecraft's that women, whether poor, respectably genteel or of the *ton*, worked to restore their 'lost dignity' through their heroic participation in the division of labour (p. 217).

The *Vindication*'s construction of the female labourer as hero adds an additional layer to the 'double discourse' that inflects Wollstonecraft's representation of labour and class difference, and might seem to lend support to revisionist accounts of Wollstonecraft's work, which have emphasized the author's commitment to a new 'aesthetics of solidarity', what Saba Bahar has recently described as a '"community of interest" [between women] necessary for a feminist politics of the future'.[37] Part of the work performed by the portraits discussed above is, indeed, to disrupt conventional social and moral hierarchies, yet they do so only to establish another, and similarly oppressive, hierarchy in its place: one which presumes the superiority of mental over manual labour. The requirement that labour afford the worker the luxury of reflection in order to be recuperable as valuable work necessitates the dismissal of various forms of labour, including service, prostitution, complacent domestic management and a host of manual employments undertaken by men and women, as mere drudgery. The 'confusing alterity' of this, at least *triple*, discourse on women's work is as much a product of the author's textual politics as it is of her views on class. For Wollstonecraft, female labour *can* be recuperated, and indeed must be recuperated if women are to be raised from their state of abjection, but only to the extent that its recuperation underscores the author's commitment to the intellectual versus manual labour binary.

Commonly, this argument is played out in Wollstonecraft's work in depictions of labouring-class men, whose manual toil is often associated with mental degradation, and whose failings as citizens are frequently presented as analogous to those of women of society's upper ranks. According to *A Vindication of the Rights of Woman*, the mind of the physically 'robust' male labourer was as 'quiescent' as the idle gentlewoman's was 'spaniel-like' (p. 107, p. 102). That men's labour is more frequently associated with intellectual degeneration than women's labour in Wollstonecraft's writing is linked to the specialist nature of much men's work, a specialism which Wollstonecraft understood as cultivating a 'vulgar' narrowness of preoccupation that, like aristocratic absorption in trifling accomplishments, transformed potentially rational subjects into 'creatures of habit and influence' (*VRM*, p. 16). The devastating consequences of this deracination through specialization are presented at their most extreme in *An Historical and Moral View of the Origin and Progress of the French Revolution* (1794), in which the French labouring class are figured as 'machines', brutalized not only by an oppressive class system but also by the monotonous drudgery of the work they were forced to undertake in order to survive:[38]

> Commerce . . . overstocking a country with people, obliges the majority . . . to enrich the proprietor, [and] renders the mind entirely inactive. The time, which a celebrated writer says, is sauntered away, in going from one employment to another, is the very time that preserves the man from degenerating into a brute. . . . [T]hus are whole knots of men turned into machines, to enable a keen speculator to become wealthy; and every noble principle is eradicated by making a man pass his life in stretching wire, pointing a pin, heading a nail, or spreading a sheet of paper on a plain surface. (pp. 233–4)

The 'celebrated writer' to whom Wollstonecraft refers is, of course, Adam Smith, who in Book I of *The Wealth of Nations* argued against traditional working practices that obliged the 'country workman . . . to change his work and his tools every half hour, and to apply his hand in twenty different ways almost every day of his life'. Smith cast such traditions as both morally irresponsible and economically inefficient on the grounds that they rendered the labourer 'slothful and lazy, and incapable of any vigorous application'.[39] For Smith, participation in the division of labour through the execution of specialist tasks separated man from brute; for Wollstonecraft, however, such intense absorption in narrow activities sunk humankind below the beasts by blunting workers' imaginations and rendering them incapable of achieving the degree of rational reflection that only leisure, or an application to multiple employments, facilitated.

Although Wollstonecraft's attack on the deracinating effects of labour might seem at odds with her earlier valorizations of manual work in the portraits of the female labourer as hero and her idealization of the male professional, whose mental 'strength' derived from his 'having all his efforts directed to one point', it in fact stands in a complementary relationship to her views on gender, labour and professionalization as articulated in *A Vindication of the Rights of Woman* and elsewhere. The heroic female labourer's work and the male professional's specialism are valuable because they are rational – spurred by maternal benevolence and the cool eye of reason respectively – and because they provide the stimulus for intellectual growth. Working men's specialisms, by contrast, are degrading because they are so closely tied to the 'sensual and consequently selfish' needs of the body that 'impede that gradual progress of improvement, . . . the perfection of reason, and the establishment of rational equality' (*HMV*, p. 234). Immersed in physical activities, the principal end of which was to 'support the body' at the expense of mental cultivation, the male labourer more nearly resembled idle women of leisure than did his female working-class counterparts or his professional male superiors. The fashionably dissipated mother of Mary, the eponymous heroine of Wollstonecraft's first novel (1788), was as much a 'machine' as the brutalized pin-makers and wire-stretchers of *An Historical and Moral View*.[40]

Taylor has observed that the extreme form of degradation experienced alike by labouring men and women of leisure in Wollstonecraft's works is politically 'debilitating rather radicalizing', with both parties figuring as 'an invidious public presence' that had to be exorcised for the sake of the nation's moral and economic health.[41] Although the rich and the poor are presented in *A Vindication of the Rights of Woman* as being similarly incapable of securing their liberation from the particular forms of servitude they endure, the uncomfortable linking of their plight is, none the less, shown to have radical potential in its ability to galvanize those readers who, like the Female Philosopher herself, were untainted by the tedium of specialist manual labour and immune to the seductions of fashionable pleasures. Between the description of the woman-of-fashion-turned-shopkeeper and its author's famous plea that women be allowed to study politics, to practise as physicians and midwives and to enter in '[b]usiness of various kinds' (p. 218), for instance, there appears a vehement attack on political representation, which strategically aligns women of a 'superiour cast' with labouring men for precisely this political end. If women of the middle and upper ranks were to be allowed to 'pursue more extensive plans of usefulness and independence', then it was essential, Wollstonecraft maintained, that they enjoyed political representation:

> But, as the whole system of representation is now, in this country, only a convenient handle for despotism, they need not complain, for they are as well represented as a numerous class of hard working mechanics, who pay for the support of royalty when they can scarcely stop their mouths with bread. How are they represented whose very sweat supports the

> splendid stud of an heir apparent, or varnishes the chariot of some female favourite who looks down on shame? (p. 217)

Wollstonecraft's association of non-labouring-class women with sweaty, 'hard working mechanics' on the grounds of a common lack of political representation suggests that we might qualify Keen's claim that professional authors of the 1790s were more likely to 'subsume' their 'morally degenerate' inferiors 'as part of their reformist project' than to characterize them as a 'group whose social grievances might legitimately inspire their own radical reformist ambitions'.[42] Wollstonecraft claimed, by contrast, that it was only by identifying the 'shame' of poverty upon which the 'female favourite' looks unfeelingly as a national embarrassment that society could look to a future in which such 'monuments of folly' would be 'levelled by virtue' (pp. 217–18).

The revolutionary tenor of this call to arms is unmistakable, but its force dissipated when the labouring poor are subsequently revealed by Wollstonecraft to be undeserving objects of our concern after all. The 'contempt and indignation' the philosopher-author feels as she looks upon the 'gothic grandeur' of Whitehall's guards is matched only by that she experiences when describing the 'gaping' labouring-class 'crowd' who are dazzled by the 'stupid pomp' of wealth to which they unthinkingly contribute through the sweat of their brow and the payment of taxes (p. 217). The 'refinements of luxury' debase the high as much as the 'vicious repinings of envious poverty' reduce the low, leaving only the 'middle class' to carry out the work of restoring national 'virtue' (p. 218). The real injustice, according to *A Vindication of the Rights of Woman*, is not that women, like the labouring classes, are unjustly debarred from political representation, but that middle-class women, so much more capable than their labouring-class counterparts of fulfilling the demands of active citizenship, should be treated as if they were as inferior as society's most degraded members.

Such moments in the *Vindication* illustrate that, while the newly professionalized discourse of labour enabled Wollstonecraft to rehabilitate the female sex by redefining the terms in which they could participate in the making of the nation's cultural and economic wealth, this rehabilitation did not entail a reimagining of the class hierarchy that structured the division of labour as surely as the gendered hierarchy Wollstonecraft disputed. Widening opportunities for middle-class women's participation in the division of labour necessitated that those for the labouring classes be closed off, as the following section from *A Vindication of the Rights of Woman* makes clear:

> Men order their clothes to be made, and have done with the subject; women make their own clothes, necessary or ornamental, and are continually talking about them; and their thoughts follow their hands. It is not the making of necessaries that weakens the mind; but the frippery of dress. For when a woman in the lower rank of life makes her husband's and children's clothes, she does her duty, this is her part of the family business; but when women work only to dress better than they could otherwise afford, it is worse than sheer loss of time. To render the poor virtuous they must be employed, and women in the middle rank of life, did they not ape the fashions of the nobility, without catching their ease, might employ them, whilst they themselves managed their families, instructed their children, and exercised their own minds. (p. 144)

By making her family's clothes, the labouring woman demonstrates her virtue, not only by expressing her willingness to play her 'part in the family business', but by executing 'her duty' in life by allowing those of higher rank to commit themselves to pursuits more worthy than self-adornment.[43] The virtue the needleworker acquires through labour is not that 'active' virtue that Wollstonecraft would reserve, here at least, for 'women of a superiour cast' alone; for the dignity ascribed to her labour is unrelated to the nature of the work itself. Although the 'making of necessaries' is presented as being essential to domestic comfort, its larger significance lies in preventing the 'virtuous poor' woman from degenerating into idleness and vice. This argument is uncomfortably similar to that made in the various conduct books the *Vindication* critiques and which I discussed in this book's introduction: that the virtue of women of leisure could be preserved only if their leisure time was carefully policed and filled up with appropriate 'employments'. Yet, Wollstonecraft evidently saw no contradiction between her rejection of the conduct book's efforts to enforce genteel women's submission and her deployment of similar strategies to guarantee the subordination of the labouring classes. Indeed, such subordination was necessary, she continued, if middle-class women were to fulfil their intellectual potential: 'Gardening and experimental philosophy, and literature, would afford them subjects to think of and matter for conversation, that in some degree would exercise their understanding' (p. 144). The improving mental labour of the middle-class woman is predicated upon the degrading physical toil of her inferiors.

If, as Lucinda Cole suggests, Wollstonecraft viewed women as a 'class, who, given their status as wives or barely employable persons within a market economy, [we]re always already dependent upon the arbitrary power of others, upon their charity, institutions, values and norms',[44] then she realized that a recuperation of their work, as mothers, wives, shopkeepers and businesswomen, might raise them from abjection. But it is important to distinguish the means of the *Vindication*'s argument – the recuperation of labour – from the ends of that argument – the recuperation of women as useful citizens. As the passage discussed above suggests, the burden of this renegotiation of women's contribution to the nation's moral and political economies rested heavily upon the shoulders of labouring-class women (and to a lesser extent upon labouring-class men), who had to work not only to support themselves and to preserve their virtue but to allow their superiors to carry out the greater affective, cultural and intellectual work that, within Wollstonecraft's newly reconfigured division of labour, fell exclusively to them. Ultimately, the *Vindication* seeks to valorize women's manual labour in order that it can throw into relief the greater cultural and intellectual work – those 'extensive plans of usefulness and independence' – in which middle-class women might engage.

The 'unmoved spectator': reflecting on labour in *Letters Written During a Short Residence*

Reviewers of *A Vindication of the Rights of Woman* seized upon the vocabulary of labour through which Wollstonecraft sought to rehabilitate the female sex, measuring the text's success, or less commonly its failure, according to the criteria for valuable work it outlined. The *Monthly Review*, for example, although critical of 'Miss W.'s plan' that women should assume 'an active part in civil government' and be 'prohibit[ed]' from 'employ[ing]' themselves in those 'elegant labours of the needle', determined that the *Vindication*'s author had earned a 'right to a distinguished place' in 'the class of philosophers'.[45] Her efforts to raise woman 'from a state of degradation and vassalage, to her proper place in the scale of existence' was, the reviewer agreed, 'important business' well executed.[46] The substantial review that appeared in the April and June issues of the *Critical Review* for 1792 likewise allowed Wollstonecraft to set 'the example of the language' it would use in assessing the polemic's merits.[47] The conclusions it reached, however, were quite different from those arrived at in the *Monthly*. Far from proving 'that the female mind [was] equally fitted for the more arduous mental operations; that women [we]re equally able to pursue the toilsome road of minute, laborious investigation', the reviewer claimed that the

Vindication only legitimized women's degradation further. Structurally deficient, and comprised of 'vague inconclusive reasoning, strung together with little art, and no apparent plan',[48] Wollstonecraft's work failed to meet even its own standards of professionalism, the reviewer claimed, forcing him to conclude that the author's 'best friends' could not 'wish that her work should be remembered'.[49]

The *Critical*'s review is as notable for the vitriol of its attack as it is for the way that it turns Wollstonecraft's standards of professionalism against her work. Its author was damning in his assessment of Wollstonecraft's intentions in writing the polemic, which he understood not as an attempt to encourage women 'to labour to improve the morals of their fellow-citizens' by reforming themselves (*VRW*, p. 66) but as a plan to improve the lot of all women in order to allow those few who had the potential to raise themselves above the rest of their sex to do so. Should Wollstonecraft's plans for 'national education' be implemented, the reviewer warned, the effects on the domestic economy would be devastating: 'the state would lose 10,0000 useful domestic wives, in pursuit of one very indifferent philosopher or statesman'.[50] Although clearly motivated by anti-feminist prejudice, the *Critical*'s pronouncements upon the unacceptable level of wastage produced by Wollstonecraft's 'revolution in female manners' cannot be entirely dismissed out of hand. It is, of course, astonishing that any reader of the *Vindication*, no matter how unsympathetic, could read Wollstonecraft's agenda as posing a threat to marriage or maternity, which, as many of its readers have noted, are among the more 'conservative end[s] of Wollstonecraft's agenda for women'.[51] None the less, the reviewer's insinuation that the *Vindication*'s primary aim is not the redefinition of the 'business' of all women's lives but the making of a Female Philosopher, who would occupy a privileged position within the new division of labour the *Vindication* constructed, is more than a little astute. For as we have seen, the most valuable work of all, according to Wollstonecraft, was not that which could supply the immediate wants and psychological needs of those who undertook it for pecuniary support, but that which had the power to enlarge and console the superior minds of those intellectual labourers who made it their business to reflect upon it.

The figure of the philosophical or 'professional' spectator – an observer who, as John Barrell observes, is deemed uniquely capable of viewing the division of labour from a position of disinterest because he lacks an occupational identity determined by the 'economy of exchange'[52]

– looms large in Wollstonecraft's writing. In one of his earliest incarnations, he can be found in the guise of the eponymous child-hero of *Young Grandison* (1790), Wollstonecraft's free translation of a Dutch text by Madame de Cambon.[53] Under the tutelage of their mentor, Dr Bartlett, Charles (Grandison) and his fellow child protagonists are encouraged 'to learn to value the labours of the poor, and the useful employments of life' by undertaking a series of visits to various 'manufactories' and the houses of rural labourers (p. 278). The children's immediate responses to the scenes of honest industry they witness – verbal demonstrations of sympathy and the dispensing of charitable gifts – fulfil the expectations of Romantic-era writing for children. Their longer-term response to labouring-class life is less predictable, however. The children learn not only how 'to value the labours of the poor' but also how 'to reason about [the labouring class], and to admire the goodness of God displayed in the ingenuity of man' (p. 278). For Charles, these insights lead not only to moral edification but also to intellectual growth. The child, Wollstonecraft suggests, is father of the philosopher: although the young hero accepts that an 'improved mind' might not be considered as economically 'useful' as the work of 'mechanics', Charles learns that the intellectual labour in which he participates when he reflects upon rural industry has an inestimable currency and generates an involuntary 'respect' that is unknown to the man 'occupied in manual labour' alone (p. 281).

The young Grandison is a (perhaps unlikely) prototype for the figure of the Female Philosopher, a figure who, as Adriana Craciun has recently observed, would occupy a central place in later Wollstonecraft works, particularly in *An Historical and Moral View* and *Letters Written During a Short Residence*.[54] Underpinning Wollstonecraft's self-fashioning as a Female Philosopher, as *Young Grandison* implies, was the work of Adam Smith, and, particularly, his model of the 'professional spectator', the man 'who being attached to no particular occupation . . . [had] leisure and inclination to examine the occupations of other[s]'.[55] Wollstonecraft made few direct allusions to *The Wealth of Nations* in her work, certainly fewer than she made to *The Theory of Moral Sentiments* (1759).[56] Yet, despite her attacks upon the deracinating effects of occupational specialization in *An Historical and Moral View* and her career-long critique of what Angela Keane has termed 'the gendered contradiction of capitalism',[57] Smith's spectatorial paradigm was crucial to Wollstonecraft's authorial self-presentation as 'a philosopher', who looked upon society with 'the cool eye of reason' (*HMV*, p. 6).

The Smithian spectator and Wollstonecraftian Female Philosopher are connected by their privileged, yet ambiguous, position within the division of labour. The construction of the professional spectator was, as Barrell has argued, founded upon a contradiction. The 'knowing subject' from whose vantage point the division of labour was understood and rendered coherent in eighteenth-century writings on social organization and the making of the nation's wealth could not, 'within the terms of the discourse, . . . conceivably exist': in a society in which everyone had 'an occupational interest', it was impossible that anyone could lay claim to the impartial 'perception of occupational difference' that made the science of political economy possible. In order to circumvent this problem, political economic theorists, including Smith, were forced to insist upon a 'simple division, which is never clearly articulated, between manual labour and intellectual labour, and thus between those whose labour is visible, and who can be seen doing things, and those whose function Smith describes as "not to do any thing, but to observe every thing"'.[58] The spectatorial activities of the Smithian professional and the Wollstonecraftian Female Philosopher modelled partly in his image had to be legitimized as labour even while they 'elude[d] the constraints of specific [occupational] discourses'.[59]

Wollstonecraft's awareness of, and willingness to negotiate, such contradictions can be seen clearly in the preface to *An Historical and Moral View*. Like the professional spectator who creates order out of the atomization produced by the division of labour, the philosopher-historian possesses a mind – 'unsophisticated by old prejudices' and enlarged by the 'enlightened sentiments of masculine and improved philosophy' – that is capable of penetrating the 'calamitous horrors' produced by 'faction[alism]'. Where once such a disinterested perspective would have been characterized as the prerogative of an aristocratic and leisured elite, Wollstonecraft presented the philosophical objectivity to which she aspired in this ambitious project as work in its own right. Only those dedicated to the cultivation of a robust 'intellectual vigour' could 'guard against the erroneous inferences of sensibility' and 'superstition', she argued (p. 6). The Female Philosopher's role as an interpreter of the 'grand theatre of political changes' gave her a privileged position within 'polished society', yet the 'task' of attaining that position was 'arduous and melancholy' (pp. 6–7). Indeed, her 'task' was all the more 'arduous and melancholy' than that of professional spectator, Wollstonecraft implied, because she was a woman; or rather, because, as a woman, the Smithian discourse of the division of labour through which she sought to legitimize her authority as a philosopher-historian was implicitly masculine and thus unavailable to her.

Wollstonecraft's double-edged response to *The Wealth of Nations* – her indebtedness to its spectatorial paradigm and linking of virtue and labouring productivity, on the one hand, and her critique of the gendered implications of Smithian economics, on the other – was echoed in the works of a number of women writers in the period. Like these figures, who, as Kathryn Sutherland explains, were equally committed to interpreting Smithian political economy for a 'general public' and to appropriating its discourse for women, Wollstonecraft drew on the political economist's work but confronted the 'exclusively masculine . . . narrative of work' it constructed.[60] *An Historical and Moral View* seeks to resolve this implicit tension by presenting the intellectual labours of the Female Philosopher as equally 'vigorous' as those of the professional spectator, yet superior because refined by the 'feminine' attributes of responsiveness 'to nature', an 'amelioration of temper' and an adherence to the 'principles of humanity' (p. 6). As such, and like Wakefield's *Reflections*, Wollstonecraft's text 'disputes' the Smithian account of labour it also 'communicates'.[61] At stake in Wollstonecraft's disputation of the Smithian narrative, as Keane suggests, was the question of the validity of 'prevailing models of "value"' which produce[d] not only sexual and class-based inequality but which place[d] a distorted premium on the body'.[62] Denied the opportunity to seek out productive employment, middle-ranking women's role within the division of labour, as conceived in texts such as *The Wealth of Nations*, was to stimulate the consumer culture and to contribute indirectly to the making of the nation's wealth through their reproductive function. Wollstonecraft vehemently contested political economy's figuring of women primarily as 'generator[s] of desire', agents of 'reproduction' and, hence, as the capitalist economy's 'most degraded subject[s]',[63] but none the less found in the Smithian model of the professional spectator a compelling authority for her own interventions into late eighteenth-century debates on the economy and the labour market. Moreover, at a time when the legitimacy of the republic of letters was drawn from the discourse on the division of labour – in which authorship was recast as the pursuit of industrious mental labourers rather than of the polite and the leisured – the Smithian paradigm provided a secure foundation for her assertion of her own 'value' as an intellectual labourer and as a Female Philosopher.[64]

Mary A. Favret has noted that in her private correspondence, Wollstonecraft commonly figured 'imaginative production' as the 'intellectual equivalent' of productive, manual work.[65] In the published works, her perception of authorship as labour is most commonly evident in her repeated attempts to discriminate between legitimate and illegitimate models for intellectual production – between knowledge that was situated within and that which existed outside the division of labour – and the rightful or bogus agendas these models served. *A Vindication of the Rights of Men*, for example, is as much an assault upon Edmund Burke's outdated understanding of the role and responsibilities of authorship as it is an assault upon his quasi-feudal political views. Indeed, these two aspects of Burke's thinking are intimately connected for Wollstonecraft, who found a direct link between the 'slavish paradoxes' that littered *Reflections on the Revolution in France* (1790) and 'the spirit of tyranny' the text set out to defend (p. 10). Burke's 'affluence' rendered him 'shortsighted', Wollstonecraft contended; his work ethic was so unprofessional that his essay appeared completely devoid of 'method' and 'vulgar' in its 'antipathy to reason' (p. 16, p. 10). Burke's 'affectation' of literary merit could be countered, Wollstonecraft argued, only by the author's commitment to rigorous application, to establishing 'first principle[s]', and, thus, to the work of writing itself (p. 10).

It was the philosopher's 'business', as she wrote in *Letters Written During a Short Residence in Sweden, Norway and Denmark*, to set 'the imagination to work', to 'promote inquiry and discussion' and to take a 'such a dispassionate view of men as will lead [her] to form a just idea of the nature of man'.[66] Her repeated troping of intellectual production through the vocabulary of labour is by no means casual. Authorship was undoubtedly perceived as 'work' by Wollstonecraft; however it was work of a distinct kind, defined not only in opposition to the 'desultory' ruminations of the leisured elite, for which Burke stood, but also in contrast to the unreflective labours undertaken by the lower classes and by those engaged in trade and commerce (*VRM*, p. 13). The philosopher's intellectual toil, though frequently characterized in terms derived from the discourse of the division of labour, was as far removed from the endeavours of that 'class of people, who, working to support the body, ha[d] not had time to cultivate their minds' as it was from the 'vulgar' efforts of so-called men of genius, who were 'born in the lap of affluence', but had never had their 'invention sharpened by necessity' (*VRM*, p. 16). Yet, if intellectual production was defined in opposition to manual work, then it was also uncomfortably contingent upon the mechanical 'labour' of society's poorest members, who, in 'only seeking a subsistence', afforded others the opportunity to pursue 'the cultivation of the arts and sciences, that lift man so far above his first state' (*Letters*, p. 288). Like the labouring masses in *The Wealth of Nations*, whose bewilderingly diverse pursuits call for the rational eye of the professional spectator, these 'objects' existed for Wollstonecraft 'merely to exercise [the philosopher's] taste' (*Letters*, p. 299).

The manual labourer's function as fodder for the Female Philosopher's mental nourishment is most clearly illustrated in *Letters Written During a Short Residence*, and perhaps most vividly dramatized by Wollstonecraft's encounter with an impoverished Norwegian 'wet-nurse' who has been left by her husband and forced to work for just 'twelve dollars a year' while paying 'ten for the nursing of her own child' (p. 283). Wollstonecraft and the wet-nurse find common ground in their status as abandoned women, and as workers trying to support their daughters. The Norwegian woman's misery, conveyed through a 'melancholy ditty' whose sentiments Wollstonecraft understands despite the language barrier that stands between the women, arouses the latter's 'compassion', causing her to reflect with pain 'on the instability of the most flattering plans of happiness' (p. 283). But while it might be tempting to view this episode as a demonstration of the power of sympathy to transcend distinctions of rank, the dynamics of this cross-class encounter are, characteristically, more ambiguous.[67] The 'melancholy' provoked by the wet-nurse and other labouring-class figures in *Letters* does little to efface social, cultural or moral distance between them and their observer, since this unease derives in large part, from Wollstonecraft's sense of the overwhelmingly oppressive nature of her own 'task[s]' – her business as envoy to her former lover, Gilbert Imlay, and the burden of the intellectual labour required to document her travels – when compared with the ultimately less onerous travails of the labouring class.

The philosopher's burden, Wollstonecraft wrote in a letter to her sister Everina, was a great one, and a particularly 'heavy weight for female shoulders' to bear.[68] Her 'impassioned imagination' might have allowed her to comprehend the debasement endured, if not necessarily felt, by the desensitized labouring poor, but it also forced the Female Philosopher to acknowledge her own inability to experience the simple pleasures the working class were commonly held to enjoy in spite of their abjection (*VRW*, p. 186). The recognition of this emotional lack leads Wollstonecraft, at several points in *Letters*, to retreat into the 'Arcadia of fiction', the fabrication of which she found so objectionable in Burke's writing, and to locate in Scandinavian working life a vision of idealized labour and domestic labouring-class life that eluded those committed to a life of the mind. In viewing the pleasing prospect of 'harvest home', for instance, the author can barely conceal her envy for the consolations of what she imagines to be a harmonious familial and labouring life:

> A little girl was mounted a straddle on a shaggy horse, brandishing a stick over its head; the father was walking at the side of the car with a child in his arms, who must have come to meet him with tottering steps, the little creature was stretching out its arms to cling round his neck; and a boy, just above petticoats, was labouring hard, with a fork behind, to keep the sheaves from falling.
>
> My eyes followed them to the cottage, and an involuntary sigh whispered to my heart, that I envied the mother, much as I dislike cooking, who was preparing their pottage. (p. 315)

Wollstonecraft's characterization of the farmer's family is imbued with a profound sense of loss that reflects not only the pain of her abandonment by Imlay but also a deeper longing for the consolations and simple pleasures of a life of honest labour devoid of the pain of intellectual toil. A '*good* understanding', as she wrote in a letter to the Reverend Henry Dyson on 16 April 1787, was as much an affliction as it was a gift: it 'prevents a person's enjoying the common pleasures in this life – if it does not prepare him for a better it is a *curse*'.[69] The farmer's family, denied the opportunity to cultivate their minds, might never feel the blessings of 'a *good* understanding', but neither would they endure the curse of mental toil that Wollstonecraft felt so acutely.

It is ironic that the suppression of the mental faculties that makes various forms of manual work less valuable according to Wollstonecraft's vision of labour in the *Vindication* also makes such work curiously desirable in *Letters Written During a Short Residence*, in which the Female Philosopher's labours are presented as both a vocation and a source of disquiet. Yet the force of this irony diminishes rapidly with Wollstonecraft's wry reminder of the domestic drudgery that makes possible her idealized vision of rural working life, and from which, ultimately, she wishes to dissociate her mental labours. As in the encounter with the wet-nurse, the point at which Wollstonecraft's attention turns away from the spectacle of labour to her own intellectual work serves to reinforce, rather than to efface, the 'distance' between the philosopher-spectator and the objects of her sympathy. Possessed of a depth of feeling that is beyond the farmer's wife, who has condemned herself to a life of domestic drudgery to which Wollstonecraft would never submit, Wollstonecraft leaves this scene, just as she had earlier left the wet-nurse, without offering pecuniary aid. Yet, the Female Philosopher has been more than adequately recompensed by these encounters. The wet-nurse and the farmer's family, in 'excit[ing]' the philosopher's mind, have done their work; the 'solitary musing[s]' their plight provokes gives pain to the spectator, but, as Wollstonecraft comments later in the text, this pain is itself productive, and endows the philosopher's mind with the 'strength' it needs to carry out its important 'work' (p. 283; p. 297).

Cross-class encounters such as those explored here underscore Favret's claim that Wollstonecraft, along with a number of her Romantic contemporaries, was committed to the production of a new intellectual order, in which imagination became a hallmark of status and therefore a 'mechanism' for 'social mobility' for the middling ranks, while at the same time reinforcing distinctions between society's middling and lower orders through the differentiation of mental and manual labour.[70] The valorization of intellectual labour at the expense of manual work, a strategy that is as characteristic of *Letters Written During a Short Residence* as it is of Wollstonecraft's work more generally undoubtedly complicates the challenge to the gendered division of labour for which Wollstonecraft's work is rightly celebrated, as well as the feminist project this challenge serves. In this, and although she would take Adam Smith to task for his failure to account for women's contribution to the making of the nation's wealth, Wollstonecraft proves to be one of the economist's most devoted disciples. Despite her challenge to Smith's homocentric model of spectatorship – determinedly blind to women's contributions to the making of the national wealth – the role of the professional spectator, parasitically dependent upon the physical labours of society's lowest ranks while himself endowed with a privileged position in the division of labour, proved powerfully attractive to Wollstonecraft throughout her literary career.

Representing manual and intellectual labour in *Mary* and *The Wrongs of Woman*

From the 1790s, manual labour and working-class life became ever more visible presences within the novel. That this development, scrutinized in more detail in the following chapter, was coincident with the professionalization of the work of writing as a specialist form of intellectual labour that was defined in opposition to manual work, is unsurprising.

The fictionalization of manual labour provided authors with an opportunity to discuss pressing political debates of the day, over the social structure, poverty and population, for example. At the same time, writers' positioning of their intellectual endeavours in relation to physical toil underscored the value of literary labour (as similarly productive and socially useful), while emphasizing the former's superiority over the latter.[71] A rather more surprising effect of this trend, however, was that the more visible workers became in the non-fictional and imaginative literature of the period, the less clearly they were heard. Sandra Sherman observes that, in both radical and conservative writings from this decade, labourers and the poor were held hostage to the political aspirations of authors, who spoke on the former's behalf often to deny them fully fledged subjectivities.[72] Wollstonecraft's representation of the labouring class, her description of the men-machines in *An Historical and Moral View*, her discussion of the needleworkers in the *Vindication* and her treatment of the wet-nurse and farmer's family in *Letters Written During a Short Residence*, seem to endorse Sherman's claim that even the most radical of middle-class Jacobin writers reduced the poor to a 'dehumanized sameness', which deprived them of 'ability or authority to take hold of their affairs' at the same time that these authors pressed for 'political equality'.[73]

Yet, Wollstonecraft's treatment of labouring women was neither so wholly callous nor so disinterested as it has variously been supposed to be. As this chapter has indicated, labouring women commonly confirm for Wollstonecraft the privileged status of mental toil within the division of labour; but that claim to privilege is made only once women's right to participation in the division of labour has been asserted and their fitness for inclusion established following an extensive re-evaluation of the contribution their work might make to the economy. What emerges, then, from these texts is Wollstonecraft's sense of the uncomfortable state of mutual dependency in which the female writer and female labourer existed at the century's close. Whereas Scott and Smith made political mileage out of the imaginative connections they drew between their intellectual work as writers and other forms of paid and unpaid female labour, for Wollstonecraft, the articulation of such associations seems to be motivated more by an uncomfortable recognition of necessity than by creative choice. The female labourer, Wollstonecraft contended, needed the Female Philosopher, whose vision provided a vital corrective to the homosocial gaze of the Smithian professional spectator, to make her work visible and its value known. Equally, the Female Philosopher needed the female labourer and as an object of enquiry, the successful interpretation of which justified the former's inclusion within the republic of letters.

This interdependence, in all its complexity, is worked out most fully in Wollstonecraft's novels, in which the relationship between intellectual and manual labour is figured in the form of the affective bonds that exist between heroines and labouring-class characters. *Mary: A Fiction* (1788) contains some of Wollstonecraft's earliest published thoughts on the Female Philosopher and her relationship to manual labourers. Intended to debunk Rousseau's characterization of the 'female organs' as too 'weak' for 'arduous employment', Wollstonecraft's novel features a heroine with 'thinking powers', whose 'grandeur' of mind 'is derived from the operations of its own faculties, not subjugated to opinion; but drawn by the individual from the original source' (p. 5). Physical labour might seem an unlikely preoccupation in a novel concerned with the making of a female 'genius', but only if we view the text anachronistically with an assumption of the incompatibility of manual and intellectual labour. Labour is, in fact, a constant preoccupation of *Mary*, the horror of which pushes the heroine further towards a pursuit of the life of the intellect, but to which this putative genius is also constantly drawn back to alleviate the pain and guilt experienced by her sensible, philosophical mind.

Foreshadowing William Wordsworth's *Prelude* (1805), *Mary* locates the origins of the growth of genius in a series of early encounters with death: first a 'little chicken' which 'expired at her feet', then a dog 'hung' in a 'passion' by the heroine's father (p. 11). Even before she had any concrete 'notion of death', we learn, Mary lived 'continually in dread' lest her father's 'tyrannical and passionate' behaviour should 'frighten her mother to death' (p. 10). Her first encounter with the death of a human is that of 'a little girl who attended in the nursery' to which Mary is banished by her unfeeling mother (p. 11). Mary pays the nursery maid 'great attention', but, 'contrary to her wish', the girl is sent to the house of her mother, 'a poor woman, whom necessity obliged to leave her sick child while she earned her daily bread'. In 'a fit of delirium', and while her mother is absent, the daughter stabs herself (p. 11). The girl's death has a profound and lasting effect on Mary:

> [she] saw her dead body, and heard the dismal account; and so strongly did it impress her imagination, that every night of her life the bleeding corpse presented itself to her when she first began to slumber. Tortured by it, she at last made a vow, that if she was ever a mistress of a family

> she would herself watch over every part of it. The impression that this accident made was indelible. (p. 11).

This tragic episode confirms for the heroine the devastating consequences of the failure of maternity, a wrong that Mary initially intends to right by becoming a mother herself. But Mary is destined not to become the 'mistress of a family' and her subsequent marriage will be a sham. Her longing for a 'world *where there is neither marrying*, nor giving in marriage' (p. 73) – perhaps also her fear of the responsibility of maternity violently brought home by the young servant's death – forces her to seek out relationships, such as those with Ann and Henry, which flout heterosexual convention.[74] As a result, Mary is unable to erase the memory of the dead girl's body. Instead, she represents a constant reminder of the terrifying ease with which women's abjection turns, as it would also do in *The Wrongs of Woman* and in Charlotte Smith's *The Old Manor House* (1793), into violent self-mutilation. A tragic warning of the deracinating effects of economic and sexual injustice, the servant girl is also a spectral double for Mary: both young women are of similar age; both are susceptible to ill health; both, although for different reasons, are rejected by their mothers. Mary seeks to avoid her contemporary's fate, first, by attempting to rise above the degrading physical toil that characterized and foreshortened the nursery maid's life and, second, by embracing a life of the mind. In doing so, however, Mary finds herself constantly drawn back to scenes of labouring life, in part to make amends for her failure to prevent the girl's death, but also, I want to suggest, as an expression of guilt over the failure of her intellectual work to secure the betterment of her inferiors.

If readers feel unease in response to Wollstonecraft's positioning of manual work in relation to the work of the Female Philosopher in the texts already discussed here, then *Mary* suggests that this was a source of some anxiety for the woman of genius herself. Initially, as the heroine's 'faculties' are 'improved' by reading and the 'society of men of genius' (p. 25), Mary becomes more removed from the labouring poor, whose 'huts' surround her home (p. 15). She rises above the bodily want that subjugates her social inferiors, parasitically finding in her meditations upon the 'vicious poor' food for thought that enables her to exert such 'power over her appetites and whims, . . . that when her affections had an object, she almost forgot she had a body which required nourishment' (p. 17). Following the deaths of Ann and Henry, however, the heroine finds herself compelled to engage once again in charitable work for rural labourers and the poor (p. 41; p. 73). In a nod to Scott's mid-century fictions, the novel concludes with the heroine's retirement to the country where she 'established factories, threw the estate into small farms; and continually employed herself this way to dissipate care, and banish unavailing regret. . . . These occupations engrossed her mind' (p. 73). '[D]oing good' is a 'luxury' that assuages the heroine's guilt over the nursery maid's death and is further symptomatic of the heroine's anxiety about the merely palliative, rather than instrumental, role her mental toil plays within the division of labour and in addressing its injustices (p. 17). Mary needs the poor to stimulate her 'benevolent contemplative mind' and to provide her with a meaningful 'employment' on earth (p. 56). Although the recognition is an unwelcome one, Mary comes to realize that as a woman who has renounced marriage, and as a female genius whose commitment to the cultivation of her mental faculties as an alternative to marriage results in a debilitating delicacy of health that 'did not promise long life', she relies upon the labouring poor's abjection to render her 'useful' to society (p. 73; p. 64).

The Female Philosopher's anxious dependency upon the female labourer is returned to in *The Wrongs of Woman; or Maria*. As in *Mary*, in Wollstonecraft's unfinished novel the working woman doubles for the novel's middle-class, sensible heroine, both of whom prove through their common experience of sexual and economic exploitation that 'in a man's world all women are prostituted'.[75] The extent to which Jemima reveals the limits of Wollstonecraft's feminism and exposes the fallacy of the novel's promise to 'show the wrongs of different classes of women, equally oppressive, though, from the difference of education, necessarily various', has been a subject of intense scholarly debate, much of which has focused upon the servant-turned-warder's insistence that she live with Maria as a 'house-keeper' and '[o]n no other terms' (p. 84; p. 175). Yet even if, in Mary Poovey's words, the novel 'does *not* develop the revolutionary implications of Jemima's narrative', it is hard not to admire the boldness and uniqueness of Wollstonecraft's construction of her working-class heroine.[76] Jemima's graphic account of her systematic brutalization at the hands of her family, employers, fellow servants and clients constitutes a radical attempt to articulate a labouring-class subjectivity otherwise almost entirely absent in female-authored fiction of the later eighteenth century.[77] Equally radical is the novel's attribution of 'thinking powers' to a woman of Jemima's rank. If Jemima is distinguished by the frankness of her unflinching account of labouring life, then she is also remarkable for her erudition, as Maria repeatedly observes (p. 113). Like her genteel charge, herself the pupil of a learned and benevolent uncle, Jemima has also benefited from a close relationship with a man of letters. In order to escape life on the streets and the relentless persecution of the town watchmen, who 'harrass', assault and 'extort' money from her, Jemima accepts a client's offer 'to keep his house' near Hampstead. Modelled on Rousseau, the 'worn-out votary of voluptuousness' for whom Jemima works is also 'a man of great talents, and of brilliant wit' (p. 113). Within the libertine's house, Jemima loses 'the privileged respect of my sex', but gains other, more valuable, freedoms when her master brings home 'a literary friend or two . . . to dine and pass the night': 'I had the advantage of hearing discussions from which, in the common course of life, women are excluded'. Having entered the philosopher's house just able to spell 'and put a sentence together', Jemima gradually develops 'a moral sense' that frames the autobiographical narrative she relates to Maria and Darnford (p. 114).

The ascription of 'thinking powers' to Jemima unsettles the intellectual/manual labour binary that structures Wollstonecraft's earlier writings, and, as Bahar writes, works to dismantle 'the rupture between the abstract, disembodied and disinterested voice of philosophy and the embodied voice of experience and in so doing becomes an agent of political change'.[78] Jemima does not need the Female Philosopher to speak on her behalf. Her experiences provide a secure foundation for her insights into social and economic injustice and legitimize her attacks on public intellectuals, who profess 'to be friends to freedom, and . . . can assert that poverty is no evil' (p. 116). Like Wollstonecraft herself, the 'true genius' behind Jemima's narrative as Godwin reminds us at the novel's close, the warder has the capacity 'to develop events, to discover their capabilities, to ascertain the different passions and sentiments with which they are fraught, and to diversify them with incidents, that give reality to the picture, and take a hold upon the mind of the reader of taste, from which they can never be loosened' (p. 184). Jemima's hopes that the 'new principles' she has cultivated will facilitate her return 'to the respectable part of society' are not, as she fears, futile (p. 114). Her 'superior' 'sentiments and language' captivate Maria, thus paving the way for the most fully elaborated of the unfinished novel's draft conclusions in which Maria and Jemima live together with Maria's formerly estranged daughter in a 'partnership', which, as Taylor explains, 'if not equal, is certainly reciprocal, rooted in mutual sympathy and congruent interests'.[79] Jemima's intellectual refinement both justifies her inclusion within this utopian, meritocratic community and authorizes her presence within the novel by proving her to be a worthy 'friend' to her future mistress.

It is perhaps a fitting conclusion to a career in which the relationship between manual and intellectual labour was such a constant refrain that, in *The Wrongs of Woman*, the female labourer is herself a philosopher. Yet it is also characteristic that this effort to efface the distance between these kinds of work was to generate further prejudices and tensions that were to make the recuperation of female labour still more difficult for the generations of women writers who followed Wollstonecraft. Paradoxically, Jemima's intellectual growth has much the same effect as the genteel woman's fall into labour has in a number of nineteenth-century novels: to confirm the women's unsuitability for the work they are forced to undertake. Her finely honed 'moral sense' may enable Jemima to reflect upon her lot, but it also renders her unfit for a life of servitude that she no longer considers 'feasible' once her mental faculties have been awakened. The pity and horror Jemima's harrowing story of labouring life and poverty first elicit give way to rather different emotions as the narrative progresses and her auditors are invited to feel sympathy for the additional pain the working heroine endures as a direct consequence of the realization that her capacities far exceed her opportunities: 'I had acquired a taste for literature . . . and now to descend to the lowest vulgarity, was a degree of wretchedness not to be imagined unfelt' (p. 115). Jemima can be saved precisely because her 'sensible' mind distinguishes her from the labouring 'machine[s]' for whom she stands and speaks (p. 115; p. 117). Like the professional spectator, upon whom Wollstonecraft modelled herself in her historical and polemical writings, Jemima can emerge as a philosopher only once she has imaginatively divorced herself from the drudgery and hardship of manual labour. She is redeemed finally not by a life of hard labour but by her ability to narrate that life and to 'make her story' 'subordinate to a great moral purpose' (p. 184). Even the labouring woman-turned-philosopher, it seems, must subsume the narratives of those objects she gives voice to if her claims for the value of women's intellectual work are to be taken seriously.

Recognizing that Jemima's redemption is guaranteed by her exceptional access to a life of the mind that unfits her for menial labour does not diminish the force of *The Wrongs of Woman*'s damning critique of the late eighteenth-century labour market, but it does force a reassessment of Jemima's function as 'an agent of political change'. More importantly, perhaps, it forces a reassessment of the nature of the political change her presence was intended to effect. In *The Wrongs of Woman*, as in the second *Vindication*, the labouring woman served two agendas simultaneously: first, to indict the systematic degradation of women as beings superfluous to the political and moral economies and, second, to establish the Female Philosopher's place within the republic of letters. The tensions this chapter has identified in Wollstonecraft's treatment of manual and intellectual work – her attempt to recuperate female labour, on the one hand, while identifying it as inferior to the greater cultural and intellectual work of the Female Philosopher, on the other – are undoubtedly shaped by Wollstonecraft's class politics, but, as I have sought to demonstrate, cannot be explained away by them alone. If, as Taylor has argued, we read *The Wrongs of Woman* as a 'preview of the tensions and divisions – as well as the solidarities – that would typify later feminist movements', then it is important that we recognize that these tensions and divisions are as much manifestations of a response to specific cultural and historical circumstances that directly threatened the role of the woman writer as they are indicators of individual class politics.[80]

This recognition is particularly significant given Wollstonecraft's central place in feminist history and the responsibility she is often asked to bear for the 'biases and inequalities as well as . . . courageous complicities' that have characterized this movement.[81] In Chapters 1 and 2, I have argued that it was far from inevitable that women writers *had* to distance themselves from the grubby world of work in order to keep the purity of their literary labours intact. The morally degenerate and hyper-libidinized fictional working women, whose origins we might detect in Wollstonecraft's work were not an inevitable presence in the 1790s in the way that many scholars have suggested they had become by the nineteenth century.[82] Neither, I want to emphasize, are these representations characteristic of Wollstonecraft's work, which, as we have seen, emphasized the rehabilitative qualities of female labour for women of all classes as much as it focused on labour as a source of female degradation. After the 1790s, however, such pejorative insinuations became more persistent and more characteristic, as women writers, striving to assert their right to participation in a literary public sphere increasingly associated with the 'masculine' qualities of industry and professionalism, appropriated the female labourer to their cause. For Wollstonecraft, as for subsequent generations of authors who theorized the public role of the woman writer, the fates of the Female Philosopher and professional woman writer were inextricably, if uncomfortably, bound to that of the female labourer. However, the gains and losses both parties incurred as a result of the Female Philosopher's re-evaluation of the business of women's lives were far from commensurate with one another. Wollstonecraft's argument for women's right to a role in the nation's political and moral economies legitimately earned her a 'right to a distinguished place' in 'the class of philosophers', but it did so partly at the expense of the labouring woman, whose contributions to the 'production of value' were inferior in kind and in degree to the productions of 'true genius'. 'On no other terms' would the labouring woman's recuperation be possible (p. 174).

4

Women writers, the popular press and the Literary Fund, 1790–1830

MEN OF GENIUS, instead of being unproductive, as intimated by a popular writer, are the most productive of all the classes of mankind. Their inventions not only fix and realise themselves in some subject, and for some time, but they direct the mode of storing and setting in motion future industry; and instead of perishing in the performance, they are renovated in every renewed action of a similar nature, and endure for ever in some permanent habit, regulating the conduct, shortening the labour, and multiplying the comforts, of mankind. No error, therefore, can more strongly indicate barbarism, than that of modern political oeconomists, who affirm, the works of genius perish in the production. The inference is too atrocious – but the provision would have been merciful – that their authors should perish with them.

David Williams, *Claims of Literature* (1802)[1]

I am now in more distress than the poorest pauper or the most abject prostitute . . . & as I am a literary character no other charity applies to my case. Gentlemen some of you perchance have daughters – sisters – wives – think what would be their case if drifted away by adversity from house – horse – servants & a competence to leave the miseries of human life and live by the pen!

Men reduced from affluence may seek their fortune in the field of war, or on the ocean, but when a woman is left alone in life

'In fortune ruin'd & in mind forlorn'

she is exposed to tenfold difficulties and is debarred from any avocations.

Susan Wood to the Royal Literary Fund, 3 February 1819[2]

The Literary Fund (later the Royal Literary Fund) was established in 1790. Its primary goal was to offer monetary support to financially distressed authors and their dependants. Its secondary aim was more ambitious: to restore literature and authorship to the cultural pre-eminence the charity claimed they had all but lost as the eighteenth century drew to a close. According to David Williams, the Fund's founder and author of its belatedly published manifesto, *Claims of Literature*, the turn-of-the-century literary public sphere had become set upon a perilous and potentially terminal course. The decline of patronage, the unscrupulous practices of booksellers and the questionable standards of taste evinced by an ever growing army of readers were just some of the more important contributory factors outlined by Williams by way of explanation for the cultural devaluation of the republic of letters and its members. Yet the principal target of Williams's text was not the literary marketplace's commercialization, but rather the academic discipline that theorized and mystified this phenomenon: the science of political economy, particularly as exemplified by the work of that 'popular writer' Adam Smith.

If, as we have seen in the previous chapter, the vocabulary of the division of labour and political economy's association of industry and value helped to construct a new model of literary professionalism in the eighteenth century's final decades, then *Claims* suggested that it also threatened to undermine that model. *Claims*'s critique of *The Wealth of Nations* (1776) hinges upon the latter's notorious differentiation of productive (i.e. manual) from unproductive (imaginative or service-based) labour. As Gruffudd Aled Ganobcsik-Williams has observed, Smith himself might not have attached an 'ethical dimension' to this distinction, but, by aligning the productive with the useful, his text implied a value judgement which, in the eyes of a number of its critics, left the status of intellectual labour ambiguous to say the least.[3] In response to *The Wealth of Nations*'s problematic construction of authorship as unproductive labour, Williams countered that the verbal productions of true 'men of genius' were neither ephemeral nor useless. Like the manual labours of 'mechanics', the mental toil of authors realized itself in 'vendible commodit[ies], which last[ed] for some time at least after the labour [was] past', and which could be 'stored up to be employed, if necessary, upon some other occasion'.[4] Indeed, mental labour was infinitely more valuable than its corporeal equivalent, Williams suggested, precisely because it 'direct[ed] the mode of storing and setting in motion future industry'. A provocative rewriting of *The Wealth of Nations*, *Claims* argued that it was the disinterested, intellectual work of men of letters, rather than the self-interested trucking and bartering of commercial man, that was the invisible hand behind the making of the nation's wealth. To equate 'works of genius' with the services of menial domestics, as *The Wealth of Nations* had done, on the grounds that both 'perish[ed] in the production' was, therefore, 'barbari[c]' and 'atrocious'. The only thing more 'barbari[c]' and 'atrocious', Williams continued, was that their noble manufacturers were quite literally perishing in want while their works were 'regulating the conduct, shortening the labour, and multiplying the comforts, of mankind'.[5] It was to offer redress for the personal misfortunes and cultural calamity unwittingly engineered by political economy's devaluation of authors' inestimable contribution to the moral and money economies that the Literary Fund was established.

My second epigraph, taken from the Literary Fund's case file on Susan Wood, the little-known 'Authoress of "Literary Exercises" &c. &c. [1802] and of various works moral & pious', is just one of hundreds of examples contained in the charity's early archives of the '*mental* and *corporeal*' distress to which *Claims* alludes.[6] Wood first approached the Fund in February 1803 hoping to obtain money to publish a number of works for which she could not raise the necessary expenses herself. The printing costs of *Literary Exercises*, she explained, had been barely covered by a small family allowance given to Wood by her grandfather, and her hopes to use the profits from this slim volume to see additional titles into print had been 'cruelly destroyed'. Fearing that her literary career would be consigned to 'oblivion', Wood pleaded with the charity for financial support.[7] Her bid was unsuccessful, however, and of her ten future applications only four resulted in the award of modest sums of money.[8] Her subsequent requests for aid, submitted over a period of seventeen years, document the author's declining health during a 'long continued depression of mind & fatigue resulting from . . . embarrassments in Life'; her accumulating debts, as a consequence of which she feared she would 'loose [*sic*] her character'; and a period of near starvation during which she lived 'chiefly on potatoes and few of them'.[9] Yet, if Wood's correspondence dwelt primarily on her private misfortunes and personal credentials, she was not averse to reminding the charity that her professional activities gave her every right to be considered 'a useful member of society' and therefore deserving of the Fund's support.[10] Despite the several rejection letters she received, Wood remained modestly defiant to the end, writing to the Fund in May 1820 that 'Even as a literary character, (humble as my pretensions are), I am *entitled* to appear very differently in society' (emphasis added).[11] This was to be Wood's last application to the charity, and was met with a small award of £5. Whether, as seems unlikely, this was enough to restore her 'character' is sadly unknown.

Wood's correspondence to the Fund crafted a narrative of authorial ills that was already all too familiar to the charity's committee by the time her first application was received. Authorship, as the Fund's archives repeatedly attest, was a devastating leveller, and, with no other charities or professional organizations dedicated to the relief of literary figures at the time of the Literary Fund's founding, the means of redress for those who fell victim to the ruthless economics of the late eighteenth-century literary marketplace were few. The various forms of financial, mental and bodily distress outlined by Wood were endured by many; they affected both men and women, the famous and highly regarded (including Samuel Taylor Coleridge, Charlotte Lennox and Thomas Love Peacock) and obscure writers such as Wood and the popular, yet much derided, female authors for the circulating libraries. None the less, Wood, like a number of other women applicants to the charity, claimed to experience the privations of authorship uniquely and all the more intensely because of her sex. The loss of personal and professional reputation might be endured or even overturned by a man, but for a woman, she pointed out, such a loss was irrevocable. How tragically ironic it was, then, Wood lamented, that society afforded so few opportunities by which a woman's character and livelihood could be securely and legitimately maintained. Recalling Mary Wollstonecraft's *A Vindication of the Rights of Woman* (1792) and Mary Ann Radcliffe's *The Female Advocate* (1799), Wood argued that women's exclusion from the professions and other economically viable forms of employment inexorably led to their degradation. Authorship, commonly presented by female Fund applicants as one of only three respectable employments to which women of middling station might turn – the others being needlework and teaching – offered a potential lifeline, but frequently dashed their hopes, leaving them 'in more distress than the poorest pauper or the most abject prostitute'. Whether she attempted to live off her mind or her body, for the financially straitened woman whose education had not fitted her for manual labour, or whose upbringing made such work unseemly, there were few safeguards against a loss of 'character'.

What remains unspoken in Wood's correspondence, but is nevertheless made clear in Williams's *Claims* and in the charity's treatment of its applicants, was that the Literary Fund and the particular form of literary professionalism it constructed were complicit with the processes of marginalization that intensified the distress of its female author-claimants. The Fund's efforts to professionalize the literary marketplace, in part through its reworking of the Smithian discourse of the division of labour, were highly prejudicial to women writers, and made it ever more difficult for them to appropriate this discourse, as Sarah Scott and Charlotte Smith had done, to justify their authorial practice. The vocabulary of labour, genius and utility, so central to the model of professional authorship that emerged at the end of the eighteenth century, was not, as we have seen, intrinsically hostile to women writers, and indeed was fundamental to the authorial self-construction of some of those whose work is best know today. However as I argue below, the anxieties provoked by textual production, evident in the writing of authors such as Wollstonecraft and in the rationale of organizations such as the Literary Fund, led to the formation of new hierarchies of literary labour which made the claims of many female 'authors by profession', particularly those who trudged along on the treadmills of the popular presses, infinitely more difficult to justify than they had been for those of previous generations.[12]

This chapter focuses upon just such popular women writers to examine the multiple and fractious legacies of the debate on women's work at the turn of the century. The picture that emerges from these writers' publications and their pleas to the Fund, the archives of which provide a rich and largely unmined seam of evidence concerning the material conditions, and rhetorical construction, of authorship, is illuminating. Increasingly presented as the degraded other against which the activities of the male professional were defined, women's work, as we shall see, was to play an ever more central role in the discourse of authorship in the late eighteenth and early nineteenth centuries, to the detriment of a number of its best-loved practitioners. Moreover, as gender became increasingly constitutive of literary authority at the turn of the century, so the discourse of authorship served more insistently to reinforce constructions of gender. Some of the female applicants to the Literary Fund seemed (openly at least) to yield to these developments by assenting to the trend towards the professionalization and masculinization of the literary that would relegate their productions to the status of amateur and forgettable trifles.[13] Indeed, the number of trembling females who appeared reluctantly as authors, and who beseeched their readers and critics' tolerance for a lack of literary aptitude, appears to have increased significantly as the century progressed.[14] In spite of these developments, however, the strategies adopted by Scott and Smith still had much to offer those writers who wished to assert the cultural and intellectual value of their literary work and to contest the gendered divisions between, for example, the genius and the hack, the useful and the ornamental, the professional and the popular and the mind and the body, that were so vital to the Fund's construction of authorship. That the authors this chapter examines remain largely obscure today, despite the now considerable body of scholarship devoted to eighteenth-century women's writing, might suggest that their claims to 'literary industry or merit' carry as little weight in our era as they carried in their own.[15] My aim here is, in part, to counter such arguments by suggesting that the contributions of, for example, Eliza Parsons, Elizabeth Helme, Ann Burke, Phebe Gibbes and Mary Julia Young to the debate on women's work does, in fact, 'entitle' them, to borrow Wood's terminology, to a rightful place in the history of eighteenth-century literature and the history of authorship.

The founding of the Literary Fund: reclaiming literature and disclaiming the market

David Williams, the Dissenting clergyman and political and religious theorist, first mooted the idea for an authors' charity in a paper delivered at a meeting of Benjamin Franklin's Club of Thirteen in 1773.[16] Arguing that '[m]en of genius' were 'the greatest Benefactors of every community', Williams urged the Club's members to acknowledge the 'justice [of] a valuation of literary benefits and the public duty of assigning indemnities to useful talents reduced to poverty'. Franklin warned his friend that such arguments would have but a 'feeble' claim upon the public purse, and further cautioned that Williams's proposed project would 'require so much time, perseverance and patience, that the Anvil [would] wear out the hammer'.[17] Franklin's predictions were borne out by a decade of unsuccessful bids on Williams's part to secure support for his proposed charity from influential public figures including Charles James Fox, William Pitt and Joseph Banks, as well as Edmund Burke and, perhaps surprisingly, Adam Smith. A 'hostile' Burke met Williams's recommendations with 'execrations on authors and scribblers', adding that he could see no reason to offer financial support to a breed of men who were no better than 'pests', while Smith met the idea of a charity designed to help society's most 'unproductive' members with 'that modest diffidence', which, as Williams ruefully recollected, 'seemed to be his character'.[18]

Williams needed more than enthusiasm to prick the public's collective conscience about the conditions of authorship, and found the evidence he required to convince sceptics of the charity's necessity in the death of the elderly and respected scholar and translator Floyer Sydenham in 1787. Although the cause of Sydenham's death was disputed – fellow Platonist Thomas Taylor suggested that he committed suicide the night before he was going to be imprisoned for a small debt, while most other sources indicate that he died in prison – there is little doubt that his tragic end galvanized the support that Williams needed to embark upon his project in earnest.[19] Eighteen guineas was donated for an advertisement intended to raise subscriptions, which subsequently appeared in *The Herald*, *The World*, *The Gazetteer*, *The St. James's Chronicle* and *The General Evening Post*. Later that year, the charity's constitution was published, although the process of applying for financial aid was not formalized until the introduction of a standardized application form in 1841, a source of much confusion and frustration for claimants who often found their claims rejected on the grounds that they failed to follow procedures of which they were unaware.[20] In general, applicants were expected to provide both evidence of genuine hardship and distress, sometimes doing so in the form of third-party accounts or medical notes, and evidence of authorship, something which posed a particular problem for the many (often female) authors of pseudonymous and anonymous works. Additionally, and more problematically, author-claimants had to convince the charity's presiding committee of the merit of their publications, a task they fulfilled in various ways, including sending in copies of their works with their applications, soliciting references from well-respected members of society or, better still, from subscribers to the charity, as well as through the development of the various and sophisticated forms of authorial self-presentation discussed below. The Fund's first meeting was held on 10 May 1790 at the Prince of Wales's Coffee House in Conduit Street, London, its members principally comprising doctors, scholars and clergymen. The charity received and summarily rejected its first application by a Lieutenant Stanton, the author of an obscure work on duelling, in July 1790. In December of that year, the Fund would offer relief to its first successful claimant, a Dissenting minister, translator and writer of religious works, Dr Edward Harwood, and by 1803 it could boast the patronage of the Prince of Wales.

Despite its growing prestige and consolidating reputation in some quarters, the Literary Fund was met with derision in others throughout much of its early history. The multiple objections to the charity that were voiced during this period are revealing, and highlight the extent to, and urgency with, which moral, cultural, political and economic anxieties coalesced around the figure of the author in the late eighteenth and early nineteenth centuries. A recurrent concern of the charity's detractors was that the Fund would 'produce or foster the evil it [wa]s intended to remedy' by increasing the number of individuals attempting to become authors by profession (*Claims*, p. 108). Driving this critique was a familiar unease about the moral implications of the expansion of print culture. By providing pecuniary encouragement to those writers who could not (and perhaps deserved not) to live by their pens, the charity ran the risk of further animating what Williams acknowledged to be an already overpopulated and degraded market, dominated by the 'SICKLY SPAWN . . . of the CIRCULATING LIBRARIES'. If such institutions, as Williams conceded, were responsible for debilitating young readers' minds and bodies and for cultivating literary aspirations among those unsuited to authorial toil, then surely, dissenting voices asserted, the rewarding of literary failure could only promote a further decline in literary standards and taste (*Claims*, pp. 97–8).

Williams's invectives against popular reading habits throughout *Claims* imply that he may have harboured a certain sympathy for such arguments, yet he also feared that these objections were often little more than a convenient mask for other, more reactionary, points of view, particularly those which targeted literature's iconoclastic and potentially revolutionary tendencies during the political turmoil of the 1790s. Williams, himself a political radical offered honorary French citizenship in 1792 along with Thomas Paine, aimed to palliate such concerns, noting in *Claims* that the establishment of the Fund implied no 'censure of the government of the country' (*Claims*, p. 8), but ominously pointed out that the '[s]uperior minds' it intended to reward were such as might 'dare to call men to the examination of their principles' and to 'penetrate and analyse every thing' in a manner 'alarming to all established systems' (*Claims*, p. 15). Indeed, *Claims* was itself accused by the then Vice-President of the Literary Fund, Sir James Bland Burges, of containing 'principles subversive of religion, government and society', its publication prompting an argument between Williams and Burges that would lead to the latter's resignation.[21]

Underlying these intimately connected political, moral and cultural concerns about the Fund's establishment was, however, a still more pressing set of economic arguments that *Claims* attempted to refute. The Fund was most contentious, Williams found, because it ran counter to the logic of the Smithian division of labour. The charity's critics argued that since financial necessity was an essential spur to labour, self-betterment and economic growth, then the charity's incentivizing of literary life might 'dishonour *labour*' by fatally increasing the number of individuals devoted to unproductive work (*Claims*, p. 67). To this extent, the Fund fell foul of suspicions that, Donna T. Andrew observes, had a widespread and disabling impact on the charity movement as a whole during the later eighteenth century.[22] Yet the charity also prompted economic concerns that were specific to its literary remit, with many opponents suggesting that the charity's impact would be even more devastating than that of other philanthropic institutions, such as the Magdalen House and Lambeth Asylum, which offered temporary respite from financial deprivation and trained inmates for a life of virtuous (manual) industry once readmitted into society. To reward authorial failure was, potentially, to deter writers from pursuing a life of productive labour and might even (if rather improbably) coax manual workers, who might not otherwise have considered a literary career, into abandoning their ploughs for their pens. Even if the Fund did not actively encourage 'the sons and daughters of farmers and tradesmen' to 'commence AUTHORS', its stimulation of the literary marketplace would, critics feared, contribute to the nation's degeneration by multiplying the number of literary works that were productive only of 'ennui, nervous atrophy, or consumption' and by depriving potential citizens and workers of their 'useful capacity' (*Claims*, p. 97).

To address such concerns, *Claims* sought to convince readers that the Fund's activities would not disturb 'the balance of employments throughout the country', an improbable conjecture, Williams maintained, given that creative inspiration evaded even the most industrious of scribblers – 'genius' being furnished by 'nature and education' not 'will'.[23] The Fund aimed simply to 'enable men of genius, already educated, to exert and employ their talents . . . to the advantage and perfection of all other employments' (p. 108). In order to achieve this task, the Fund had first to establish authorship's status as productive work. Intellectual endeavour, Williams argued, was valuable precisely because it was *the* 'genius directing [all] labour' on earth (p. 23):

> Genius, talents, and labour, wisely employed, form the fund, from which every thing valuable to society is produced. All the land, and all the spontaneous productions which first constitute property, would not, without this fund, support a tenth of the present population of the world, or a hundredth part of the expences of its governments. (pp. 19–20)

The nation's vitality, as Williams wrote in his *Incidents in my own Life* (1802), rested upon the 'candour', and promotion, of 'genius', without which the 'steam engine, the cotton mill, the art of mingling tin and copper' would not exist and 'half the [country's] cotton works would be closed'.[24] The fallacy of modern political economy was its ascription of greater 'relative value' – a well-worn phrase in *Claims* – to bodily over mental endeavour. Williams acknowledged that establishing an 'equitable mode' by which intellectual labour could be assigned a value equivalent to services rendered was difficult (p. 47). Physical labour resulted in the production of 'vendible commodities', the use and/or exchange value of which was, according to Smithian equation of commodity value and the labour invested and commanded by its production, more readily measurable than the ethereal speculations produced by mental toil.[25] Yet the usefulness of the latter mode of industry, when prompted by the spirit of genius and utility upon which 'every capitalist and every adventurer draws at his pleasure' (p. 47), long outlived the former, and could be 'applied to national use' even while its authors 'and his family' inexplicably lived 'destitute and distressed' (p. 52).

Ultimately, Williams failed to identify an economic answer to the question of how to assign monetary 'equivalents' to mental labour (p. 47), but found an alternative solution in the example of the 'ORDERS AND CORPORATIONS' around which the professions of the church, the law and medicine organized themselves (p. 43). As Penelope J. Corfield has demonstrated, the eighteenth century witnessed significant growth within such 'tertiary' occupations – that is, those 'not subsumed under primary (agriculture and mining) or secondary (manufacturing) productions' – which, in turn, necessitated that its members strove for status through 'improved self-definition and organization'.[26] As a consequence, professional prestige was increasingly attached throughout the period to specialization, to self-regulation and to a 'formalized process of training and education' that controlled the number of individuals entering such lines of work.[27] Literature's aspirations to professional status already had a long history by the time that the Fund was established in 1790, the republic of letters' bid to secure prestige through self-regulation manifest, for example, in the rise of the literary review at mid-century, and the legal debates over copyright that recurred throughout the period. While such efforts undoubtedly made the literary public sphere's claims to professionalism more plausible, commentators lamented that they failed to protect its members against the infractions and pecuniary distress from which those who worked in the 'learned professions, and all the provinces of arts merely imitative' were supposedly immune.[28] Neither, they claimed, were such mechanisms sufficiently robust to counter the effects of the decline of literary patronage and pensions, and the coterminous expansion and commercialization of print culture. If, as Paul Keen observes, the professions' claims to 'moral integrity' were predicated upon their introduction of 'self-governing organizations capable of regulating the conduct of their members', then 'authors were clearly faced with the troubling fact that their profession was . . . impossibly anarchic': 'Access was wholly dependent on the increasingly easy process of being published, and the issue of standards was caught up in wider debates about the uneven tastes of modern readers.'[29] That the literary public sphere, so much more entitled to a monopoly over 'the genius and talents of a country' than the ecclesiastical, medical and legal professions, could not withstand these pressures, and that some of its most talented members would sink as a result, was, according to Williams, absurd (*Claims*, p. 44). But simply co-opting the discourse of professionalism was, he suggested, inadequate to the task of granting literature cultural and social prestige. What was needed was the kind of institutional regulation – the advocacy, esteem and support of genuinely useful and specialist knowledge by men who stood above political partisanship and 'delirium' (p. 111) – that the Literary Fund promised to provide.[30]

Key to the Fund's success, therefore, was the establishment of a set of agreed criteria by which genuine literary merit could be judged and accorded the cultural and economic recognition it deserved. *Claims* cites four principal standards for authorial excellence, pre-eminent among which is 'genius', the 'first of all human distinctions' and the 'actuating principle' of all the literary 'arts', but most particularly 'PHILOSOPHY', which concerned itself with 'the real science of principles' and commanded 'sublimity and beauty of conception' (p. 19; p. 11; p. 13). Second only to genius were 'learning' (or 'talents') and 'labour' (or 'literary industry'), which were distinguished from the former by their claims to the Fund's fourth official criterion for literary merit, 'obvious UTILITY' to society at large (p. 13).[31] These standards formed the basis for a series of discriminations between culturally valuable and non-valuable forms of mental toil that Williams suggested would enable the Fund's adjudicating committee, its subscribers and the public at large to 'distinguish the plausibilities of pretenders from the claims of genius' (p. 107).

Claims's differentiation between works of original genius and their imitative counterfeits – between works of 'literary industry' (the generally useful) and merely ornamental works – resulted in the establishment of an elaborate literary hierarchy, an intellectual division of labour that was to have an inestimable effect upon a number of the Fund's applicants, particularly upon its female claimants. At the top of this literary pecking order, and thus most deserving of the Fund's notice, were works of genius produced by those latter-days Virgils and Homers, who sought to discover 'unknown regions of science' and, through the communication of their insights, to contribute to the nation's 'common stock of knowledge' (p. 113). Since the literary marketplace commonly proved too shortsighted to sustain such visionary figures, however, the majority of men of talents who 'covet[ed] the fame of extensive utility' were forced to confine their 'learning' and 'communications' to areas of knowledge 'already discovered' (p. 113). This second class of authors included 'translators', who relied upon borrowed knowledge, but were none the less acknowledged to meet the Fund's criterion of utility. '[L]ike the inventors of navigation, or of the bridges of roads', these literary engineers made 'familiar' ideas that would otherwise be obscure to the public and thus stood as an impediment to national progress (p. 114). Inferior to these 'importers of foreign knowledge' were 'compilers, and writers of books for children'. Although merely employing 'secondary talents', such authors were capable of 'reduc[ing]' 'profound ideas' to 'simple and clear propositions', and, although they were incapable of 'add[ing] to the common stock of knowledge' themselves, they could, nevertheless, 'increase its utility by diffusion'. Ranked below compilers and writers of children's literature, and only one tier above those 'disappointed men of letters' who devoted themselves to a life of 'LITERARY INDOLENCE' and the 'passing of illiberal judgements', were 'novellists' (*sic*). Such figures, Williams grudgingly admitted, might be considered to have a legitimate claim on the Fund, despite the unspoken 'injuries' they 'commit[ed]' through their work, but only when they proved able to 'harmonize and improve the language' (pp. 114–15). The greatest achievement a novelist could boast, according to *Claims*, was to have sharpened the tools deployed by those authors who truly promoted the nation's betterment. At their best, William's concluded, these '[f]ine writers may be denominated the tailors and milliners of the intellectual world. They agreeably clothe, but do not form the ideas of genius' (p. 14).

I have dwelt on Williams's text in such detail because, in the absence of explicit information on how and why the Literary Fund arrived at the decisions it made when dealing with claimants, it provides the most thorough account of the charity's rationale and the model of intellectual labour to which its applicants were encouraged to aspire. While it would be misleading to view *Claims* as a wholly definitive statement of the Fund's views, as Williams's dramatic falling out with Burges over its contents suggests, the text's elaboration of arguments outlined in other documents published in the charity's early years, particularly its *Accounts* and 1788 *Constitutions*, and its elucidation of the case histories contained in the Fund's archive, indicates that the literary professionalism it constructed was to have a marked impact upon the treatment of early applicants. Although it is difficult to draw concrete conclusions from so vast and, in places, so patchy an archive, there is compelling evidence to indicate that no group of authors suffered more from the Fund's professional aspirations than women writers, and particularly women novelists and writers of works for children.[32]

The relative paucity of applications by women in the Fund's early years is particularly striking. Of the 105 applications made to the charity between 1790 and 1797, for example, only 11 were made by women claiming as authors in their own right.[33] This clear imbalance, even allowing for the greater number of men engaged in the various forms of textual production the Fund considered worthy of remuneration, seems to reflect the general untenability of the female claimant's position. Similarly revealing is that of the 97 successful applicants between November 1790 and March 1801 (the year in which Elizabeth Helme, whose career and works will be discussed in more detail below, made her first application to the Fund), 65 were male authors or the dependants of male authors of works of non-fiction, typically devoted to theology, political economy, various branches of science, education, history and other subjects that reflected the properly 'useful' concerns that Williams would rank among the top two tiers of the literary hierarchy outlined in *Claims*. A further three playwrights were awarded grants, as were four poets and dependents of poets (including Samuel Taylor Coleridge and Robert Burns's widow) and two members of the book trade. Only two male novelists applied to the Fund in the period, Alexander Bicknell and W. C. Proby, both of whom were infinitely more successful in their claims than most of their female counterparts, and both of whom wrote a number of works that fell within the more traditional purview of the man of letters.[34] Of the 14 non-dependent women applicants from this period, there were three actresses who had performed at Fund benefits but had never written a published word in their lives, two writers of educational works, a travel writer and a single poet, Elizabeth Bentley. Seven, including Charlotte Lennox, were novelists, and it seems no coincidence that at least five worked for William Lane's much-derided Minerva Press.[35] Of the 14, more than half were subsequently referred to an 1806 Committee of Inquiry for further investigation; their cases were all deemed 'suspect' and they were retrospectively determined undeserving and unworthy of future consideration.[36]

The Committee of Inquiry's verdicts cast a long shadow, with many of the women authors who fell foul of its pronouncements still largely unknown today. Moreover, the small body of scholarship that has been devoted to some of these women, while undoubtedly valuable for ensuring that a handful of their works have been kept alive in the critical imagination, has tended to reinforce the Fund's appraisal of popular female novelists as amateur hacks who laboured (in the pejorative sense of the term) for money, rather than striving for 'the fame of extensive utility' that *Claims* held to be demonstrative of literary excellence. Lacking literary ambition in proportion to their want of money, these women were, and often still are, perceived as having catered to the whims of idle readers through the production of works of limited cultural and intellectual significance.[37] Such, for example, is the verdict of Devendra P. Varma's otherwise sympathetic introduction to a 1968 reprint of Eliza Parsons's Minerva Press gothic, *The Mysterious Warning* (1796), in which the editor excuses the novel's 'defects and limitations' by noting that 'it was imperious necessity rather than any inclination to vanity that made Mrs Parsons take up her pen'.[38] Nigel Cross's more recent, and otherwise invaluable, account of nineteenth-century Grub Street, *The Common Writer* (1985), does little to dispel this image of Parsons as reluctant author, taking as read the modest and deferential rhetoric in which the author's applications to the Fund are sometimes, but by no means always, couched. Taking her as 'as good an example as any of a representative woman writer of the [late eighteenth] century', Cross suggests that Parsons 'occupied the middle of the second rank in fiction, perhaps a little below Charlotte Smith'. In a passage that attests to the strength of the legacy that late century theorists and reformers such as Williams left to literary scholarship, Cross concludes that 'despite flashes of quality', Parsons's works are 'hastily written, trivial and conceived with that "cynicism which gives to the public what it craves"'.[39] However, I want to suggest in the following sections that closer scrutiny both of the content of women writers' applications to the Fund and of some of their dauntingly vast literary output suggests that a more accurate picture of these women's literary aspirations and achievements can be formed if we approach their (highly strategic) self-representations with the degree of the cynicism that scholars have historically attributed to the writers themselves. Rather than confirming these authors' aversion to living by their pen, their correspondence and published works reveal the myriad ways in which they responded to, and sought to challenge, the models of literary professionalism and intellectual labour the Literary Fund promoted and which literary scholarship has helped to perpetuate.

The man of genius and the female drudge

Of all the discriminations that underpinned the Fund's professional aspirations, that which was to prove most prejudicial to women writers was the firm distinction the charity made between the properly intellectual work of literary genius and the menial hack-work produced by writers for the popular press. Most histories of genius have tended to focus upon the attribute's close association with originality and sublimity, connotations that appear to ascribe genius with ethereal or godlike qualities that seem far removed from the physically arduous mental graft described in Williams's *Claims* and many other contemporary accounts of the work of writing.[40] However, as we saw in Chapter 2, debates over copyright and intellectual property demonstrate a widespread and increasing association of genius and originality with labour in the last three decades of the eighteenth century. This trend, which, as Martha Woodmansee has argued, culminated in the birth of the '"author" in its modern sense' as 'an individual who [was] solely responsible – and therefore exclusively deserving of credit, for the production of a unique work' – crucially entailed the devaluing of lesser forms of textual workmanship in favour of a more sophisticated model of authorial practice, one which understood the act of writing as being inspired by God or the Muses, but refined by the author's intellectual toil.[41]

From the Renaissance to the early eighteenth century, Woodmansee observes, the author was primarily represented as a 'craftsman'. Although the very best of authors was considered to be, at least in part, inspired by the Muses or by God, he was 'first and foremost . . . [a] master of a body of rules, preserved and handed down to him in rhetoric and poetics, for manipulating traditional materials'.[42] As the eighteenth century progressed, however, the increasingly discredited author-craftsman was more likely to be figured as a 'manufacturer' or 'mechanic', against whose efforts the inalienable and elevated intellectual labours of the man of genius were defined. As early as 1759, Edward Young mobilized the language of manual labour not only to assert the greater value of intellectual work but also to differentiate between higher and lesser forms of textual production:

> An *Original* may be said to be of a *vegetable* nature; it rises spontaneously from the vital root of Genius; it *grows*, it is not *made*: *Imitations* are often a sort of *Manufacture* wrought up by those *Mechanics*, *Art* and *Labour*, out of pre-existent materials not their own.[43]

Young's formulation would prove resilient. The Fund rehearsed the sentiments of *Conjectures on Original Composition* in its *Papers and Documents Respecting the Society for the Management and Distribution of the Literary Fund* (1820), which distinguished between 'the manufacturer' of inferior works, 'fantastically raised to opulence', and 'the man of science, of research, and of genius' who was left 'to languish in penury' or in 'prison'.[44] Isaac D'Israeli, a subscriber to the charity, similarly reworked Young's account in his 1812 *Calamities of Authors*, which sought to dissociate 'Authors' from 'Writers' on the grounds that the latter were mere 'mechanic[s]' and could not be counted among those inspired intellectual labourers, who alone could lay claim to genius. Approaching their careers from no 'loftier motive than that of humouring the popular taste', these mere 'Writers' were held responsible by D'Israeli for having 'pollut[ed] . . . the press' and, thus, for having 'turned a vestal into a prostitute'.[45]

Calamities reveals how the conceptualization of genius as intellectual labour was deeply, indeed as Sonia Hofkosh argues, *necessarily*, implicated in wider debates surrounding genre and gender. '[C]onstrued in a gendered matrix, however muted or displaced, however invisible', the authority of the man of genius and his productions was most commonly defined in contemporary commentaries in relation to its degraded and feminized double.[46] The Fund's published documents proved no exception to this rule. Works of genius (primarily comprised of poetry, non-fictional tracts, essays and polemics), Williams argued, were capable of giving 'a new direction to the national character' and, unlike merely imitative and ornamental productions such as novels, spurred industry by increasing the nation's intellectual and cultural capital. The authors of such works were devoted solely to a life of the mind, and were 'inattentive', often tragically so, to such 'little' and domestic 'things' as bodily comfort and pecuniary need (*Claims*, p. 83). As Jean Burns wrote when applying to the Fund for financial support after her husband's death: 'The improvidence of genius is proverbial; and to the list of men of genius, by whom pecuniary attentions have been neglected, the name of Robert Burns must, unfortunately for his family, be added.'[47] Utterly unsuited to other forms of labour, men of genius were equally unfitted for a life of domestic ease or leisure, which as D'Israeli wrote, was 'rarely . . . congenial to [their] pursuits'.[48]

If literary genius was characterized by its orientation towards the public, rather than private, sphere then it was also, and ironically, defined by its scorn for the reading 'public' that was its audience. Participating in a representational trend that, as Hofkosh has elucidated, was central to the Romantic author's self-construction, the Fund and its supporters figured the turn of the nineteenth-century literary marketplace as a degradingly feminized arena, prostituted by genius's 'commodified counterfeits': namely, the illegitimate labours of the female drudges for the circulating libraries, whose cynically commercial fictions made 'all the difference . . . between the vestal and the prostitute, and the base and voracious appetites of an unreflective female readership'.[49] All too easily dazzled by the 'glitter[ing]' ephemera produced by the 'scurrilous satirist, the scribbler of factious politics [and] manufacturer of tinsel verse', the reading public was frequently imagined in the charity's public statements as an indiscriminate woman with promiscuous tastes. Although the Fund was confident that her 'erroneous' judgements would be corrected with time, the promise of future or posthumous recognition offered little consolation to those men of genius whom she so cruelly refused to court, and to whose 'pains of indigence' she was wilfully oblivious.[50]

That women, both as authors and as readers, threatened the future of literature was, Williams maintained, more than borne out by the Literary Fund's subscription lists. Although it seemed logical that '[l]iterary distress . . . [would] deeply interest the female heart', and despite the fact that the number of 'female claimants' who had turned to the charity was equal to that of male applicants, 'SEVEN LADIES ONLY' had offered the charity financial support in the eleven years between its establishment and the publication of *Claims*. Williams's explanation of this anomaly confirms his understanding of genius as a masculine preserve, defined in opposition to the domestic and the feminine. Unlike other philanthropic organizations, which could produce 'actual specimens' and 'symbols of misery' to tug at potential benefactress's heart and purse strings, the Literary Fund was unable publicly to expose the identity of applicants for fear that it would be prejudicial to their reputations and future careers. Instead, it relied upon anonymized accounts of mental distress, which, apparently, had little hold over the female imagination: no matter how accurately drawn, 'the miseries of genius' were impotent to draw the 'attention of any elevated and opulent women', Williams concluded (p. 89). That Williams makes no attempt, here, to distinguish between women applying as authors in their own right and those claiming as the dependants of deceased male writers in the catch-all designation 'female claimants' is further indicative of the Fund's conventional gendering of genius as a masculine trait.[51] Gender, not genius or literary industry, seems to have been the single most important consideration when dealing with the applications of women writers.

The fact that many women writers (and particularly women novelists) fell foul both of the intellectual/manual binary that *Conjectures* helped to construct, and of the correlative gendered and generic divisions to which it gave rise, is evident in numerous cases from the Fund's early history, but nowhere more ironically than in the case of Edward Young's granddaughter, Mary Julia Young. A novelist, poet and translator, Young applied to the Fund on 28 March 1808, citing as grounds for her case poor health and severe 'pecuniary embarrassments' as a result of her publisher declaring himself bankrupt and failing to pay her more than a tenth of the £70 owed to her.[52] Although keen to point out that in all of her novels she had 'endeavoured to render the strictest observance of relative duties indispensible to amiable and sensible characters, and to inculcate virtue, and benevolence by the most engaging examples', Young registered a profound sense of unease at the thought of attempting to obtain the charity's interest in her 'as a Novelist' alone. She sought to strengthen her case by launching a second assault upon the Fund's defences as the 'lonely Kinswoman' of 'Dr Edward Young, of Welwyn, who in almost all Countries and by all Sects is esteemed as one of the brightest ornaments of English Literature'. As a 'Voluminous scribbler' for the 'Circulating Libraries', and as an indirect consequence of the model of authorial excellence her grandfather had helped to construct, Young appears to have felt that she had less claim to the Fund's charity as an author than she did as the distressed and '*only* surviving relative' of a deceased, yet still greatly respected, man of genius. Her application was rewarded with a relatively generous award of £15, although whether this was granted in acknowledgement of her claims to literary merit as the author of *Right or Wrong, or, the Kinsmen of Naples* (1803), the novel of which Young claimed to be most proud, or as the descendant of an esteemed author who had died some thirty years earlier, is not recorded.[53]

Apparently debarred from the Fund's conception of genius both on the grounds of their gender and the genre in which they worked, it is perhaps little wonder that many of the first female author-applicants to the charity openly questioned whether their cases would be deemed eligible for consideration. Lacking Young's credentials as a 'descendant or relative of any literary character', and as the author of only 'trifling' works of fiction, the former governess Ann Burke, for example, feared that her 'case' would 'differ from any that have yet been offered to your consideration' and, as a consequence, would be discounted.[54] Burke first approached the Fund in a letter dated 9 October 1795 as the author of two novels published by G. G. J. and J. Robinson, *Ela: or, the Delusions of the Heart* (1787) and *Emilia de St. Aubigne* (1788), and as the widowed mother of a son recovering from smallpox. Burke's financial situation was desperate. Her debts, including the medical expenses incurred as a result of her son's illness, had forced her to sell many of her clothes and much of her furniture, leaving her dependent upon the charity of a small group of friends. Her case was considered three times by the Fund over the next four years, although she wrote many more letters to the charity pending the decisions of its monthly meetings, each of which increasingly plays down the modest claim she initially makes for her fiction – that her novels 'sold as well as most works of a similar nature'.[55] Latterly, defences of her work are left to a male sponsor, Dr William Thompson, who wrote to the Fund on 24 October 1797, asserting that Burke did indeed possess 'Genius', if only in relation to 'that common class of writers in the line she has pursued'. Burke herself felt more comfortable in presenting herself as a distressed mother rather than as a distressed genius, a strategy that resulted in limited success. Burke's touching pleas for her child were noted in the minutes for the November 1795 meeting, while her status as the 'Author of two novels' is mentioned only as an apparent afterthought.[56] By the time of what appears to have been her final application to the charity, Burke's identity as a writer had been entirely subsumed by that of a mother pleading for her 'lovely and innocent' son and looking to the Fund for sums that might allow her to fit herself for another, more seemly, employment.[57] By 1799, the Fund recorded that it felt that the eight guineas in total awarded to Burke exceeded the degree of talent her literary productions evidenced.[58] She was awarded five more on the condition that she would receive no further.[59] When the Fund instituted the Committee of Inquiry, Burke was listed as a suspect applicant.

Eliza Parsons, one of the Fund's more successful female author-claimants, shared Burke's sense that the 'Distress of the Widow and the Fatherless' would the more effectively appeal to the 'Hearts' of committee members than the 'small Degree of Merit' evidenced in what she also termed her 'trifling' publications.[60] Parsons's biography, as documented in a succession of applications to the charity over a period of ten years, is as dramatic as the plot of many a Minerva Press novel. The daughter of a successful wine merchant, Parsons had every reason to think that she might have 'become a Subscriber rather than a Solicitress' to the Fund.[61] As a young woman, she had made a good marriage to a 'worthy and respectable' turpentine merchant, but the couple's fortunes declined during the American Revolution, only for their remaining capital to go up in smoke, quite literally, when their Bowbridge factory caught fire.[62] Shortly afterwards, Parsons's husband contracted a 'paralytic disorder' and died, leaving Eliza with eight children to support on the £40 a year she was supposed to earn as 'Sempstress in Ordinary to the Wardrobe' of the royal household. The fact that she had received only a fraction of the money owed to her in this capacity – she noted that the Civil List was seven quarters in arrears by the summer of 1796[63] – compelled Parsons 'by dire necessity' to avail herself 'of the Fashion of the times' and 'earn [her] daily bread' by writing novels.[64] Her debut fiction, *The History of Miss Meredith*, was published in 1790, two years before her first application to the Fund; by the time she made her last application to the charity in 1803, and despite 'repeated Misfortunes' and a succession of debilitating illnesses and injuries that 'blunt[ed] the edge of genius', she had authored some 65 volumes.[65] But even so arduous and 'painful [a] period of mental labour' could not prevent Parsons from being arrested for debt and imprisoned in the King's Bench at the age of 62, where she was forced to succumb to the indignity and privations of 'poverty', the 'worst crime', she discovered, a woman of her station could commit.[66]

Reading Young's, Burke's and Parsons's applications alongside one another, reveals the extent to which female author-applicants shared a common rhetoric that emphasized the correspondents' fall from gentility, their domestic integrity and their authorial reluctance. However, the formulaic nature of their correspondence with the Fund belies both the rhetorical complexity of their authorial self-constructions, its very derivativeness a sign of disingenuousness and the subtlety with which these writers attempted to challenge the Fund's model of professional authorship through vindications of their intellectual and domestic labours. Like a number of Fund applicants, Parsons had become fully conversant with the conventional language of writerly humility she would adopt in her Fund applications through her authoring of a series of prefaces for her novels. While such prefatorial conventions, particularly when deployed by women writers, have traditionally been read as sincere declarations of authorial modesty, or as evidence of a lack of literary ambition, recent work, particularly that of Gérard Genette, has provided new models for understanding the complexity, and deconstructing the fictiveness, of such strategies. In *Paratexts* (1987), Genette reveals how writers' attempts to grapple with the difficulty of putting '*a high value on* the text without antagonizing the reader by too immodestly, or simply too obviously, putting a high value on the text's author', led to the development of an elaborate 'rhetorical apparatus of persuasion' encoded in paratextual material such as the preface, and characterized, broadly, by a contrived dissociation between a text's 'subject (always praiseworthy) and its treatment (always unworthy)'.[67] Thus, while authors accepted that a work's 'importance' and 'usefulness' had to be established for their work to be read and to be read properly, they also understood that declarations of their '*talent*' or '*genius*' had be jettisoned as 'taboo'.[68] Authorial labour, to recast Genette's argument in eighteenth-century terms, had to be presented as subservient to the greater utility the writer's work might serve.

Although Genette's study is not concerned with the gendered implications of its conclusions – that, for example, women writers were doubly stymied by the constraints of authorial propriety and thus were forced to develop distinctive strategies for negotiating these impediments – his analysis of the prefatorial 'rhetoric of value-enhancement' none the less has much to offer the study of female-authored prefaces in the eighteenth and nineteenth centuries and, by extension, the applications of female Fund claimants.[69] When looked at through this lens, the slippery rhetoric of Parsons's preface to *Miss Meredith* provides clear insights into her subsequent epistolary exchanges with the Fund. Part of an elaborate paratextual framework – which also comprises a dedication and a subscription list that boasts Elizabeth Montagu, Horace Walpole and the Prince of Wales among its numbers – the preface to this novel opens with its author standing before the 'public eye with trembling anxiety' lest her readers should charge her with 'Vanity' for having had the 'presumption of writing after a BURNEY, a SMITH, a REEVE, a BENNET, and many other excellent female novelists'.[70] Parsons 'utterly disclaims' such imputations of literary ambition, declaring that she wrote her novel only to support her 'numerous family' after her fall from 'affluence'. Casting her illustrious forebears and contemporaries as the moral benefactors of their age, Parsons positions herself in her preface as a charitable object, who, in an ironic anticipation of her position as a Fund applicant two years later, was reliant upon 'the benevolence of the public' and trusted her 'inducements for presuming to publish' might 'shield 'MISS MEREDITH from every shaft of criticism' (I, p. v).

Echoes of Frances Burney's preface to *Evelina* (1778) resound strongly, here, and indicate that Parsons recognized, as Jacqueline Pearson notes that a number of her contemporaries did, that Burney offered 'an exhilaratingly enabling model of female authorship, not only promising cultural and financial capital, but also suggesting that novel-writing and reading were by no means incompatible with genteel respectability'.[71] Parsons's self-characterization as a modest and re-assuringly deferential writer is clearly indebted to Burney; so too are her claims that she demurely followed in the footsteps of an illustrious list of novel writers to whose achievements she was unequal. Yet *Miss Meredith* also reveals some important departures from Burney's model, which suggest that Charlotte Smith – that astute manipulator of the contemporary politics of authorship – offered a still more 'enabling' model for Parsons and other Fund claimants. Unlike the author of *Evelina*, Parsons published *Miss Meredith* under her own name. Whereas Burney famously dedicated her novel to no one (or rather, to the two dashes that concealed the name of her father), Parsons was proud to 'shelter the first feeble efforts of [her] pen' under the patronage of the Marchioness of Salisbury (I, p. i). And despite her assumption of authorial inferiority (one of many 'sacrifices' that, as Genette writes, are often painful to the writer's 'amour propre', but generally 'pay off'), Parsons conveys much more overt confidence as a woman and as a writer than Burney does.[72] A far cry from the Burneyesque deferential daughter who, whether sincerely or not, asks forgiveness of the 'Author of [her] Being' in *Evelina*'s dedicatory poem for her temerity in taking up her pen, Parsons is as unapologetic as Smith about her decision to support her children through the work of writing. Still more revealing, perhaps, is Parsons's telling rewriting of Burney's decision to locate her first foray into the 'republic of letters' in relation to the careers of 'Rousseau, Johnson, Marivaux, Fielding, Richardson, and Smollett'.[73] 'Trembling' though she may have claimed to be, Parsons wanted her work to be read in the context of an established female literary genealogy, which, she suggested, had been characterized by 'excellence' and demanded respect.

Parsons's fluency in the mutually constitutive discourses of authorship and gender that circulated in the later eighteenth century, and evident in the preface to *Miss Meredith*, would play a vital role in her applications to the Fund, which similarly challenged these discourses' conventions without exceeding the bounds of feminine propriety. Indeed, like Burke and Young, Parsons proved particularly adept at exploiting the Fund's common failure to distinguish between author-applicants and dependant-applicants in its formulation 'female claimants', using her claims as a woman to mitigate those she made as an author. Thus in her second application to the Fund, Parsons wrote:

> a spirit oppressed gives little scope for the power of fancy or fertility of Imagination requisite in all works of fiction; therefore at this time when 'my daily labour must earn my daily bread' the difficulties I labour under are doubly distressing, affect my health, and blunt the edge of genius. The Public have honoured my writings with generous Approbation infinitely more than I could hope for, but as necessity always obliges me to sell the Copy rights [*sic*], my Advantages are trifling to what the Publisher gains.[74]

This skilfully argued passage is immersed in contemporary debates on the manual/intellectual labour binary, the literary marketplace, and the power and authority of genius, even while it is reassuringly framed by Parsons's account of the 'difficulties' she laboured under as a widowed mother. Ostensibly, Parsons appears to subscribe to the Fund's model of authorship as wholeheartedly as she seems to subscribe to the late eighteenth-century ideology of domesticity. As in the Fund's publications, writing is troped, here, as work, work which is, moreover, as valuable and as physically demanding as manual labour, but which is also degraded by the trucking and bartering of the literary marketplace. Parsons's declaration that her 'Genius' has been 'blunt[e]d' and her 'Imagination' rendered infertile by corporeal and financial distress serves further to underscore the Fund's conviction that the 'fruits of dire necessity, and of literary leisure, are, however, extremely different' – a truth that Williams argued was proved by the inferiority of the ubiquitous novels for the circulating libraries (*Claims*, p. 79). An adept ventriloquist of the emergent discourse of literary professionalism, Parsons acknowledges 'the gendered matrix' within which genius was constructed while subverting its logic. Rather than an agent in the literary sphere's degradation, an author of promiscuously circulating texts, Parsons casts the popular woman novelist as one of its unrecognized victims, unwillingly prostituted not only by a market that takes away women's rights to ownership of their intellectual labours when it forcibly transforms their private property into publicly tradable goods but also by the new discourses of genius and literary professionalism, the authority of which was constructed through the systematic degradation of the supposed hack-work of women writers.[75]

That Parsons's application is as much an implicit critique of the Fund's conception of genius as it is an explicit condemnation of the nefarious practices of the book trade is further demonstrated by her account of the relationship between personal distress, physical illness and literary excellence. It is well documented that the figure of the distressed genius, prepared to die for his art, achieved cult-like status in the literary and visual culture of the Romantic period, during which the physiology of genius, as Clark Lawlor has recently documented, was an abiding preoccupation.[76] Many theorists of genius's corporeal manifestations posited that intense periods of intellectual production led to a consumptive degeneration of the authorial body because they depleted 'energy' needed for 'vital' physiological functions.[77] D'Israeli went so far as to estimate in *Calamities of Authors* that 'over-study' and 'intellectual enthusiasm' were responsible for the death of 'half the rising genius of the age'.[78] The widely held connection between intense intellectual application and a loss of bodily vigour gestures towards genius's pejorative association with the feminine (with the excessive, the unruly and the passionate), an association that the work of Andrew Elfenbein has done so much to illuminate.[79] But if the mental labours of the man of genius were feminizing, then their inscription upon his ailing body was, paradoxically, a sign of intellectual strength and masculine purpose that subsumed, and thus neutralized, genius's more alarming feminine characteristics.[80] In the words of D'Israeli, the man of genius's career could be likened to 'plucking a few brilliant flowers from the precipices, while the reward terminates in the honour', a description that does double work in its rendering of genius as simultaneously feminine and heroic.[81]

The ambiguous gendering of genius pointed to an irony that Parsons and a number of Fund applicants felt keenly: that this attribute became more difficult for women to lay claim to precisely as it became more explicitly associated with the feminine.[82] Where the physiological signs of male genius were inextricably yoked to intellectual production, and perceived as indicators of cultural authority and value as a consequence,[83] their female equivalents were more commonly associated with an excessive desire or hysterical, consumptive sensibility, of the kind to which Wollstonecraft's female genius Mary temporarily succumbs when her lover dies and her 'reason' gives way to 'phrensy' and 'enthusiastic devotion'.[84] By redefining the conventional relationship between bodily suffering and mental toil – intellectual labour is robbed of its vitality by corporeal infirmity in Parsons's application rather than itself being productive of physical illness – Parsons casts both the man of genius whose mental toil writes itself on to his abject body, and the woman of genius who lives as a slave to her passions, as narcissists. After all, only those who have the luxury of being able, like Wollstonecraft's professional male, selfishly to direct all their 'efforts . . . to one point' can succumb to such all-consuming maladies.[85] Thus, as we shall see, Parsons concurred with Smith that domestic life, with all its distractions and consolations, might make the work of writing all the more onerous, but it also prevented the author from acceding to that egotism which, though sometimes taken as a sign of intense literary application, was incompatible with the virtues of disinterestedness and utility that the Literary Fund, and she also, held to be markers of 'genius'.

'[B]eing a domestic woman' and mothering the novel

Parsons *is* 'representative' of female applicants to the Literary Fund, but not, as Cross suggests, because she is typically modest and lacking in ambition. On the contrary, her correspondence and fiction display a more genuinely representative desire of female Fund applicants to prove that they were 'not', in Catherine Bayley's words, 'unworthy object[s]' of the charity's consideration, while also demonstrating a characteristic willingness to tackle head on later eighteenth-century constructions of authorship and their gendered implications.[86] Like Wollstonecraft, female claimants to the Fund were willing to appropriate the new model of literary professionalism for themselves, often alluding to their own genius and to the 'arduous' nature of their intellectual labours. Unlike Wollstonecraft, however, they rarely articulated such aspirations without qualification. Parsons, as we have seen, obliquely laid claim to 'genius' only by admitting that its force had long since been 'blunt[ed]' by misfortune, while Elizabeth Macauley, a former actress and author of various miscellaneous works, hoped that the Fund would find '*traits* of Genius and Talents' in her work, but evidently feared that they would be so obscure that they would evade the charity's notice.[87] Similarly, Phebe Gibbes, probably the most spirited of the Fund's early female author-applicants, fully endorsed Williams's assertion that writing was, as she 'had ever called it', '*Literary Industry*' and '*Mental Toil*' of a highly productive kind, but was careful to point out that she was and always had been a 'domestic woman, and of a withdrawing turn of Temper'.[88]

The applications of those women who failed to make such demonstrations of moral integrity were given predictably short shrift by the charity's presiding committee. Where the genius of male authors such as Burns was demonstrated, rather than compromised, by their excess and profligacy, the merits of the woman writer could be proved only by indisputable evidence of domestic virtue.[89] Eliza Norman, the author of the rare and appropriately entitled *The Child of Woe* (1789), should have known that her applications were doomed to failure when she mysteriously admitted that her financial distress had arisen from 'combined causes, in which indiscretion forms a part'.[90] Her first application was rejected; her second, made some years later, was rewarded a minimum, and somewhat dismissive, three guineas. In 1806 Norman's name accompanied Burke's on the list of suspect cases. Most female applicants were more canny than Norman, however, and few failed to comment on their domestic credentials, fully aware, as the novelist Mary Ann Newman knew, following Charlotte Smith's *Elegiac Sonnets*, that 'to a *woman* "the post of honour is a private station"'. Domestic life provided a 'safe retreat' from calumny, and Newman declared that she would 'most thankfully have lived & died' within this sphere had it not fallen upon her to provide for her seven fatherless children through the 'regrett[able]' act of writing novels.[91] Many other Fund claimants would similarly seek refuge in the languages of domesticity and maternity in their applications for aid, but, as Parsons's knowing letters indicate, the languages of female privacy and propriety offered much more than a retreat from the hostile and gendered lexicon of authorship the Fund helped to construct. Female applicants' protestations of domestic integrity and maternal devotion are less signs of feminine reserve, I want to suggest, than the criteria for an alternative and explicitly feminine construction of authorship intended to rival the Fund's homocentric model of intellectual labour in its claims to productiveness, utility and cultural value.

Recent scholarship has illuminated the complex ways in which the discourses of domesticity and maternity fed into women writers' self-construction during the Romantic era and early nineteenth century.[92] By this period, as Susan Stanford Friedman has argued, the metaphorical links between artistic and reproductive creativity were well established. Whether 'rejected as repulsive or celebrated as creative, women's procreativity . . . was perceived through an androcentric lens as a mindless, unconscious, uncontrolled act of the body' that 'perpetuated' the gendered mind-body, male-female, artist-mother split 'it attempted to transcend through analogy'.[93] But if the creation/procreation analogy was 'overdetermined', then it was also fundamentally unstable; by forcing women writers to 'confront the patriarchally imposed essential dilemma of their artistic identity', it afforded them the opportunity to legitimize their artistic practice 'by unifying their mental and physical labour' in a manner that seemed to be non-threatening because reassuringly feminine.[94] That this masking of creative desire beneath the guise of procreative responsibility has, in the case of the popular women writers examined here, commonly been taken for a lack of intellectual or artistic aspiration exposes a failure of imagination on the part of their readers, and the rather depressing longevity of the gendered assumptions that have historically undermined women's efforts to appropriate metaphors of reproductive labour to legitimize their authorial work.

Crucial to these efforts, as Parsons's preface to *Miss Meredith* and as Newman's allusion to the preface to the sixth edition of *Elegiac Sonnets* indicate, was the work of Charlotte Smith. Somewhat ironically, given Smith's disdain for the circulating libraries run by Lane and other literary 'tradesmen', she was to prove a particularly empowering model for female Fund applicants.[95] Smith, as we saw in Chapter 2, worked strenuously throughout her career to deny the divisions supposed to exist between manual, intellectual and affective labour, both through her careful cultivation of a model of embodied authorship, which imprinted the labour of writing and of wife- and motherhood on to the pages of her publications, and through her insistence that 'reproduction' should be taken as a key third term in the debate on the relationship between different models (productive or otherwise) of labour. Domesticity, as we have seen, was work for Smith, as it was for many of her characters, but work that authorized, rather than compromised, her professional labours. It was 'in *observance*', not out of neglect, of her domestic duties as a woman and as a mother that Smith turned to authorship.[96] Fearful for the welfare of her children in a world rendered corrupt by economic and social injustice, Smith cast her writing career as politically necessarily, as well as financially expedient, and thus imagined authorship as a logical extension of the work of motherhood itself.

Diane E. Boyd has suggested that Smith's construction of a '"mother-writer" author function', while a concerted effort 'to transgress pervasive ideological structures like the codified cultural spaces of public/private and the cultural representations of professional/drudge', was a treacherous strategy. Smith's sustained reflections on her 'biological and economic responsibilities as a mother' gave 'the public a way to discuss *her*, not *her work*'. Thus, she 'inadvertently lodged herself in the drudge camp of the professional/drudge sphere', a danger that she successfully bypassed, Boyd concludes, only in her later children's fiction, where Smith expresses 'a desire to eschew the encumbrance of her material conditions' through public demonstrations of the mechanics of the book trade and a willingness to meet its demands as a professional writer.[97] My own reading of Smith's professional aspirations and achievements departs somewhat from Boyd's. None the less, Boyd's account of the limitations of the '"mother-writer" author function' Smith deployed is helpful for understanding the constraints under which the female Fund applicants, who espoused a similar model of authorial self-presentation, laboured. This is particularly the case given the extent to which such strategies have overshadowed these writers' literary reputations. It doesn't, however, explain why these writers persistently emphasized, rather than attempted to 'eschew[,] the encumbrance . . . of [their] material conditions' in their fiction. Various answers to this question are suggested by the works produced by female Fund applicants. In the preface to *Clara and Emmeline; or, the Maternal Benediction* (1788), for example, the novelist, translator and schoolteacher Elizabeth Helme made no attempt to conceal the financial imperatives and domestic responsibilities that compelled her to write:[98]

> A celebrated Actress [Sarah Siddons] produced three reasons for leaving her Bath friends; now I have *five* as powerful *reasons* to induce me to write, beside a natural inclination for the employ. The weak and unprotected ever meet with favor from the generous and brave; then be merciful to my CLARA and EMMELINE, and the already-conferred obligation will be doubled on a heart that (I thank Heaven) is susceptible of gratitude.[99]

Inverting Sarah Scott's self-presentation in *Millenium Hall* as her readers' benefactor, and much like Parsons in *Miss Meredith*, Helme strategically positions herself in the preface to *Clara and Emmeline* as a charitable object. Forced to write to support her children, she appears not to aspire to the empowered position of gift-giver; instead, Helme claims that she is an obligated and grateful recipient of the public's and critics' generosity. Helme's self-objectification certainly played into the hands of critics who wished to talk about her character rather than about her work at the same time that it helped to mitigate reviewers' often dismissive responses to the various kinds of popular fiction Helme wrote. The *Critical Review*, for example, noted of *Clara and Emmeline*: 'In this second attempt, an attempt to which our fair author was urged by five reasons proportionately more powerful, because more numerous, than the three reasons of Mrs. Siddons for leaving Bath, she has not equalled her former work', the incredibly popular *Louisa: or, The Cottage on the Moor* (1787). As a mother, the reviewer contended, Helme was a paragon; as an author, however, she was guilty of 'errors' and 'inaccuracies' that made the reader 'start back with disgust'.[100]

The mother/writer dyad that structures the *Critical*'s review seems to take its cue from the novel itself; yet, in perceiving motherhood not as a crucial aspect of its author's self-construction but as a biological function, and one that is, moreover, at odds with Helme's career as an author, it misreads her work. The reference to Siddons in the novel's preface, like Parsons's nod to Charlotte Smith in *Miss Meredith*, is crucial here. Interpreted sympathetically by the reviewer as a sign of motherly devotion, the foregrounding of Siddons, a woman whose reputation as an actress and as a woman was absolutely bound up with her performance of motherhood, also opens up the possibility that Helme self-consciously stages maternity in the preface to *Clara and Emmeline* in order to legitimize her appearance in the potentially unfeminine role of writer, a reading of the text that is supported by Helme's rather less than modest assertion that authorship is an 'employ' for which she has a 'natural inclination'.[101]

The word 'natural' is freighted with meaning, here. For those inclined to believe Helme's protestations that she wrote only for financial reasons, the phrase might simply suggest that the author, serendipitously, has an instinctive bent for writing. More alert readers, however, attuned to the connection between performance and maternity alluded to in the reference to Siddons, might see that motherhood is being deployed by Helme as a mask that renders acceptable an occupation – authorship – that is as 'natural' as childbearing, but artificially constructed as maternity's illegitimate other. Extending the (pro)creation metaphor further in the following sentence, Helme suggests that her characters – '*my* CLARA and EMMELINE' (emphasis added) – are as much her offspring as her five biological children.[102] As for Smith, whose children drove, but also competed with, her authorial labours – Helme uses maternity to reconcile her domestic and professional identities, to signal the seriousness with which she viewed her authorial work, and to write herself out of the 'drudge camp' of the professional/drudge binary Boyd describes. By self-sacrificially casting her beloved progeny (Clara and Emmeline) into the world, Helme transforms herself from the pitiable, charitable object she at first appeared in the opening lines of the preface into a Scott-like moral benefactor, whose 'maternal benediction', to return to *Clara and Emmeline*'s subtitle, tends to the improvement of its young readers.[103]

Unlike female dependant-claimants, whose worth was established in terms of their domestic relationship to a (usually) male writer, and unlike male applicants, for whom the tedious demands of domestic life were, at best, a burden and a distraction, the likes of Helme and Parsons, as well as Burke and Gibbes, used their domestic situations to stress their needs as women while maintaining their autonomy as writers. If, as Laura Runge has argued, writing from the position of 'explicit femaleness' was both a necessity and a liability for women – an expectation they were ill advised to counter, but a shortcut to 'trivialization and marginalization' when met[104] – then numerous Fund applicants attempted to avoid these perils by casting their domestic virtues as the basis for an alternative model of literary labour to that espoused by the reviews and institutions such as the Literary Fund. Metaphors of (pro)creativity, such as those used by Helme, return writing to the body while neutralizing the potential threat implied by such a move. The maternal, domestic writing body gives the lie to the equation of female literary activity and prostitution which, as we have seen, was widely implied in Fund documents and general commentaries on the late eighteenth- and early nineteenth-century literary marketplace. Simultaneously, the mother-author function supplants egotism, as a hallmark of intellectual labour as defined by the Fund, with a notion of authorial (and decidedly feminine) selflessness that performs vital cultural work for which women are uniquely suited.[105] The 'self-sufficing power of absolute *Genius*', as Coleridge described it in Book I of *Biographia Literaria* (1817), is replaced, here, with a model of authorship based upon self-sacrifice, as the female author releases her literary progeny into the world with a mixture of pride and trepidation.[106] Above all, however, she does so with a view to the public good, of adding to 'the common stock of knowledge' through the bestowal of culturally useful, indeed culturally vital, maternal benedictions and advice.

Maternity and moral utility are commonly liked in the applicants of female claimants. Phebe Gibbes, for example, defended her numerous textual productions as '*well conceived Effort*[*s*], of *Public Utility*'. The fact that Gibbes wrote to support herself and her family did not lessen her commitment 'to convey some moral and usefull Hunts . . . to young and Inexperienced Minds'.[107] The former governess turned biographer, children's writer and novelist Mary Pilkington similarly attempted to justify her transformation of 'those Talents which had been cultivated for Amusement into the Means of Support' on the grounds of her maternal public mindedness: all of her publications, she wrote, were 'devoted to the improvement of the rising Generation'.[108] Refuting accusations that their work was merely ornamental, as *Claims* had suggested and the reviews commonly argued, female applicants almost universally asserted the utility of their texts, a utility that was inextricably linked to their authors' identity as exemplary mothers, into whose care the nation's future should be trusted. The public function of the woman writer, many of these authors claimed, derived precisely from her domestic and private virtues; her disinterested advice served to counter a range of social and cultural problems, such as inadequacies in education and parental negligence, and promised to nurture the nation as a consequence.

The woman writer's public role as surrogate mother, better equipped than many biological parents to raise the next generation of citizens, is, moreover, a recurrent strain in novels produced by Fund applicants, in which good mothers are commonly and conspicuously absent. That so many heroines of late eighteenth- and early nineteenth-century fiction are motherless, or deprived of maternal love, during a period in which motherhood's reification as a marker of subjectivity and status was reaching its height, is a conundrum that the work of Ruth Perry has done much to solve. The (good) mother's absence from such texts derives, Perry argues, from multiple causes, including matters 'of literary expediency', and 'deeper' concerns regarding women's powerlessness and the 'existential lack of grounding for narrative in the world'.[109] Less 'easy to interpret', perhaps, is the pervasiveness with which the loss of the biological mother is compensated for by the intervention of mother substitutes.[110] Among the many surrogate mother-types Perry examines (including biological and 'fictional' aunts), one, however, remains largely overlooked: the mother-*author* who creates, and guides the reader through, her text.[111] This figure is particularly important in Parsons's fiction. *Miss Meredith*, for example, follows the lives of two women who make disastrous matches as a consequence of a lack of sufficiently forceful or reliable maternal figures. Emma has so little respect for her mother's wishes that she marries in opposition to them, and finds herself tied to a womanizing gambler as a result; the motherless Harriet, meanwhile, marries in accordance with her father's wishes, but in opposition to her heart, and is equally unhappy. *Miss Meredith* concludes with Parsons's assertion that should her novel 'incline young women to reverence themselves' and 'impress their minds with a conviction of the blessed effects which arise from filial piety . . . then the author's labours will be amply rewarded' (II, p. 205). The plot, however, works against this simplistic moral. Harriet's inability to find happiness despite acceding to her father's wishes suggests that Parsons's novel is ultimately less concerned with promoting 'filial piety' than with championing the need for proper maternal guidance. In the absence of reliable biological parents, Parsons presents herself as a surrogate mother to her readers. In a distinctly feminine counterpoint to Williams's man of letters, she dispenses her knowledge and wisdom as a mother to encourage a 'uniform adherence to virtue' in a bid to reform the age (II, p. 205).

Parsons would return to the subject of the mother's vital social role throughout her career, but most extensively and politically in *The Convict, or the Navy Lieutenant* (1807). Parsons's last novel is an intricately plotted tale, which looks back to Mary Hays's *The Victim of Prejudice* (1799) and Wollstonecraft's *The Wrongs of Woman; or Maria* (1798) in its focus upon the oppression of women through the parallel plots of a mother and daughter. Ellen, the mother and eponymous convict, first appears in the novel prior to her execution for stabbing the father of her two-year-old child Fanny, who is subsequently taken, along with a manuscript documenting the mother's tragic life, under the care of the kindly naval lieutenant Henry Thompson. 'The crimes, the wrongs and sorrows of Ellen', like the memoir penned by Wollstonecraft's Maria, is written with the intention of impressing upon her daughter the wrongs of woman, and of teaching the child 'to shun the voice of delusion, the arts of assumed tenderness, the specious reasoning, oaths, and vows of the vile seducer, who seeks to draw from the paternal roof, to violate the first great duty implanted in our hearts, of love and filial duty'.[112] Ellen's account, which remains unread by Fanny until the novel's final pages, reveals that, as a young woman, she had entered into a secret marriage to a young aristocrat, who left her once she fell pregnant. Before long, Ellen discovered that her marriage was not, in fact, legal, but not before she had been drugged and raped by a Major Freeland, to whom she had been offered by the man she once called husband. Some time after giving birth to her daughter, Ellen hears of her seducer's return to England, and stabs him. The rest of the novel follows Fanny through a series of trials, indirectly linked to her mother's original crime of disobeying her parents and marrying in secret. Fanny is beset by predators at every turn, and, although she is possessed of 'a good and ingenious mind', and remains ignorant of her mother's 'story' until the end of the novel, it appears that her destiny will replicate that of her parent (III, p. 246). Men plot and scheme against Fanny at every turn; each attempt to evade their advances merely plunges the heroine into another seduction plot until the novel's resolution in which Fanny is reconciled with her mother and her would-be seducer is revealed to be her own father. (The very much alive Ellen, it transpires, had been granted a timely pardon when it was revealed that her victim had not been fatally injured after all.) The mother dies soon after her reconciliation with her daughter, and the remorseful father leaves Fanny a sum of £20,000 before embarking for the Continent, thus enabling the heroine to marry the man she loves.

Although *The Convict* is a tale brimful of attempted murder, suicide, incest, rape and exploitation, its most shocking aspect is surely the role that the novel's many mother-substitutes play in the heroine's narrowly avoided destruction. The first woman to whose care Fanny is entrusted by Thompson is Mrs Barton, the wife of a former ship's surgeon, who uses the money received for the child's upkeep to buy herself clothes. When she accidentally learns of Fanny's dubious parentage she violently assaults the child and her own husband when he tries to protect the girl. Fanny is then passed on to a Mrs Fitzwilliam, whose initially tender feelings towards her charge soon wane as a result of the plotting of her nieces. Subsequently forced 'to procure her subsistence by industry and labour', Fanny endures the 'slavery' of being a lady's maid in the house of a female gambler, who subjects her servant to the sexual advances of one of her creditors in lieu of a debt (IV, p. 147). When Fanny leaves Lady Overton for a job as a companion to Mrs Canning, she believes she has finally 'found an asylum', only to learn that her employer is complicit with a scheme to engineer her rape. It is significant that the multiple female and patriarchal plots in which Fanny becomes unwittingly embroiled are thwarted only with the revelation of her mother's 'story', a word that haunts Fanny, who longs to know her mother's narrative, but is all too aware that others' knowledge of it would lead to her abjection and prevent her lover from wanting to marry her.

The relationship between a woman's 'story' and her moral authority was one that concerned a number of Romantic-era writers, particularly Hays, who, in *The Victim of Prejudice*, used the maternal memoir and the parallel mother–daughter plot to reinforce the inevitability of women's subjugation within a capitalist and patriarchal society.[113] But unlike Hays's novel, in which Mary Raymond's knowledge of her mother's history is 'suffocat[ing]' and fails to prevent her own demise,[114] in *The Convict*, the maternal narrative is liberating, since it enables the heroine to resist the plot Ellen's story foreshadows and thus empowers her to break free from the 'magic circle' of female oppression.[115] In this respect, Parsons's novel is more obviously indebted to Wollstonecraft's

The Wrongs of Woman, in which, as Laurie Langbauer argues, the autobiographical narrative the heroine addresses to her daughter expresses the author's 'view of the possibilities of women's writing'. Ellen's tale, like Maria's, 'takes the place of – in fact, becomes – [her own] experience', the legacy of which is passed on by the author to the lost daughter and the novel's readers.[116] The cross-generational transmission of women's stories, *The Convict* argues, was the only way to prevent the exploitative circulation of their bodies; the generation and dissemination of such narratives was, above all, the work of the mother-author.

To read the novels of women applicants to the Literary Fund in tandem with their non-fictional correspondence with the charity is not to insinuate that these authors' imaginative works are autobiographical in any simple sense, although a number of their prefaces implicitly invite readers to view their works in this way; neither is it to suggest that their pleas are inherently fictional. It is, however, to acknowledge the highly complex and mutually reinforcing relationship between these women's personal and professional lives. Assuming the role of the mother-author collapsed such distinctions, proving, as Smith had done, the arbitrariness of the division between women's affective work as wives and nurturers and their intellectual labour as authors. This decidedly female species of genius suggested that the roles of 'proper lady' and 'woman writer', to return to Mary Poovey's formulation, were crucially linked, rather than fundamentally opposed, its cultivation allowing writers such as Helme and Parsons to deny the supposed incompatibility of domesticity and authorial genius, utility and productivity disseminated in the Fund's publications. In the process, these writers established a model of intellectual labour that was authoritative and uniquely women's own. Popular women novelists refused to 'eschew the encumbrance of [their] material circumstances' as embattled mothers and writers precisely because it was in these encumbrances that the source of their personal strength and claims to professional regard lay.

Representing work and authorship in the popular novel

The deployment of the discourse of maternity in novels and pleas by Literary Fund applicants underlines Anne K. Mellor's argument that Romantic women writers' accommodations to 'the construction of the proper lady as a modest, domestic woman . . . confined to the private sphere' should not be taken as proof of 'the ultimate triumph of a patriarchal domestic ideology'.[117] The popular women writers discussed here exploited, rather than conceded to, 'domestic ideology', building their literary authority on the basis of their credentials as wives and mothers and, in the process, revealing the ties that bind the private to the public and the moral economy of the home to the political economy of the state. Connecting these far from separate spheres is women's work, a subject that receives unprecedented treatment in the popular fiction of the 1790s. Although, as this book has demonstrated, work was never absent from the eighteenth-century novel, paid labour certainly became a more ubiquitous concern as the century drew to a close. It is no coincidence that as the domestic ideal became more thoroughly embedded within both the rhetoric of fiction and the female author's self-presentation, work became an ever more abiding preoccupation of the female-authored novel. Neither is it coincidental that women writers' near obsessive turn to the subject of labour was coterminous with the republic of letters' deployment of women's work as the degraded other against which men's professional labour was defined. Recognizing that work (having to, not having to, working well, working badly) was constitutive of their gendered and professional identities, women writers looked to the subject of labour to redefine themselves and their careers.

Fiction, as Edward Copeland argues, provided one of few available forums in which 'the potential of [female] employment' could be canvassed in the late eighteenth century; and women writers confronted 'the unhappy prospects' of paid work 'with a Bakhtinian cacophony of voices'. Through the din, however, Copeland detects three distinct cries, which articulate diverse 'fictions of employment': that of 'genteel fiction', which 'reject[ed] employment completely', 'didactic fiction', which 'embrac[ed] it with the fervour of the Christian martyrs, and Minerva fiction, [which took] it on with stoicism and cold fury'.[118] Copeland links these differences between fictional modes to their authors' economic backgrounds and their experiences of labour itself. The fact that sometime Minerva writers such as Parsons and Helme, a wine merchant's and a schoolmaster's daughter respectively, 'skirt[ed] the lower edges of the middle class', in which didactic novelists (such as Pilkington) and genteel novelists (such as Burney) were more securely placed, thus comes to account, in Copeland's reading, for the 'canny assessment of employment for women' that characterizes many of the novels published by the Press.[119]

Numerous Fund applicants came from the lower middling sort, undertaking forms of paid work that the income from their literary activities was intended merely to supplement, rather than to replace. And a number of women claimants indicated that they applied for financial aid, not to advance their hopes of authorial success but to fit them for more respectable and supposedly less precarious employments, such as teaching or needlework.[120] Yet, the archives of the Literary Fund frustrate attempts to link women writers' class and publishing affiliations (fluid as both were) or their choice of textual form (the didactic or fashionable novel, for example) to the attitudes towards work that their writing evidences. Parsons, for example, assisted her husband in the management of their turpentine factory, while Helme married a schoolmaster and worked as a teacher herself. However, Parsons was also employed, as we have seen, by the royal household as Sempstress in Ordinary, and, like Helme, published a number of novels with presses other than the Minerva, which display her didactic intentions and genteel aspirations, not to mention her professional ambition. Similarly, so-called genteel and didactic writers (some, including Mary Pilkington, were surely both) were not averse to using the Minerva Press when it proved an expedient way of placing their novels.[121]

The unpredictability of these writers' personal and professional situations is reflected in their typically polyphonic representations of labour. Some of Parsons's characters, for example, articulate a genteel disdain for manual work not unlike that explored in such poignant detail in Frances Burney's *The Wanderer* (1814). In the 'genteel' and Burneyesque *Miss Meredith*, the hero encounters in France a former gentleman-turned-woodcutter, who conventionally figures labour as a fall:

> O, Sir, you who have a feeling mind, may judge what a life mine is for a man of family; a man of sentiment! The low-born peasant, by daily labour, earns his bread, and tastes contentment – but [not] the man of noble birth, unused to laborious occupations, and pampered with the luxuries of life . . . when he is sensible that this scanty pittance depends on his life only; and that when he dies, those he holds most dear will be exposed to beggary and contempt . . . . (I, pp. 130–1)

Comparing this episode to the encounter between the French vine grower and the eponymous hero of Charlotte Smith's later *Marchmont* (1796) is revealing. In both, manual labour is associated with 'contentment', but only while the labourer remains blind to the degradation his work is understood to produce in the minds of members of the genteel classes. Charlotte Smith's novel, as we have seen, encourages the reader to read against the grain of such assumptions about manual work, by ridiculing the hero's self-indulgent emotional displays, by exposing his failure to support his family through his own labour and, most importantly, by contrasting his attitudes to work and to the labouring class with those of his more pragmatic wife to be, Althea Dacres. No such dissenting voice exists in *Miss Meredith*, but it does in other novels by Parsons, in which heroines, like Smith's, prove much better able than their male counterparts to negotiate the tensions between gender, rank and labour. In *The Convict*, for instance, Parsons presents an altogether different model of paid employment, much more nearly indebted to the mid-century fictions of Scott than to the plays and novels of Burney. Fanny may be unjustly 'fated to procure my subsistence by industry and labour' (IV, p. 147), but she has 'no objection to work' (IV, p. 124). The 'repugnance' she feels when forced to accept a position as a '*lady's companion*' is not a rejection of employment per se, but of those forms of work, which, as *The Adventures of David Simple*'s (1744) Cynthia and *The History of Sir George Ellison's* (1766) invisible domestic servant Mrs Alton had found, degraded women by exploiting their domestic skills and subjecting them to the 'whims and caprice' of others and unable to 'speak [their] own sentiments' (IV, p. 123). A state of 'absolute servitude' was infinitely preferable, Fanny suggests, to such forms of 'slavery', since the former allowed for the possibility of economic and psychic independence denied to those 'automaton[s]' employed in supposedly more genteel and suitably feminine employments such as companionship or governessing (IV, p. 123).

Elsewhere, Parsons promotes a georgic model of labour, according to which work is imagined as a civilizing force that marks national (and imperial) progress, and industriousness is presented as the hallmark of 'self-making' and a source of reformative agency.[122] In *The Valley of St. Gothard* (1799) labour and the independence it affords distinguish the truly virtuous man and woman of feeling from the dissipated leisure classes: where wealth, the narrator comments, produces 'disease, inquietude, lassitude and the most baneful passions, the sons of nature and temperance, accustomed to labour, to exercise, and to a boundary of their wishes . . . enjoy health, vigor, peace of mind, and that tranquillity of soul, unknown to pupils of the gay world'.[123] As in *The Convict*, in which Fanny is eventually reunited with her mother and marries her lover, labour finds in its just reward in *St. Gothard*. Alexis, an orphaned Swiss goatherd, is given an education by a compassionate man of feeling and eventually marries the daughter of an English lord in whose eyes the young man's humble origins only further prove his worth as a potential son-in-law.

Alexis's story, like that of Fanny in *The Convict*, forms part of a recurrent strain in popular novels of the late eighteenth century and virtually obligatory in the novels of Literary Fund applicants: the making, or remaking, of the self through labour. A particularly resonant example, in which this self-(re)making is linked not only to labour but specifically to the labour of writing, occurs in Burke's *Adela Northington* (1796), a novel in which the titular heroine is alerted to the plight of a father and daughter reduced to penury. After undergoing a series of trials, injustices and familial tragedies, parent and child support themselves tirelessly for nine years through a combination of 'the labours of [the father's] pen' and the daughter's 'industry', only to be falsely arrested and imprisoned for debt at the malicious instigation of the man who had earlier married, but subsequently disowned, the daughter. At this point, the work of father and daughter is impotent to secure their independence; however, the relation of the story of their fall and of their endeavours to work themselves out of the poverty to which they have been unjustly reduced through literary and manual industry awakens the charitable interest of Adela and her guardians, and the father and daughter are placed in a comfortable lodging before eventually being restored to their rightful place within society. In light of the dire financial situation Burke was in when she wrote the novel, and it is probable that *Adela Northington* is the unpublished work she claimed to have 'in hand' when she first applied to the Literary Fund in 1795, it is tempting to read this plot, as we might the labour plots of *The Valley of St. Gothard* and *The Convict*, as a form of fictional wish-fulfilment on the part of its author. Within the realm of the novel, at least, 'labours of [the] pen' and the narration of personal misfortune will bring the financial redress the author herself sought so determinedly, and elusively, in real life.[124]

A different kind of self-making through the work of writing occurs in Helme's children's book *Instructive Rambles Extended* (1800), a work that, like its predecessor, *Instructive Rambles* (1798), is structured as a set of fictional excursions in London and its 'adjacent villages' undertaken by the Richardson children and their companion and mother-substitute, Mrs Sidney. One of the last of the stories in this two-volume work follows the children's friendship with Rosa, a 'gentoo slave' whom they encounter placing flowers on the grave of her former mistress. The children are frightened by Rosa's appearance, a fear which Mrs Sidney attempts to allay by explaining that skin colour is arbitrary: 'were *you* by any accident to be thrown into their country, you would be equally disgusting to the natives, as those unhappy people are now to you'.[125]

Concerned that she has not fully stamped out the children's prejudice, Mrs Sidney enjoins Mary to listen to, and subsequently to transcribe, the former slave's life story.

Rosa's narrative begins in the South Asian province of Ratipore, where she is raised under the nurturing guidance of her mother and industrious father. Throughout her early years, Rosa's father labours 'incessantly at the cultivation of his rice', so much so that he not only sees his family 'furnished in plenty' but is able 'to supply a neighbouring factory belonging to the English' (II, p. 132). This life of plenitude and self-sufficiency is destroyed when white settlers enter into business negotiations with Rosa's father and introduce him to the luxuries and indolence of European life. He takes to drink and refuses to 'labour . . . and toil for a paltry subsistence' (II, p. 137). His rice fields are neglected and animals trample the existing crops. Rosa tries to 'repair all [the] damages' wrought by her father's idleness through her labour, but her efforts prove futile; neither can they save the young woman's mother who is tragically killed by a snake bite (II, p. 138). Georgic industry is, thus, thwarted by a European pastoralism that is productive only of cultural degeneracy, and Rosa is subsequently sold into slavery before being taken to England by a compassionate woman, where she is baptized as a Christian.[126] What is particularly interesting about 'The History of a Gentoo Slave' is the way in which the text explicitly connects Rosa's exemplary manual labours with the 'arduous task' of writing undertaken by Mary (II, p. 127). The novel indicates, moreover, that the labours of the slave and her author are not only analogous but mutually reinforcing: in polishing the slave's language and idiom, Mary renders her story more 'worthy [of] reflection', while the lessons derived from constructing the narrative of Rosa's labour 'exercise' and 'improve' the young writer's 'mind' (II, p. 128).

Helme's implicit association of the act of writing and the manual labours of the slave recollects her earlier *The Farmer of Inglewood Forest* (1796), in which the state of dependency in which the author and slave live is figured through the common language of engraving. In the novel's dedication, Helme declares that her obligation to her patron, Mrs Hastings, is 'impressed on my mind in characters never to be effaced', a metaphor to which the novel returns when the boy slave Felix is spared from branding by the intervention of Henry: '"my young master . . . bore me off, my back unmarked, but his goodness is engraven in far more indelible characters"'.[127] As in *Inglewood Forest*, the connection drawn in *Instructive Rambles Extended* between the position of author and slave serves as much to vindicate the author as it does the text's argument for the amelioration of slavery. For as 'The History of a Gentoo Slave' progresses, the parallels the text draws between literary and manual labour become less significant than the differences that characterize these activities. When Mr Richardson, the father, praises his daughter's work in crafting Rosa's story, Mary modestly suggests that her efforts offer no 'proof of genius' since the narrative's shape and content are not of her own making (I, p. 162). The effect of this disavowal, like so many of those made by Fund applicants, is more complex than it first appears, however. Mary's renunciation of genius, on the grounds that she is merely an amanuensis, allows Helme, as the true author of the work, to claim it for herself. As such, 'The History of a Gentoo Slave' can profitably be read as an attempt to recuperate authorship in fiction through a reworking of the division of labour not unlike that attempted in *Claims of Literature*. Like Williams's manifesto, *Instructive Rambles Extended* establishes writing as an analogue for labour in order to argue for the transformative and socially useful role of literature, before subordinating mechanical to intellectual work within the strict labour hierarchy the text constructs in order to assert authorship's primacy as a morally useful, politically educative and ultimately civilizing form of labour. The Literary Fund may have provided limited redress for novelists such as Burke, Helme and Parsons, but, through their vindications of reproductive, paid and authorial labour, they could at least find a poetic justice in their fiction.

The self-reflexive novels explored in this chapter complicate claims that popular fiction of the late eighteenth century registers a gauge of tension between employment, station and self-respect measurable 'by the almost complete impenetrability of the only employment that authors [could] be guaranteed to know first hand: novel-writing itself'.[128] Nevertheless, it is certainly the case that, as work became an ever more common preoccupation of the novel, and as the discourse of labour became ever more central to the professionalization of authorship, so women writers' reflections upon the work of writing became more thoroughly encoded. The relative obliqueness of the strategies adopted by Literary Fund applicants as they strove to theorize their literary work, when compared with the bolder efforts of the likes of Scott, Smith and Wollstonecraft, is, in no small part, an indication of the undoubted complexity of their attitudes towards labour. None of the writers explored in this study approached the subject of work without ambivalence, but the financially compromised female applicants to the Literary Fund evidently felt the perceived tensions between their gender, their social status and their professional activities more keenly than the other figures examined in this book. Yet while it might be tempting to view these writers' representations of work biographically, as symptomatic of their all-too-real experiences of economic hardship and the inequities of the gendered division of labour, this would be to misjudge these writers' formulation of the relationship between their personal and professional lives. Moreover, to argue such would be to misrepresent the strategic and sophisticated use these writers made of both the discourses of privacy and publicity to meet their individual needs and to realize their occupational aspirations in the face of a new political economy of authorship in which the woman writer's position was becoming increasingly untenable.

There is a tragic irony in the story that Fund applicants' novels and pleas tell about the narratives of labour and authorship with which this book is concerned: that the valorization of the work of writing would ultimately find its victims among a group of authors – women novelists – who had played such an important part in its development and contestation. Yet, the strategies of resistance and self-vindication identifiable in the applications and works of Literary Fund claimants demonstrate that the charity was much more than the 'institutional repository of abandoned hope' it has been said to have been.[129] On the contrary, the Fund provided a focal point for the professional ambitions of a group of women who took their work as writers seriously and who made that work one of the principal subjects of their prose. To read these women's claims for their writing alongside their reputations as unambitious and second-rate writers, more deserving of our sympathy as women than of our acknowledgement as authors, is to reveal the unreliability of some of the assumptions that have underpinned the narratives we have told about women's writing in the long eighteenth century, assumptions which, in many cases, have their origins in eighteenth-century paradigms that women writers actively set out to reject. Although the contributions made by popular women novelists to the ongoing debate about women's work were, perhaps, more modest than those made by the authors discussed in other chapters, and despite the fact that their still obscure status today seems to signal the effectiveness of 'the Great Forgetting' that the professionalization of intellectual labour inaugurated, they were not, as Catherine Bayley wrote, 'unworthy object[s]' of the Fund's charity, neither are their works undeserving of scholarly enquiry. Bayley's claims for her literary work, like that of so many of her fellow Fund applicants, demand to be taken seriously.

Coda: reading labour and writing women's literary history

> [O]ur efforts in writing eighteenth-century women's literary history are now hampered less by a lack of awareness of the problem [of the professionalization of literature] than by our resistance to rethinking women writers' and readers' positions toward, and implication in this defining moment in women's literary history, wherein they were purportedly being relegated to the footnotes and margins of the central narrative, soon to be erased from it altogether.
>
> Betty A. Schellenberg, *The Professionalization of Women Writers in Eighteenth-century Britain* (2005)

As Betty A. Schellenberg reminds us, despite three decades of ground-breaking feminist scholarship, the project of writing women's literary history is still, to an extent, overshadowed by the critical narratives about professionalism, gender and the literary that were being constructed and contested in these writers' own lifetimes, and which subsequent generations of scholars have resisted rethinking.[1] My own effort to break down this resistance has been to explore women writers' negotiation of a series of defining moments in literary history through their responses to the manual/intellectual labour axis around which this history unfolded, and to which that history is still – often prejudicially for women writers – subject. By making work, in its various forms, visible in eighteenth-century writings by women, my intention has not been simply to uncover something that has always been there. Rather, I have attempted to offer some account for eighteenth-century studies' unwillingness fully to acknowledge labour's crucial, if vexed, presence in imaginative and non-imaginative prose of the period and, further, to suggest the costs (of underestimation and misrepresentation, for example) of colluding with assumptions about gender, work and women's writing that would play such a vital part in the 'Great Forgetting' of female authors in the nineteenth century.

The effects of allowing labour to figure more centrally in our analysis of eighteenth-century fiction and authorship are various. Such a manoeuvre, for example, forces us to reassess the narratives that we have told about constructions of gender, gentility and genre in this period; equally importantly, perhaps, it encourages us to interrogate some of our (post-Romantic) anxieties about intellectual labour: is 'inspiration' polluted by our Burneyesque 'hard fagging'? Can there be worth without work, for example? A further effect – one which I had not anticipated when I began this project and which might usefully bear brief elaboration here – is this strategy's possible impact upon questions of genealogy and the writing of women's literary history itself. In a recent essay on continuities in the 'picturing [of] benevolence' in novels from Sarah Fielding's *Adventures of David Simple* (1744) to Elizabeth Inchbald's *Nature and Art* (1796), Donna Landry demonstrates that women's writing represents something of a special case, one which suggests 'alternative periodizations to traditional literary historical ones'.[2] If this claim is borne out by eighteenth-century fictional representations of philanthropy from 1750 to 1830, then it is equally proved by women writers' representations of labour in the literature same period. To think about the work of Charlotte Smith and Mary Wollstonecraft as being in dialogue with one another, as this book has done, is hardly unusual, but to present these writers' thinking as being shaped by, and in productive conversation with, the novels of much earlier and less obviously radical authors such as Sarah Fielding or Sarah Scott is rather more so.[3] To write about Wollstonecraft in the context of the popular women novelists she so often derided in the pages of the *Analytical Review* is more unusual still. And yet, as we have seen, the continuities between Scott's attack on men's usurpation of female trades and the arbitrariness of the gendered division of labour in her 1750s novels and the similar arguments made by Mary Ann Radcliffe, Priscilla Wakefield and Mary Wollstonecraft in their 1790s polemics are striking. So too, is the shared conviction that all of the women writers discussed in this book had in the potential of women's manual, intellectual and affective labour to provoke cultural, economic and social reform. Read as part of a longer history of writing about labour (one that can accommodate both eighteenth-century sentimental fiction and the Romantic novel, as well as both conservative and radical feminisms), Wollstonecraft's arguments about active citizenship and the necessity of women's participation in the division of labour as workers, mothers and philosophers seem less exclusively a product of the 1790s than they have often appeared to be. Rather, we might see *A Vindication of the Rights of Woman* (1792), like Smith's *Marchmont* (1796) or the letters and popular novels of the Literary Fund applicants, as evidence of the longevity of a mid-century moment – persistent in the face of the transformations that occurred in the labour and literary marketplaces during the second half of the long eighteenth century – in which women's labour can be imagined as a source of pride and cultural optimism. A full assessment of the legacies of mid-century women writers including such figures as Scott and Fielding, as well as Mary Collier, Jane Collier, Elizabeth Griffith, Elizabeth Justice and Charlotte Lennox, is the work of another project, but it is one which I am now more than ever convinced would be worth the effort. Suffice it to say here that the resonances between different generations of women writers' work on work gives us an exciting opportunity to rethink at least some of the organizing principles – particularly those surrounding questions of chronology and politics – that have underpinned histories of women's writing of this period.[4]

In claiming such continuities, my aim is not, however, to efface difference or the historical and cultural specificity of the representation of labour in the texts under discussion here. Scott, Smith, Wollstonecraft and the various women applicants to the Literary Fund do not speak with one voice when they speak about women's work. And, indeed, their individual negotiations of this tricky subject are fraught with contradictions and inconsistencies that reveal the weight of the issues with which they grappled and the multiple and conflicting stakes they had invested in them. None the less, by recognizing these women's collective participation in this debate on women's work, common ground is exposed. By lifting the veil of 'Inchantment', to borrow a metaphor from Fielding's *The Adventures of David Simple* (1744), we can see that eighteenth-century women writers were deeply invested in questions surrounding labour and its relationship to their own status as writers and as women, and much more willing to interrogate, to dispute, or to exploit for their own advantage, shifts in the division of labour and the literary marketplace than has often been allowed.[5] The cost of failing to recognize these investments is high. To deny the presence of labour in female-authored texts from this period is, this book has suggested, to deny women writers' provocative and formative presence within a series of pressing political, economic and literary debates – on the connections and disconnections between manual, affective and intellectual work, on the justness of gendered division of labour, on the (in)compatibility of domestic and professional life and on the cultural and economic status and value of women's work – that shaped eighteenth-century culture as surely as they shape our own.

Notes

Introduction

1 Samuel Crisp to Frances Burney, 1779. *The Early Journals and Letters of Fanny Burney. Volume III The Streatham Years: Part I, 1778–1779*, ed. Lars E. Troide and Stewart T. Cooke (Oxford: Oxford University Press, 1994), p. 352.
2 Frances Burney to Samuel Crisp, 22 January 1780. *The Early Journals and Letters of Fanny Burney. Volume IV The Streatham Years: Part II, 1780–1781*, ed. Betty Rizzo (Oxford: Oxford University Press, 2003), p. 7.
3 *The Early Journals and Letters of Fanny Burney. III*, p. 48.
4 Frances Burney to Dr Charles Burney, c. 13 August 1779, *ibid.*, p. 345. On the suppression of the play see Margaret Anne Doody, *Frances Burney: The Life in the Works* (Cambridge: Cambridge University Press, 1988), pp. 66–98.
5 On the relationship between economics, print and authorship in the period see: George Justice, *The Manufacturers of Literature: Writing and the Literary Marketplace in Eighteenth-century England* (Newark: University of Delaware Press, 2002); Clifford Siskin, *The Work of Writing: Literature and Social Change in Britain, 1700–1830* (Baltimore and London: The Johns Hopkins University Press, 1998); James Thompson, *Models of Value: Eighteenth-century Political Economy and the Novel* (Durham, NC: Duke University Press, 1996); and Martha Woodmansee, *The Author, Art, and the Market: Rereading the History of Aesthetics* (New York: Columbia University Press, 1994). Studies that focus particularly on how shifts in the literary marketplace affected constructions of gender include Catherine Gallagher, *Nobody's Story: The Vanishing Acts of Women Writers in the Marketplace, 1670–1820* (Berkeley and Los Angeles: University of California Press, 1994); Catherine Ingrassia, *Authorship, Commerce, and Gender in Early Eighteenth-century England: A Culture of Paper Credit* (Cambridge: Cambridge University Press, 1998); Paula McDowell, *The Women of Grub Street: Press, Politics, and Gender in the London Literary Marketplace, 1678–1730* (Oxford: Clarendon Press, 1998); and Linda Zionkowski, *Men's Work: Gender, Class, and the Professionalization of Poetry, 1660–1784* (New York and Basingstoke: Palgrave Macmillan, 2001).

6 On Pope's views on 'literary labour' and his concern for 'the class and gender status that it conferred upon professional writers' see Zionkowski, *Men's Work*, pp. 115–23. On Pope and patronage see Dustin Griffin, *Literary Patronage in England, 1650–1800* (Cambridge: Cambridge University Press, 1996), pp. 147–54.

7 As Kristina Straub has commented in relation to Burney's *Evelina*: 'The relationship between eighteenth-century, middle-class women and their work is . . . complicated and made difficult to define because the lines drawn between tasks we would be inclined to see as recreational – mere hobbies or amusements – and tasks performed out of a sense of obligation or duty – "work", in short – are often blurred in eighteenth-century writing.' *Divided Fictions: Fanny Burney and Feminine Strategy* (Lexington: The University Press of Kentucky, 1987), p. 79.

8 In *Common Ground: Eighteenth-century English Satiric Fiction and the Poor* (Stanford, CA: Stanford University Press, 1997), Judith Frank shows how representations of the labouring classes inevitably 'set off tremors in representations of the non-labouring gentleman' who must negotiate his difference from, and similarities to, his social inferiors (p. 17). Zionkowski's *Men's Work* is specifically concerned with the question of poetic labour and the pressure that the commercialization of the literary marketplace exerted upon contemporary discourses of masculinity and rank. Chapter 2 returns to the question of men's work in the form of Charlotte's Smith parodic treatment of men's fall into labour.

9 Sarah Jordan, *The Anxieties of Idleness: Idleness in Eighteenth-century British Literature and Culture* (Lewisburg: Bucknell; and London: Associated University Presses, 2003).

10 Penelope J. Corfield, *Power and the Professions in Britain 1700–1850* (London and New York: Routledge, 1995), p. 24; p. 174. See also Geoffrey Holmes, *Augustan England: Professions, State and Society, 1680–1730* (London: George Allen and Unwin, 1982).

11 Corfield, *Power and the Professions*, p. 204.

12 John Barrell, *English Literature in History 1730–1780: An Equal, Wide Survey* (London, Melbourne, Sydney, Auckland, Johannesburg: Hutchinson, 1983), pp. 17–50.

13 Siskin, *The Work of Writing*, p. 107.

14 Corfield, *Power and the Professions*, p. 188.

15 The first quotation is taken from Thomas Gisborne's *An Enquiry into the Duties of Men in the Higher and Middle Classes of Society in Great Britain, Resulting from their Respective Stations, Professions, and Employments* (London: B. and J. White, 1794), p. 85. The second quotation is from Gisborne's *An Enquiry into the Duties of the Female Sex* (London: T. Cadell and W. Davies, 1797), p. 2.

16 Steven Wallech, '"Class Versus Rank": The Transformation of Eighteenth-century English Social Terms and Theories of Production', *Journal of the History of Ideas*, 47: 3 (1986): 409–31.

17 One of the most influential studies among the vast body of literature that traces the middle class's rise, and one which is of particular relevance to this study, is Leonore Davidoff and Catherine Hall's *Family Fortunes: Men and Women of the English Middle Class, 1780–1850* (London: Routledge, 1995). Other studies which have pointed to the earlier emergence of a middle class include: Peter Earle, *The Making of the English Class: Business, Society and Family Life in London, 1660–1730* (London: Methuen, 1989); Holmes, *Augustan England*; Margaret Hunt, *The Middling Sort: Commerce, Gender and the Family in England, 1660–1750* (Berkeley and London: The University of California Press, 1995); Paul Langford, *A Polite and Commercial People: England, 1727–1783* (Oxford: Oxford University Press, 1989); and John Smail, *The Origins of Middle-class Culture: Halifax, Yorkshire, 1660–1780* (Ithaca: Cornell University Press, 1994).

18 Earle, *The Making of the English Middle Class*, pp. 4–10.

19 *Ibid.*, p. 3.

20 On Scott's biography see Betty Rizzo, *Companions Without Vows: Relationships Among Eighteenth-century British Women* (Athens and London: University of Georgia Press, 1996), pp. 295–319.

21 Gary Kelly, 'Introduction', *A Description of Millenium Hall and the Country Adjacent*, ed. Gary Kelly (Peterborough, Ontario: Broadview, 1995), p. 11.

22 See Loraine Fletcher, *Charlotte Smith: A Critical Biography* (Basingstoke: Palgrave Macmillan, 2001).

23 Charlotte Smith, *Desmond: A Novel*, ed. Stuart Curran, reprinted in *The Works of Charlotte Smith*, 14 vols (London: Pickering and Chatto, 2005–7), V, p. 4.

24 Edward Copeland, *Women Writing About Money: Women's Fiction in England, 1790–1820* (Cambridge: Cambridge University Press, 1995), p. 202.

25 See Janet Todd, *Mary Wollstonecraft: A Revolutionary Life* (New York: Columbia University Press, 2000).

26 Mary Wollstonecraft, *A Vindication of the Rights of Woman*, reprinted in *The Works of Mary Wollstonecraft*, ed. Janet Todd and Marilyn Butler with Emma Rees-Mogg, 7 vols (London: Pickering and Chatto, 1989), V, p. 75.

27 Wallech, '"Class Versus Rank"', p. 410.

28 Barbara Taylor, *Mary Wollstonecraft and the Feminist Imagination* (Cambridge: Cambridge University Press, 2003), p. 167.

29 Copeland, *Women Writing About Money*, p. 165.

30 Eliza Parsons to the Royal Literary Fund, 18 December 1792. *Archives of the Royal Literary Fund: 1790–1918*, 145 reels (London: World Microfilms Publications, 1981–84), Reel 1, case 21.

31 Among the most important recent studies of labouring-class poetry, not including single author studies, are John Goodridge, *Rural Life in Eighteenth-century English Poetry* (Cambridge: Cambridge University Press, 1995) and William J. Christmas, *The Lab'ring Muses: Work, Writing and the Social Order in English Plebeian Poetry* (Newark: The University of Delaware Press, 2001). Studies with a particular focus on gender, work and labouring-class poetry include Donna Landry, *The Muses of Resistance: Labouring-class Women's Poetry in Britain, 1739–1796* (Cambridge: Cambridge University Press, 1990) and Susanne Kord, *Women Peasant Poets in Eighteenth-century England, Scotland and Germany: Milkmaids on Parnassus* (Rochester, NY, and Woodbridge: Camden House, 2003).
32 Christmas, *The Lab'ring Muses*, p. 20.
33 Copeland, *Women Writing About Money*, p. 161. Among the genteel novelists who shunned the world of work, Copeland counts Burney, Jane Austen and Maria Edgeworth, as well as the subjects of Chapters 2 and 3 of this book, Charlotte Smith and Mary Wollstonecraft.
34 *Ibid*., p. 162.
35 Anna Seward, *The Letters of Anna Seward written between the Years 1784 and 1807*, 6 vols (New York: AMS Press, 1995), II, p. 287.
36 Copeland, *Women Writing About Money*, pp. 163–4.
37 Ann Van Sant, 'Crusoe's Hands', *Eighteenth-century Life*, 32: 2 (2008), p. 131.
38 Sandra Sherman, *Imagining Poverty: Quantification and the Decline of Paternalism* (Columbus: The Ohio State University Press, 2001), p. 1.
39 *Ibid*., p. 1. I am thinking of novels such as Fielding's *The Adventures of David Simple* (1744) and *The History of the Countess of Dellwyn* (1759), to which I return in Chapter 2, Lennox's *Henrietta* (1758), in which the heroine undertakes paid work rather than accede to her aunt's wish that she convert to Catholicism, and Burney's *The Wanderer* (1814).
40 Mary Hays, *Memoirs of Emma Courtney*, ed. Marilyn L. Brooks (Peterborough, Ontario: Broadview, 2000), p. 65.
41 Margaret Anne Doody in her 'Introduction' to *The Wanderer* comments that, in its preoccupation with manual labour, the novel foreshadows concerns that reached full articulation only in 'the social novels of the late 1830s and early 1840s'. Frances Burney, *The Wanderer*, ed. Margaret Anne Doody, Robert L. Mack and Peter Sabor (Oxford and New York: Oxford University Press, 1991), p. xxxii.
42 The key text, here, is Nancy Armstrong's *Desire and Fiction: A Political History of the Novel* (New York and Oxford: Oxford University Press, 1987), pp. 75–6.
43 On eighteenth-century concepts of time see, for example, Stuart Sherman, *Telling Time: Clocks, Diaries and English Diurnal Form, 1660–1785* (Chicago and London: The University of Chicago Press, 1996). On the

internalization of clock time by the middle classes see Hunt, *The Middling Sort*, pp. 53–6. On the Christian and conduct-book imperatives for gentlewomen to make good use of their time see Jordan, *The Anxieties of Idleness*, pp. 84–122.

44 Lady Sarah Pennington, *An Unfortunate Mother's Advice to her Absent Daughters; In a Letter to Miss Pennington* (London: S. Chandler, 1761), p. 20.

45 Scott, *Millenium Hall*, p. 244.

46 Samuel Richardson, *Clarissa, or, the History of a Young Lady*, ed. Angus Ross (Harmondsworth: Penguin, 2004), Letter 529 (Miss Howe to John Belford, Esq.), pp. 1469–71.

47 Armstrong, *Desire and Domestic Fiction*, p. 14; p. 60; pp. 75–81.

48 *Ibid.*, p. 61.

49 *Ibid.*, p. 79.

50 *Ibid.*

51 Harriet Guest, *Small Change: Women, Learning, Patriotism, 1750–1810* (Chicago and London: The University of Chicago Press, 2000), pp. 85–6n24.

52 In *Common Ground*, Frank argues for a more nuanced understanding of the relationship between the gentle classes and the poor, observing that the former were 'particularly susceptible to identifications' with the latter 'because theirs too was a status group defined in relation to labour – specifically lack of labour' – the recognition of which fact was commonly registered and forestalled through the medium of satire. In her discussion of *Cecilia* (1782), Frank urges us to reconsider domesticity's relation to labour, reading the sentimental affect that threatens to overwhelm Burney's heroine as resulting from, and analogous to, the poor's dispossession as a result of the reorganization of labour in the later eighteenth century (p. 131). Frank's ingenious reading of the novel and my rather different take on how women writers figured the relationship between labour and domesticity is worked through in Chapter 2.

53 Guest, *Small Change*, p. 85.

54 Sarah Fielding, *The Adventures of David Simple and Volume the Last*, ed. Malcolm Kelsall (Oxford: Oxford University Press, 1987), pp. 52–3. The husband of the exemplary woman who prompts this observation constantly belittles and berates his wife. He appears in a chapter of the novel the title of which declares that such 'Examples' of domestic 'abuse' are to be found only in 'very low life' (p. 50). Interestingly, though, in *Volume the Last* (1753), David and Valentine are guilty of precisely the same failure to recognize women's domestic labour. The 'Business of Housewifry' (*sic*) which underpins the idyllic but (not coincidentally) doomed community described in *David Simple*'s sequel appears to the novel's heroes to be 'done by Enchantment', as if 'Household Management had never employed [the women's] Thoughts' (p. 316).

55 Sarah Scott, *A Journey Through Every Stage of Life*, ed. Gary Kelly, in *Bluestocking Feminism: Writings of the Bluestocking Circle, 1738–1785*, 6 vols (London: Pickering and Chatto, 1999), V, p. 22.

56 Jane Spencer, *The Rise of the Woman Novelist: From Aphra Behn to Jane Austen* (Oxford: Blackwell, 1986), p. 20; Janet Todd, *The Sign of Angellica* (London: Virago, 1989), p. 126.

57 A particularly useful survey of this material and its implications for the study of eighteenth-century women's writing can be found in Betty A. Schellenberg, *The Professionalization of Women Writers in Eighteenth-century Britain* (Cambridge: Cambridge University Press, 2005), pp. 1–9.

58 My terms, of course, are taken from Mary Poovey's *The Proper Lady and the Woman Writer: Ideology as Style in the Works of Mary Wollstonecraft, Mary Shelley, and Jane Austen* (Chicago and London: University of Chicago Press, 1984).

59 Copeland, *Women Writing About Money*, p. 190.

60 Frank Donoghue, *The Fame Machine: Book Reviewing and Eighteenth-century Literary Careers* (Stanford, CA: Stanford University Press, 1996), pp. 160–1.

61 Siskin, *The Work of Writing*, particularly pp. 103–29.

62 In *The Crisis of Literature in the 1790s: Print Culture and the Public Sphere* (Cambridge: Cambridge University Press, 1999), Paul Keen argues that the professionalization of the literary public sphere in the 1790s was in large part dependent upon the casting of 'Women, the lower orders, and that anomalous group, colonial subjects' as 'the beyond of the republic of letters – social domains which could not be trusted with the cultural authority that ought to accrue to an informed reading and writing public' (p. 137). See also his chapter on the 'masculine women' who sought to counter their marginalization, pp. 171–205.

63 Siskin, *The Work of Writing*, p. 222.

64 Schellenberg, *The Professionalization of Women Writers*, p. 9.

65 The question of representation is not commonly foregrounded in historical studies of women's work. One recent notable except is Isabelle Baudino, Jacques Carré, Cécile Révauger, eds, *The Invisible Woman: Aspects of Women's Work in Eighteenth-century Britain* (Aldershot: Ashgate, 2005). Only Cheryl Turner's *Living by the Pen: Women Writers in the Eighteenth Century* (London: Routledge, 1992) offers a sustained treatment of women's work as writers in relation to other forms of female employment.

66 Alice Clark, *The Working Life of Women in the Seventeenth Century* (New York: Dutton, 1919); Ivy Pinchbeck, *Women Workers and the Industrial Revolution, 1750–1850* (London: Routledge, 1930).

67 Bridget Hill, *Women, Work and Sexual Politics in Eighteenth-century England* (London: UCL Press, 1994).

68 Harriet Bradley, *Men's Work, Women's Work: A Sociological History of the Sexual Division of Labour* (Cambridge: Polity, 1989), pp. 7–32.
69 Bridget Hill, 'Women's History: A Study in Change, Continuity or Standing Still?', in *Women's Work: The English Experience 1650–1914*, ed. Pamela Sharpe (London, New York, Sydney and Auckland: Arnold, 1998), p. 53.
70 See for example, Maxine Berg, 'What Difference Did Women's Work Make to the Industrial Revolution?', *History Workshop Journal*, 35 (1993): 22–44; Pamela Sharpe, *Adapting to Capitalism: Working Women in the English Economy, 1700–1850* (Basingstoke: Palgrave Macmillan, 1996); Amanda Vickery, *The Gentleman's Daughter: Women's Lives in Georgian England* (New Haven and London: Yale University Press, [1998] 2003).
71 Hill, *Women, Work and Sexual Politics*, p. 263.
72 Katrina Honeyman, *Women, Gender and Industrialisation in England, 1700–1870* (Basingstoke: Macmillan, 2000), p. 32.
73 Davidoff and Hall, *Family Fortunes*, p. 272.
74 *Ibid*., pp. 272–315.
75 Hannah Barker, *The Business of Women: Female Enterprise and Urban Development in Northern England, 1760–1830* (Oxford: Oxford University Press, 2006); Vickery, The Gentleman's Daughter.
76 *Ibid*., p. 7. Barker, in *The Business of Women*, makes a slightly different point to Vickery's, but comes to a similar conclusion. She argues: 'factors traditionally thought to discriminate against women's commercial activity – particularly property laws and ideas about gender and respectability – did have significant impacts upon female enterprise. Yet it is also evident that women were not automatically economically or socially marginalized as a result . . . . The woman of business might be subject to various constraints, but at the same time, could be blessed with a number of freedoms, and a degree of independence, that set her apart from most other women – and many men – in late Georgian society' (p. 10).
77 For an account of the effects that late eighteenth-century political economic discourse had upon the construction and experience of labouring-class women, in particular, see Deborah Valenze, *The First Industrial Woman* (New York and London: Oxford University Press, 1995), pp. 128–40.
78 Stephen Duck, *The Thresher's Labour*, in *The Thresher's Labour (Stephen Duck) and The Woman's Labour (Mary Collier)*, with an introduction by Moira Ferguson (Los Angeles: William Andrews Clark Memorial Library, 1985), lines 168–9; 154–5.
79 Landry, *Muses of Resistance*, pp. 56–7.
80 Valenze, *First Industrial Woman*, pp. 129–40.
81 Laurie Ellinghausen, *Labour and Writing in Early Modern England, 1567–1667* (Aldershot and Burlington, VT: Ashgate, 2007), p. 22.
82 Kathryn R. King, 'Of Needles and Pens and Women's Work', *Tulsa Studies in Women's Literature*, 14: 1 (1995), p. 80.

83 *Ibid.*, p. 81.

84 Jane Barker, *The Galesia Trilogy and Selected Manuscript Poems of Jane Barker*, ed. Carol Shiner Wilson (Oxford and New York: Oxford University Press, 1997), p. 143.

85 King, 'Needles and Pens', p. 79.

86 Adam Smith, *An Inquiry into the Nature and Causes of the Wealth of Nations*, ed. W. B. Todd, 2 vols (Indianapolis: Liberty Fund, 1981), II, p. 787.

87 A different kind of book on labour and women's writing in this period would find room to discuss at length the works of writers including Mary Brunton, Mary Hays, Clara Reeve and Mary Robinson, and might extend its generic boundaries to look at the poetry of the likes of Felicia Hemans and Letitia Landon. Part of this book's project is to urge the benefits of making labour a central category of our analysis of writing in this period more widely.

88 On Burney and the cultural work of gender see Straub, *Divided Fictions*, and Frank's chapter on *Cecilia*, affect and charity in *Common Ground*, pp. 127–64. On Burney and authorship see Justice, *The Manufacturers of* Literature, pp. 195–233; and Schellenberg, *The Professionalization of Women Writers*, pp. 141–61.

89 On 'gentry capitalism' see Gary Kelly, 'Bluestocking Feminism', in *Women, Writing and the Public Sphere, 1700–1830*, ed. Elizabeth Eger, Charlotte Grant, Clíona Ó Gallchoir and Penny Warburton (Cambridge: Cambridge University Press, 2001), pp. 163–80.

90 Charlotte Smith to Dr Thomas Shirley, [22 August 1789], *The Collected Letters of Charlotte Smith*, ed. Judith Phillips Stanton (Bloomington and Indianapolis: Indiana University Press, 2003), p. 23.

91 Siskin, *The Work of Writing*, pp. 210–27.

Chapter 1

1 Sarah Scott, *A Description of Millenium Hall and the Country Adjacent*, ed. Gary Kelly (Peterborough, Ontario: Broadview, 1995), p. 111. Subsequent references will be given in the text.

2 Dorice Williams Elliott's *The Angel out of the House: Philanthropy and Gender in Nineteenth-century England* (Charlottesville and London: University Press of Virginia, 2002) contains a particularly interesting account of philanthropy in *Millenium Hall* (see pp. 33–53).

3 Gary Kelly, 'Bluestocking Feminism', in *Women, Writing and the Public Sphere, 1700–1830*, ed. Elizabeth Eger, Charlotte Grant, Clíona Ó Gallchoir and Penny Warburton (Cambridge: Cambridge University Press, 2001), pp. 163–80.

4 Notable exceptions include Diane E. Boyd's discussion of *Millenium Hall* and *Sir George Ellison* in 'Working Fictions: Representations of Middle-class Working Women in Eighteenth-century Fiction' (unpublished PhD

thesis, Auburn University, 2002) and April London's discussion of *Millenium Hall* in *Women and Property in the Eighteenth-century English Novel* (Cambridge: Cambridge University Press, 1999), pp. 111–21.

5 On Scott's indebtedness to contractualism see Alessa Johns, *Women's Utopias of the Eighteenth Century* (Urbana and Chicago: University of Illinois Press, 2003), pp. 91–109. *Millenium Hall*'s grounding in classical republican thought and sentimental notions of community is explored by Mary Peace in '"Epicures in Rural Pleasures": Revolution, Desire and Sentimental Economy in Sarah Scott's *Millenium Hall*', *Women's Writing*, 9: 2 (2002): 305–16. On the scope and limits of Scott's utopianism see Ruth Perry, 'Bluestockings in Utopia', in *History, Gender, and Eighteenth-century Literature*, ed. Beth Fowkes Tobin (Athens: University of Georgia Press, 1994), pp. 159–78; and Vincent Carretta, 'Utopia Limited: Sarah Scott's *Millenium Hall* and *The History of Sir George Ellison*', *The Age of Johnson*, 5 (1992): 303–26.

6 Judith Still, *Feminine Economies: Thinking Against the Market in the Enlightenment and the Late Twentieth Century* (Manchester and New York: Manchester University Press, 1997), p. 112.

7 On the literary representation of women in business see Elizabeth Kowaleski-Wallace, *Consuming Subjects: Women, Shopping, and Business in the Eighteenth Century* (New York: Columbia University Press, 1997), pp. 111–43.

8 Sarah Fielding, *The Adventures of David Simple and Volume the Last*, ed. Malcolm Kelsall (Oxford: Oxford University Press, 1987), p. 160. The influence of Fielding's feminist critique upon Scott's utopianism is documented by Johns in *Women's Utopias* (particularly pp. 89–90) in an argument which is underscored by Donna Landry's forthcoming 'Picturing Benevolence Against the Commercial Cry, 1750–1798: or, Sarah Fielding and the Secret Causes of Romanticism', in *The History of British Women's Writing, Volume V, 1750–1830* (Basingstoke: Palgrave Macmillan). While not refuting this model of influence, this chapter complicates it significantly by putting Scott's 1750s fiction – not part of Johns's or Landry's studies – squarely into the frame. Once considered a part of this narrative, novels such as Fielding's *The History of the Countess of Dellwyn* (1759), a work that is rather different in content and tone from *David Simple*, emerges not so much as a source for *Millenium Hall* but as a response to Scott's earlier utopian fiction.

9 Fielding, *David Simple*, p. 166.

10 Anon., *The Histories of Some of the Penitents in the Magdalen-House*, ed. Jennie Batchelor and Megan Hiatt (London: Pickering and Chatto, 2007), p. 43.

11 Deborah Valenze, *The First Industrial Woman* (New York and Oxford: Oxford University Press, 1995), pp. 13–28.

12 Sir John Fielding, *A Plan for a Preservatory and Reformatory for the Benefit of Deserted Girls and Penitent Prostitutes* (London: R. Francklin, 1758), p. 4.
13 See Donna T. Andrew, *Philanthropy and Police: London Charity in the Eighteenth Century* (Princeton: Princeton University Press, 1989), pp. 98–134.
14 Fielding, *Plan*, pp. 1–2.
15 Bernard Mandeville, *A Modest Defence of Publick Stews: or, An Essay upon Whoring* (London: A. Moore, 1724), p. 4.
16 Fielding, *Plan*, p. 3.
17 *Ibid*., p. 3.
18 Anon., 'A New Method for making Women as useful and as capable as men of maintaining themselves, as the men are; and consequently preventing their becoming old maids, or taking ill Courses, By a Lady', *Gentleman's Magazine*, 9 (1739): 525–6.
19 Jonas Hanway, *A Plan for Establishing a Charity-House, or Charity-Houses for the Reception of Repenting Prostitutes to be Called the Magdalen Charity* (London: n. pub., 1758), p. 29.
20 *Ibid*., p. 32.
21 *Ibid*., p. 38.
22 Valenze, *The First Industrial Woman*, p. 25.
23 This resemblance is noted by Peace in '"Epicures in Rural Pleasures"' and by Elliott in *The Angel out of the House*. Contemporary correspondence also shows that Scott, at the very least, would have known the anonymous 'Lady' who wrote the sentimental novel *The Histories of Some of the Penitents in the Magdalen-House* (1760) and may even have been its author. See Batchelor and Hiatt's introduction to *The Histories*, pp. xx–xxiii.
24 Elliott, for example, has argued that *Millenium Hall* 'helped to establish philanthropy as a defining characteristic of the domestic woman', while presenting charity as an appropriately feminine alternative to the more conventional domestic work of wifehood and motherhood (*The Angel out of the House*, p. 34).
25 Sarah Scott, *The History of Cornelia*, with an introduction by Caroline Franklin (London: Routledge/Thoemmes Press, 1992), p. 50. Subsequent references will be given in the text.
26 Sarah Scott, *A Journey through Every Stage of Life*, ed. Gary Kelly, in *Bluestocking Feminism: Writings of the Bluestocking Circle, 1738–1785*, ed. Gary Kelly, 6 vols (London: Pickering and Chatto, 1999), V, p. 111. Subsequent references will be given in the text.
27 Fielding, *David Simple*, p. 26. For an intriguing reading of Cecilia's relationship with the poor see Judith Frank, *Common Ground: Eighteenth-century Satiric Fiction and the Poor* (Stanford, CA: Stanford University Press, 1997), particularly pp. 138–42. Frank's account is engaged with more fully in Chapter 2.

28 Labour is a theme within the novel's other inset narratives, but I focus here upon the first tale, here, because of the primacy given to this particular story by its narrator – who claims it is the most important and most salutary of those she will relate – and because of the absolute centrality of labour to this particular narrative and its argument.

29 Cornelia is accomplished in such feminine arts as needlework and music, but has also received an education in the 'sciences' as well as 'Greek and Latin' (pp. 3–5).

30 Gillian Skinner, *Sensibility and Economics in the Novel, 1740–1800: The Price of a Tear* (Basingstoke: Palgrave Macmillan, 1999), pp. 59–90.

31 David Hume, 'Of Refinement in the Arts', in *Selected Essays*, ed. Stephen Copley and Andrew Elgar (Oxford and New York: Oxford University Press, 1993), pp. 169–70.

32 Harriet Guest, *Small Change: Women, Learning, Patriotism, 1750 1810* (Chicago and London: The University of Chicago Press, 2000), p. 279.

33 See, for example, Skinner, *Sensibility and Economics in the Novel*, especially, p. 126; and E.J. Clery, *The Feminization Debate in Eighteenth-century England: Literature, Commerce and Luxury* (Basingstoke: Palgrave Macmillan, 2004), particularly pp. 1–12.

34 Hume, 'Of Refinements in the Arts', p. 172.

35 It is significant that the occupation to which Scott first turns to challenge the notion of labour as fall should be one of the dressmaking trades, trades in which *A Journey*'s Louisa and *Millenium Hall*'s Miss Mancel also work in various capacities. Millinery, dressmaking and plain-working were among the most widely condemned employments in eighteenth-century literature, even though (or perhaps because) such trades were among the largest employers of women for much of the century. See Jennie Batchelor, *Dress, Distress and Desire: Clothing and the Body in Eighteenth-century Literature* (Basingstoke: Palgrave Macmillan, 2005), chapter 2.

36 In their peculiarly effective blending of male and female attributes, Scott's heroines prefigure Anna, the eponymous heroine of Anna Maria Bennett's *Anna: or, Memoirs of a Welch Heiress* (1785) whose 'hermaphroditic' character Skinner discusses in *Sensibility and Economics in the Novel*, pp. 117–33.

37 Johns has observed that Mrs Bilson's movement from millinery to companionship makes '[c]onversation a respectable, saleable commodity' and, by extension, 'legitimized female publication, both morally and economically' (*Women's Utopias*, p. 86).

38 Sarah Fielding, *The History of the Countess of Dellwyn*, 2 vols (London: A. Millar, 1759), I, p. 180. Subsequent references will be given in the text.

39 Skinner, *Sensibility and Economics in the Novel*, p. 32.

40 On the centrality of notions of the commonwealth to mid-century fiction, particularly that of Sarah Fielding, see Landry's forthcoming 'Picturing Benevolence'.

41 Eve Tavor Bannet has identified such novelistic faith in women's moral ascendancy as characteristic of the 'Matriarchal feminism' espoused by a number of eighteenth-century female authors who celebrated women's superior virtues, but stopped short of the radical vindications of women's rights and calls for social and economic reform championed in the 'Egalitarian' writings of the likes of Smith and Mary Wollstonecraft. *The Domestic Revolution: Enlightenment Feminisms and the Novel* (Baltimore: The Johns Hopkins University Press, 2000), pp. 209–20. *A Journey* troubles Scott's identification as a 'matriarchal feminist', not only because of the novel's assault upon cultural constructions of gender but also because of its critical representation of the domestic economy.

42 Leonora's adoption of male dress to find work – a strategy that leads to countless women falling in love with her – has its real-life counterpart in Charlotte Charke's *A Narrative of the Life of Mrs Charlotte Charke* (published a year after *A Journey* in 1755), in which the actress recounts her efforts to attempt to support herself and her child when her stage career founders.

43 Perry, 'Bluestockings in Utopia', p. 162.

44 Johns, *Women's Utopias*, pp. 52–5.

45 Still, *Feminine Economies*. Johns touches briefly on the gift paradigm in relation to her analysis of *Millenium Hall*, arguing that the novel adumbrates modern gift theory in so far as Scott was critical of how notions of gratitude and obligation were deployed to mask various political and economic interests (*Women's Utopias*, p. 106). A more extensive treatment of the novel in terms of gift theory is provided by Julie McDonegal's 'The Tyranny of Gift Giving: The Politics of Generosity in Sarah Scott's *Millenium Hall* and *George Ellison*', *Eighteenth-century Fiction*, 19: 3 (2007): 291–306. McDonegal argues that 'Scott's novel enacts a fantasy of authority that, through presenting the woman as a powerful agent in the gift economy, seeks to empower gentry women through aligning generosity with the feminine'. This utopian manoeuvre, she concludes, merely serves the economic interests of the gentry, and replicates the social order by masking 'interested relations' as 'elective relations of reciprocity' (pp. 292–3; p. 306). By focusing on the function of labour as gift, my own account differs from McDonegal's and leads me to conclude that the novel's failure to fulfil its utopian promise lies not in its treatment of female labourers but in its inability to afford some of the community's dependent gentlewomen the same freedom through the exchange of gift-labour that their lower ranking counterparts enjoy.

46 See, particularly, Cynthia Klekar and Linda Zionkowski, eds, *The Culture of the Gift in Eighteenth-century England* (New York and Basingstoke: Palgrave Macmillan, 2009).

47 Mary Douglas, Introduction to Marcel Mauss, *The Gift: The Form and Reason for Exchange in Archaic Societies*, trans. W. D. Halls (London and New York: Routledge, 1990), p. xi.

48 Mauss, *The Gift*, p. 4.
49 Phebe Lowell Bowditch, *Horace and the Gift Economy of Patronage* (Berkeley and London: University of California Press, 2001), pp. 48–9.
50 Still makes a similar distinction between market and gift economics. If the market is 'impersonal', 'casual' and free, then the gift economy, she reminds us, is characterized by exchanges that 'effect a kind of bonding' and in which '[t]he economic aspect is neither predominant nor isolatable' (*Feminine Economies*, pp. 14–15).
51 See, for example, Georges Bataille, 'The Notion of Expenditure', in *Visions of Excess: Selected Writings, 1927–1939*, ed. Allan Stoekl and trans. Allan Stoekl with Carl Lovitt and Donald M. Leslie Jr (Minneapolis: University of Minnesota Press, 1985); Pierre Bourdieu, *The Logic of Pratice*, trans. Richard Nice (Cambridge: Polity Press, 1990); Jacques Derrida, *Given Time. 1. Counterfeit Money*, trans. Peggy Kamuf (Chicago: University of Chicago Press, 1992); and Luce Irigaray, 'Women on the Market', in *This Sex Which Is Not One*, trans. Catherine Porter with Carolyn Burke (Ithaca: Cornell University Press, 1985), pp. 170–91.
52 Even Still, who makes an eloquent case for retaining some faith, at least, in the gift's radical possibilities, acknowledges that 'the more strictly the gift is understood (as *outside* the economic), the harder it is to imagine a giving subject' (*Feminine Economies*, p. 13).
53 Cynthia Klekar, '"Her Gift Was Compelled": Gender and the Failure of the "Gift" in *Cecilia*', *Eighteenth-century Fiction*, 18: 1 (2005), p. 114.
54 Linda Zionkowski, 'The Nation, The Gift, and the Market in *The Wanderer*', in Klekar and Zionkowski, *The Culture of the Gift*, pp. 180–2.
55 Sir James Steuart, *An Inquiry into the Principles of Political Economy: Being an Essay on the Science of Domestic Policy in Free Nations*, 2 vols (London: A. Millar and T. Cadell, 1767), I, pp. 2–3.
56 Johns argues that Scott was attracted to contractualism – because it 'made possible a sociopolitical space for female subjects' – but was critical of its more 'problematic aspects', notably its obscuring of the 'sexual contract on which it depends' (*Women's Utopias*, p. 92).
57 Sarah Scott, *The History of Sir George Ellison*, ed. Betty Rizzo (Kentucky: The University of Kentucky Press, 1996), p. 16, p. 78. Subsequent references will be given in the text.
58 Ironically, it is Hintman's strategic abuse of the practice of gift exchange that first alerts the community's founders to the benefits it might confer upon women. Louisa attempts to pass on her benefactor's gifts to her friend, Miss Melvyn, who initially refuses them for fear that to do so would be to take 'advantage' of Miss Mancel's 'youth' (p. 93), as Hintman does. Eventually however, she learns that when gifts are given between equals, they have the power to break down boundaries and barriers and to forge alliances that protect against the kinds of sexual and economic exploitation both women

experience. The beneficiary of a disinterestedly given gift 'taste[s] not only the comforts arising from it to themselves, but share[s] the gratification of a benefactor, from reflecting on the joy they give to those who have conferred it: thus the receiver of a favour from a truly generous person, "by owing owes not, and is at once indebted and discharged"' (pp. 93–4).

59 McDonegal, 'The Tyranny of Gift Giving', p. 295.

60 Irigaray's critique of Lévi-Strauss's reading of the role of marriage as a form of gift exchange in *Elementary Structures of Kinship* (1949) is outlined in 'Women on the Market'.

61 On women's role as agents of charity in the eighteenth century, and charity's role in reinscribing 'masculine and hierarchical values', see Klekar, '"Her Gift was Compelled"', pp. 107–26. For feminist critiques of the gift see: Irigaray, 'Women on the Market' and Hélène Cixous, 'Sorties: Out and Out: Attacks/Ways Out/Forays', in Hélène Cixous and Catherine Clément, *The Newly Born Woman*, trans. Betsy Wing (Minneapolis: University of Minnesota Press, 1987), pp. 63–132. On the figure of the toadeater (particularly in reference to the work of Sarah Fielding and Jane Collier) see Betty Rizzo, *Companions Without Vows: Relationships Among Eighteenth-century British Women* (Athens and London: University of Georgia Press, 1996), pp. 41–60; and Audrey's Bilger's introduction to Jane Collier's *The Art of Ingeniously Tormenting* (Peterborough [Ontario]: Broadview, 2003), pp. 17–28.

62 As Johns suggests, Scott was critical of jurisprudential discourse's assumption of 'the fact of women's unpaid work' (*Women's Utopias*, p. 57).

63 Fielding, *David Simple*, p. 115.

64 *Ibid.*

65 Lewis Hyde, *The Gift: Imagination and the Erotic Life of Property* (London: Vintage, 1999), p. 106.

66 *Ibid.*, p. 50.

67 Most influentially, Gary Kelly has argued that the novel offers the fullest articulation of the ideology of 'gentry capitalism' that lay at the heart of 'Bluestocking feminism'. Gentry capitalism is described by Kelly in his introduction to *Millenium Hall* as 'the application of capitalist practices of entrepreneurship, investment, and modernization to the agrarian economy of the landed estate' (p. 11).

68 As Alfred Lutz observes of the novel's sequel, Ellison is a man torn by his efforts to exercise civic virtue while gratifying the desires of *homo oeconomicus*. Ultimately, Lutz argues, Ellison fails in his endeavours: 'the rhetoric of virtue, pushed by both civic man and the man of sensibility, enacts a textual displacement of economic realities', which simply serves to underscore 'the hierarchies on which commercial capitalism depends'. 'Commercial Capitalism, Classical Republicanism, and the Man of Sensibility in *The History of Sir George Ellison*', *SEL*, 39: 3 (1999), pp. 567–8.

69 Boyd, 'Working Fictions', p. 120.

70 Hume, 'On Commerce' (1752), in *Selected Essays*, p. 166. On the effect that such arguments had on conceptions of labour, poverty and charity in the later eighteenth century see Andrew, *Philanthropy and Police*, p. 141.

71 As both Elliott (*Angel out of the House*) and Peace ('"Epicures in Rural Pleasures"') note, *Millenium Hall* is almost puritanical in its denial of the force of bodily and sexual pleasure, a price which both determine too high for the women to pay for their emancipation. In terms of the novel's labour plot, however, the fact that the community is single-sex is crucial to the novel's critique of the heterosexual economy's dependence upon the exploitation of female labour, and particularly of domestic labour.

72 London, *Women and Property*, p. 116.

73 This literary manoeuvre foreshadows the aesthetic strategics adopted by painters of rural landscape and rural labour such as George Stubbes, whose 'strikingly tidy' and ennobled labourers are discussed by John Barrell, in *The Dark Side of the Landscape: The Rural Poor in English Painting, 1730–1840* (Cambridge: Cambridge University Press, 1980), pp. 25–31.

74 London, *Women and Property*, p. 116.

75 Still, *Feminine Economies*, pp. 114–16.

76 This is an example of what Hyde refers to as the 'tyranny of the gift': where the giving of gifts is exploited to enforce social obligations (*The Gift*, p. 137).

77 McDonegal, for example, has argued that if Scott 'withdraws gentry women from a system that oppresses and exploits them, she nevertheless reproduces a comparable system between Millenium Hall's female proprietors and the district's labouring classes' ('The Tyranny of the Gift', p. 300).

78 Hyde maintains that charity has no place within the gift economy because 'the recipient of a gift, should, sooner or later, be able to give it away again. If the gift does not really raise him to the level of the group, then it's just a decoy.' Charity reinforces the 'boundary of class' whereas the logic of gift economy, ideally, works to efface such distinctions (*The Gift*, pp. 137–8).

79 In making the claim that the novel treats female workers more equitably than their genteelly (and therefore unsuitably) educated superiors, I want to argue that recognizing labour's centrality to the gift economy of the novel's community significantly complicates scholarly accounts which have argued that Scott's class politics have irrevocably undermined her more radical gender politics. For a particularly interesting Foucauldian reading of Scott's class politics see Johanna M. Smith, 'Philanthropic Community in *Millenium Hall* and the York Ladies' Committee', *Eighteenth Century: Theory and Interpretation*, 36: 3 (1995): 266–82.

80 Johns reads Mrs Alton's description of her life as her brother's servant as indicative of Scott's belief that 'interpersonal exchanges are not removed [from] but continuous with commerce and must be viewed in that light in

order to introduce justice and a fair movement of resources'. Mrs Alton's insistence that her situation in her brother's house represented no 'balance between obligations conferred and repaid' demonstrates, Johns suggests, Scott's advocacy of 'the need for fair exchange' in 'human relationships' (*Women's Utopias*, pp. 107–8).

81 As Derrida suggests, once a gift (and the obligation it entails) is recognized as such, 'all that remains is debt and obligation'. These 'conditions of possibility of the gift . . . define or produce the annulment, the annihilation, the destruction of the gift. . . . For there to be a gift, there must be no reciprocity, return, exchange, countergift, or debt' (*Given Time*. 1, p. 12).

82 In part this can be explained by the erasure of the thorny issue of class within the idealized textual economies Scott imagines. If Scott's attempt to claim the gift for women falters because of the gift's historic misapplication by paternalist and patriarchal societies, then in the egalitarian reader/writer relationships her novels establish, in which texts are explicitly exchanged between friends and equals, she is able fully to demonstrate the gift's emancipatory potential.

83 An important exception to this rule, discussed in more detail below, is Betty A. Schellenberg's chapter on Scott's historical novels in *The Professionalization of Women Writers in Eighteenth-century Britain* (Cambridge: Cambridge University Press, 2005), pp. 76–93, which examines Scott's self-representation as an author.

84 Indeed, it is possible that some of the prefatory material that accompanies the novels was authored by her publishers rather than by Scott herself.

85 Schellenberg, *The Professionalization of Women* Writers, p. 77.

86 *Ibid*., p. 93.

87 Susan Sniader Lanser, *Fictions of Authority: Women Writers and Narrative Voice* (Ithaca and London: Cornell University Press, 1992), pp. 16–17. Lanser is making a distinction between writers who use an authorial voice that draws attention to itself, and to the process of fiction-making, and those writers who 'engage exclusively in acts of representation'.

88 Bowditch, *Horace and the Gift Economy of Patronage*; Hyde, *The Gift*; Angela Keane, 'The Market, the Public, and the Female Author: Anna Laetitia Barbauld's Gift Economy', *Romanticism: The Journal of Romantic Culture and Criticism*, 8: 2 (2002): 161–78.

89 Hyde, *The Gift*, p. xi.

90 Frances Burney, *Cecilia; or Memoirs of an Heiress*, ed. Peter Sabor and Margaret Anne Doody (Oxford: Oxford University Press, 1988), p. 944.

91 Hyde, *The Gift*, p. xii.

92 *Ibid*., p. xii.

93 *Critical Review*, 1 (1756): 97–8.

94 On this common strategy see Zionkowski, *Men's Work*, pp. 10–23.

95 James Ralph, *The Case of Authors by Profession or Trade* (1758), reprinted with *The Champion* (1739–40), with an introduction by Philip Stevick (Gainesville, FL: Scholars' Facsimiles and Reprints, 1966), p. 2; p. 22.

96 Oliver Goldsmith, *An Enquiry into the Present State of Polite Learning in Europe* (London: R. and J. Dodsley, 1759), p. 127.

97 Sarah Scott to Elizabeth Montagu, 28 November [1761], The Huntington Library, Montagu Collection, MO 5287.

98 Scott to Montagu, [January] 1754, The Huntington Library, Montagu Collection, MO 5238.

99 Scott to Montagu, [31 January 1763], The Huntington Library, Montagu Collection, MO 5300. Scott's negotiations of the terms of the sale of *Sir George Ellison* would produce similar regret. Andrew Millar's 'readiness' to accept the work convinced Scott that she could have asked for 'ten pounds more' than the hundred pounds secured in total for the first and second edition, a disappointment Scott tried to shrug off when she declared how 'glad' she was to have 'washd my hands' of the novel. 30 January 1766, The Huntington Library, Montagu Collection, MO 5319.

100 This construction of authorial disinterestedness was maintained, in part, by Scott's unwillingness publicly, and sometimes privately, to acknowledge her texts as her own work. Scott would, for example, divulge the fact that she had written *The History of Gustavus Ericson* (1761) to her father only two years after it had been published, and only then because she learned that he had praised *Millenium Hall*. Scott to Montagu, April 1763, The Huntington Library, Montagu Collection, MO 5301.

101 Schellenberg, *The Professionalization of Women Writers*, p. 15.

102 Another approach to this problem is that adopted by Eve Tavor Bannet, who reads the 1740s and early 1750s correspondence between Scott and Montagu alongside *A Journey*. Considering the formal and thematic connections between these two modes of 'life-writing', Bannet argues that Scott's correspondence and novel 'echo and supplant one another in ways which . . . suggest that women's displaced re-presentation and re-examination of personal concerns in autographic novels can itself be viewed as a necessary, even cathartic, stage in their journey through life'. 'Lives, Letters and Tales in Sarah Scott's *Journey through Every Stage of Life*', *Age of Johnson*, 17 (2006): 233–59.

103 Outside this highly idealized textual economy the gift falters. One of the ironies of Scott's career is that life failed to imitate art. While *Sir George Ellison* would see the hero emulating the Millenium Hall society in the creation of a series of philanthropic projects, Scott was herself unable to use the money generated by her writing career to fulfil her own ambition to establish and maintain real-life communities along the lines of those imagined in her fiction. Unable to escape the fetters of obligation, Scott remained precariously dependent, upon the generosity of relatives, friends

and her writing career for financial support until her death in 1795. On the thwarted Batheaston and Hitcham projects see Rizzo, *Companions Without Vows*, pp. 295–319.

104 Charlotte Lennox, *Henrietta*, ed. Ruth Perry and Susan Carlile (Lexington: The University Press of Kentucky, 2008), p. 134.

Chapter 2

1 Sir Walter Scott, *Miscellaneous Prose Works of Sir Walter Scott*, 28 vols (Edinburgh: Robert Cadell; E. Whittaker and Co., 1834–36), II, 68–9. In fact, this biography is a composite of Scott's own observations on Smith's life and career and a biographical sketch offered to Scott by Catherine Ann Dorset, Smith's sister.

2 John Locke, *Two Treatises of Government* (London: A. Millar, 1764), pp. 216–17.

3 See, for example, Curran's introduction to *The Poems of Charlotte Smith*, ed. Stuart Curran (Oxford and New York: Oxford University Press, 1993); and 'Charlotte Smith and British Romanticism', *South Central Review*, 11: 2 (1994): 64–78.

4 Loraine Fletcher's *Charlotte Smith: A Critical Biography* (Basingstoke: Palgrave Macmillan, 2001) contains readings of all the novels, while most are given at least some attention in Jacqueline M. Labbe's recent and splendid edited collection *Charlotte Smith in British Romanticism* (London: Pickering and Chatto, 2008). Carrol L. Fry's *Charlotte Smith: Popular Novelist* (New York: Arno Press, 1980) is the only book-length study on the fiction to date. Among other important chapters and articles on the fiction are Mary Anne Schofield, '"The Witchery of Fiction": Charlotte Smith, Novelist', in *Living by the Pen: Early British Women Writers*, ed. Dale Spender (New York: Teachers College Press, 1992), pp. 72–88; Kathryn R. King, 'Of Needles and Pens and Women's Work', *Tulsa Studies in Women's Literature*, 14 (1995): 77–93; Jacqueline M. Labbe, 'Metaphoricity and the Romance of Property in *The Old Manor House*', *Novel: A Forum on Fiction*, 32 (2001): 216–31; Katherine Binhammer, 'Revolutionary Domesticity in Charlotte Smith's *Desmond*', in *Women, Revolution and the Novels of the 1790s*, ed. Linda Lang-Peralta (East Lansing: Michigan State University Press, 1999), pp. 25–46; and Angela Keane's chapter on Smith in *Women Writers and the English Nation in the 1790s* (Cambridge: Cambridge University Press, 2000): 81–107.

5 *The Analytical Review* (July 1788), in *The Works of Mary Wollstonecraft*, ed. Janet Todd and Marilyn Butler with Emma Rees-Mogg, 7 vols (London: Pickering and Chatto, 1989), VII, pp. 26–7.

6 Edward Copeland, *Women Writing about Money: Women's Fiction in England, 1790–1820* (Cambridge: Cambridge University Press, 1995), p. 47.

7 *Ibid.*, p. 50.

8 Smith to Joseph Cooper Walker, 9 October 1793, *The Collected Letters of Charlotte Smith*, ed. Judith Phillips Stanton (Bloomington and Indianapolis: Indiana University Press, 2003), p. 80. This is an allusion to Henry Fielding's *Joseph Andrews* (1742) in which Barnabus is described as loving 'Sermons no better than a Grocer doth Figs'. *Joseph Andrews and Shamela*, ed. Thomas Keymer (Oxford: Oxford University Press, 1999), p. 69.

9 Jacqueline M. Labbe, *Charlotte Smith: Romanticism, Poetry and the Culture of Gender* (Manchester: Manchester University Press, 2003), p. 8. On the performative qualities of Smith's poetry see also Adela Pinch, *Strange Fits of Passion: Epistemologies of Emotion, Hume to Austen* (Stanford: Stanford University Press, 1996), pp. 51–71.

10 Sarah Zimmerman, 'Charlotte Smith's Letters and the Practice of Self-presentation', *Princeton University Library Chronicle*, 53: 1 (1991), p. 65.

11 Labbe has also presented the fiction in this way, arguing that Smith's dissatisfaction with novel writing was a recognition of the limitations of the genre. If poetry provided a forum in which to explore 'interiority in a recognizably "Romantic" way', the novel allowed her only to 'dramatize' her biography is such a manner that it closed the crucial gap between author and persona she so successfully strove to maintain in the poetry (*Charlotte Smith*, p. 8).

12 Charlotte Smith, *Desmond: A Novel*, ed. Stuart Curran, reprinted in *The Works of Charlotte Smith*, 14 vols (London: Pickering and Chatto, 2005–7), V, p. 4. Subsequent references will be given in the text.

13 My discussion of Smith's complex presentation of authorship as (dis)embodied labour is indebted to Labbe's account of embodiment in *Elegiac Sonnets*. However, my argument departs from Labbe's in two crucial ways: first, by identifying a broadly similar and similarly complex account of authorship as embodied activity in the novels; second, by identifying labour as the crux of Smith's authorial self-construction.

14 By perceiving authorship as an embodied activity and by emphasizing the economic imperatives that shape textual production, Smith constructed a model of authorship that could scarcely be more different from that constructed by Sarah Scott, despite the authors' shared commitment to questions surrounding women's work and the status of authorship as intellectual labour.

15 Charlotte Smith, *The Old Manor House*, ed. Ina Ferris, reprinted in *The Works of Charlotte Smith,* VI, p. 46. Subsequent references will be given in the text.

16 King, 'Of Needles and Pens', pp. 86–7.

17 This episode has a parallel in Elizabeth Inchbald's *Nature and Art* (1796) in which the seduced Hannah Primrose is forced to support herself and her illegitimate child through the only employment initially open to her, tending

and feeding the cattle of a farmer, whose subsequent death leaves Hannah again vulnerable to the prejudice of others. In stark contrast to Monimia, and faced with the reality of rural labour in a way that Monimia is not, Hannah finds herself 'ill suited to her occupation'. Though 'born of peasants', she has been 'nursed with a tenderness and delicacy' that renders her unfit for the work she has to undertake. *Nature and Art*, ed. Shawn L. Maurer (Peterborough, Ontario: Broadview Press, 2005), p. 123.

18 On changes in agricultural labour and their implication for women workers in the later eighteenth century see K. D. M. Snell, *Annals of the Labouring Poor* (Cambridge: Cambridge University Press, 1988), pp. 15–66.

19 Schofield, '"The Witchery of Fiction"', p. 184.

20 On the question of romance see also Jacqueline M. Labbe's introduction to the Broadview edition of *The Old Manor House* (Peterborough, Ontario: Broadview, 2002), pp. 19–26.

21 Kate Davies and Harriet Guest, 'Introduction', *Marchmont*, reprinted in *The Works of Charlotte Smith*, IX, p. xxiv.

22 Charlotte Smith, *Marchmont*, p. 416. Subsequent references will be given in the text.

23 Keane, *Women Writers and the English Nation*, p. 86; p. 102.

24 See above, pp. 12–13.

25 Davies and Guest, 'Introduction', p. xiii.

26 *Ibid.*

27 Charlotte Smith, *Emmeline, or the Orphan of the Castle*, ed. Judith Stanton, reprinted in *The Works of Charlotte Smith*, II, p. 100.

28 Charlotte Smith, *Montalbert: A Novel*, ed. Stuart Curran and Adriana Craciun, reprinted in *The Works of Charlotte Smith*, VIII, p. 31. Subsequent references will be given in the text.

29 In *Montalbert*, Rosalie also avoids service, although she is forced to endure a series of terrifying ordeals, including an earthquake, kidnapping and imprisonment in an Italian castle, from which she is rescued only for her jealous husband to kidnap their child, fearing that his wife is having an affair with her rescuer. Unsurprisingly, Rosalie endures a period of insanity before reconciling with her husband.

30 Davies and Guest, 'Introduction', p. xvi.

31 In *Emmeline*, Burney's novel is read to the eponymous heroine and her older companion, Mrs Stafford, by Fitz-Edward, an episode which is discussed briefly by Loraine Fletcher in her introduction to the Broadview edition of the novel (Peterborough, Ontario: Broadview, 2003), pp. 16–17.

32 Frances Burney, *Cecilia; or Memoirs of an Heiress*, ed. Peter Sabor and Margaret Anne Doody (Oxford: Oxford University Press, 1999), p. 659.

33 Judith Frank, *Common Ground: Eighteenth-century Satiric Fiction and the Poor* (Stanford, CA: Stanford University Press, 1997), p. 28.

34 *Ibid.*, pp. 28–9.

35 As Frank demonstrates, affective response is persistently described in Burney's novel in the same vocabulary – that of singleness and variety, direction and dissipation – in which labour is imagined in the literature of the period. *Ibid.*, pp. 138–42.

36 *Ibid.*, p. 137.

37 Burney, *Cecilia*, p. 659.

38 Adam Smith, *An Inquiry into the Nature and Causes of the Wealth of Nations*, ed. W. B. Todd, 2 vols (Indianapolis: Liberty Fund, 1981), II, p. 787.

39 Sandra Sherman, *Imagining Poverty: Quantification and the Decline of Paternalism* (Columbus: Ohio State University Press, 2001), p. 253. Marchmont's response to the problem of labouring-class deracination contrasts starkly with that of *Desmond*. Indeed, Smith's fourth novel complicates Sherman's argument about the later eighteenth-century novel's inability to acknowledge the labouring class as anything other than an undifferentiated underclass. Although *Desmond* stops short of imagining the kind of 'complex' labouring-class subjectivities, the absence of which Sherman laments, it none the less forcefully counters those who would deny the labouring poor sensibility and intellect in order to maintain the status quo and alleviate their collective guilt. In this earlier novel, it is society's highest, not lowest, members who live in the 'calm stupor of ignorance', with 'hearts so indurated by their success of fortune, that they are insensible to generosity, and even justice!' *Desmond*, p. 150.

40 Althea alludes directly to Thomas Paine's *Rights of Man* (1791) when she reflects that 'if only a third or a fourth of the sums yearly raised' to fund wars were 'applied to the mitigation of the sufferings of the aged and the infant poor, every labouring man might then labour for the rich, yet possessing him a certain degree of comfort; the country would become more populous, and of course, more powerful to resist all encroachment from nations less wise'. Attribution noted in Davies and Guest's edition of the novel, p. 442, n. 28.

41 *Marchmont*'s argument that women possess 'more fortitude' in adversity 'than men' was one to which Smith's fiction frequently turned (p. 386), and is often proved by a heroine's willingness to labour. When, for example, the newly married Monimia of *The Old Manor House* finds herself in 'as great poverty' as she had endured as Mrs Rayland's upper-servant, she is forced to carry out her new employment in a linen warehouse in secret for fear that she should wound her husband's 'pride'. Like the partially sighted Marchmont, Orlando sees that his wife is 'always busy', but refuses to admit the truth that is plainly before him: that his wife is working to support them, while Orlando allows himself to become engrossed by 'troubled spirits' (p. 424).

42 Diane Long Hoeveler, *Gothic Feminism: The Professionalization of Gender from Charlotte Smith to the Brontës* (University Park, PA: The University of Pennsylvania Press, 1998), pp. 27–50.

43 Charlotte Smith, *Marchmont: A Novel*, 4 vols (London: Sampson Low, 1796), IV, n.p.

44 The role that maternity and reproductive labour play in Smith's authorial self-construction, as well as its influence upon her contemporaries and successors, is returned to in more detail in Chapter 4.

45 Smith to Dr Thomas Shirley, [22 August 1789], *Collected Letters*, p. 23.

46 The relationship between Smith's personal and professional selves has been explored by Diane E. Boyd, who argues that Smith drew on her personal affairs in her letters and novels 'to transgress ideological structures, like the codified cultural spaces of public/private and the cultural representations of professional/drudge'. '"Professing Drudge": Charlotte Smith's Negotiation of a Mother-writer Author Function', *South Atlantic Review*, 66: 1 (2001): 145–66.

47 This quotation, originally from Joseph Addison's *Cato* (1713), appears in the preface to the sixth edition of *Elegiac Sonnets* (*The Poems of Charlotte Smith*, p. 6).

48 Clifford Siskin, *The Work of Writing: Literature and Social Change in Britain, 1700–1830* (Baltimore and London: The Johns Hopkins University Press, 1998), p. 133.

49 Zeynep Tenger and Paul Trolander, 'Genius versus Capital: Eighteenth-century Theories of Genius and Adam Smith's *Wealth of Nations*', *Modern Language Quarterly*, 55 (1994), p. 171.

50 Paul Keen, *The Crisis of Literature in the 1790s: Print Culture and the Public Sphere* (Cambridge: Cambridge University Press, 1999). Keen's arguments about women's position within the republic of letters in the 1790s will be interrogated more fully in Chapter 3.

51 Siskin, *The Work of Writing*, p. 224.

52 On the power of the reviews see Siskin, *The Work of Writing*, pp. 224–5.

53 Laura Runge, 'Churls and Graybeards and Novels Written by a Lady: Gender in Eighteenth-century Book Reviews', *Corvey CW3 Journal*, 1 (2004) <www2.shu.ac.uk/corvey/cw3journal/Issue%20one/runge.html>.

54 *Anti-Jacobin Review*, 1 (1798), p. 189. This review is cited in Runge's 'Churls and Graybeards'.

55 Preface to the sixth edition of *Elegiac Sonnets*, reprinted in *The Poems of Charlotte Smith*, p. 8.

56 *Analytical Review*, 20 (1794), p. 255. This review is cited in Runge, 'Churls and Graybeards'.

57 *Critical Review*, 8 (1793): 44–54.

58 Scott's own views on the relation of labour to writing are discussed in Kathryn Sutherland's 'Fictional Economies: Adam Smith, Walter Scott and the Nineteenth-century Novel', *ELH*, 54 (1987): 97–127.

59 Keen, *The Crisis of Literature in the 1790s*, p. 174.

60 Smith to Sarah Rose, 15 June 1804, *Collected Letters*, p. 627. We might see in Smith's letter an echo of the penultimate stanza of Mary Collier's *The*

Woman's Labour (1739), in which Collier directly counters Duck's use of heroic imagery to describe men's work and disparage women's labour: 'While you to *Sisyphus* yourselves compare, / With *Danaus' Daughters* we may claim a Share; / For while *he* labours hard against the Hill, / Bottomless Tubs of Water *they* must fill.' Mary Collier, *The Woman's Labour*, in *The Thresher's Labour (Stephen Duck) and The Woman's Labour (Mary Collier)*, with an introduction by Moira Ferguson (Los Angeles: William Andrews Clark Memorial Library, 1985), lines 239–42.

61 Smith, *The Wealth of Nations*, pp. 330–1.

62 One of Adam Smith's most vocal detractors was David Williams, founder of the Literary Fund, whose critique of *The Wealth of Nations* is elaborated at some length in his 1802 *Claims of Literature*. Williams's attack on Smithian economics is explored in Chapter 4.

63 Smith, *The Wealth of Nations*, II, p. 783.

64 Hays's *The Victim of Prejudice* (1798), for example, had explored the prejudice a genteel woman encounters when seeking to support herself by her own labour. The relationship between manual and intellectual labour was also taken up by Hays, most notably in a series of articles for the *Monthly Magazine*.

65 Mary Hays, 'Mrs Charlotte Smith', in *Public Characters of 1800–1801* (London: Richard Phillips, 1807). Subsequent references will be given in the text.

66 Smith to Mary Hays, 26 July 1800, *Collected Letters*, p. 351.

67 Preface to Volume II of Elegiac Sonnets. The Poems of Charlotte Smith, pp. 9–10.

68 Charlotte Smith, *Celestina*, ed. Kristina Straub, reprinted in *The Works of Charlotte Smith*, IV, p. 121.

69 Isaac D'Israeli, *An Essay on the Manners and Genius of the Literary Character* (London: T. Cadell, 1795), p. 52.

70 As Angela Keane observes, Smith's novels 'transform displaced wanderers into cosmopolitan communities living by New World freeholds' (*Women Writers and the English Nation*, p. 106).

71 Tenger and Trolander, 'Genius versus Capital', p. 171. The 'antagonism' between genius and labour that Tenger and Trolander identify was by no means universally acknowledged, however. Indeed, as I explore in Chapter 4, a number of late eighteenth- and early nineteenth-century texts imagined genius as intellectual labour, although, in doing so, they commonly made clear distinctions between this properly intellectual work and the inferior modes of textual labour engaged in by the literary 'mechanic' or 'hack'.

72 Charlotte Smith, *The Banished Man*, reprinted with *The Wanderings of Warwick*, ed. M. O. Grenby, reprinted in *The Works of Charlotte Smith*, VII, p. 275. Subsequent references will be given in the text.

73 Charlotte Smith, *The Wanderings of Warwick*, p. 98. Subsequent references will be given in the text.

74 Smith was not, of course, alone in her rejection of the bluestockings. As Norma Clarke observes, the 'Bluestocking ideal did not survive the combined impact of political upheaval and commercial expansion', and the term became a 'pejorative' one well before the end of the eighteenth century. *The Rise and Fall of the Woman of Letters* (London: Pimlico, 2004), p. 9.

75 Smith to Hays, 26 July 1800, *Collected Letters*, p. 350.

76 The poem Walsingham recites, 'The night flood rakes upon the stony shore', would become sonnet 66 in *Elegiac Sonnets*.

77 On Smith's attack on Cowley see Grenby's introduction to *The Wanderings of Warwick*, pp. xvii–xviii.

78 The *OED* indicates that the term 'professional' was first used to identify someone engaged in one of the learned or skilled professions in 1793. The earliest example of the word being used to describe an individual who follows an occupation as his profession, life-work or means of livelihood is 1798.

79 Smith, *Collected Letters*, p. 256.

80 See Susan Eilenberg's 'Copyright's Rhetoric and the Problem of Analogy in the British Eighteenth Century Debates', in *Romanticism and the Law*, ed. Michael Macovski (Romantic Circles Praxis Series: March 1999) <www.rc.umd.edu/praxis/law/eilenberg/sebg.htm>; Mark Rose, *Authors and Owners: The Invention of Copyright* (Cambridge [MA] and London: Harvard University Press, 1993). On the author as original genius and proprietor see also Martha Woodmansee, 'The Genius and the Copyright: Economic and Legal Conditions of the Emergence of the "Author"', *Eighteenth-century Studies*, 17 (1984): 425–48.

81 Eilenberg 'Copyright's Rhetoric'.

82 Catherine Gallagher, *Nobody's Story: The Vanishing Acts of Women Writers in the Marketplace, 1670–1820* (Berkeley and Los Angeles: University of California Press, 1994), pp. xix–xx.

83 Smith to William Davies, 18 February 1802. *Collected Letters*, pp. 403–4.

84 Gallagher, *Nobody's Story*, p. xxii.

85 Smith to Thomas Cadell, 22 August 1790. *Collected Letters*, p. 27.

86 Fletcher, *Charlotte Smith*, p. 222.

87 Smith to James Upton Tripp, 4 April 1794, *Collected Letters*, p. 107.

88 Smith to Joseph Walker, 25 March 1795, *Ibid.*, p. 103.

89 Rose, *Authors and Owners*, p. 114.

90 On the question of copyright see also Eilenberg, 'Copyright's Rhetoric'; and Woodmansee, 'The Genius and the Copyright'.

91 The unavailability of Locke's theory of property to women has been widely commented upon. In a particularly interesting article on the fiction of Sarah Fielding and Sarah Scott, Sara Gadeken has argued that women writers' turn to utopian models of female community can fruitfully be understood as a critique of Locke's homocentric models of property and the social contract. Sara Gadeken, '"A Method of Being Perfectly Happy": Technologies of Self

in the Eighteenth-century Female Community', *The Eighteenth-century Novel* (2001): 217–35.

92 Smith to Thomas Cadell, 22 August 1790. *Collected Letters*, p. 27. Similar arguments had been used by critics of perpetual copyright against understanding intellectual labour as authorial property. The author of the anonymous *An Enquiry into the Nature and Origin of Literary Property* (London: William Flexney, 1762), for example, wrote: 'If [an author's] Works were to become a Property, they might be taken in Execution for Debt. Creditors would ravish Dramatic Writers their half-formed Tragedies, from Clergymen their pious Discourses, the Spiritual Food of their respective Flocks. A Moral Essay might go in Discharge of a Debt contracted in a Bagnio'. To recognize intellectual labour as property was to risk diminishing its value by making it equivalent to 'Stay-Tape, Buckram and Canvas, or Legs of Mutton, Calf's-Heads, and other Articles, which usually compose a Taylor and a Butcher's-Bill' (pp. 34–5).

93 Smith to Thomas Cadell and William Davies, *Collected Letters*, p. 295. For a discussion of Catharine Macaulay's *Modest Plea for the Property of Copyright* (1774) and the genealogy of the trope of writing as mental farming and harvesting see Rose, *Authors and Owners*, pp. 105–7.

94 Smith to Thomas Cadell, 22 August 1790. *Collected Letters*, p. 27.

95 Smith to Thomas Cadell and William Davies, 5 January 1796, *ibid.*, p. 218. Smith's dislike of the circulating libraries is humorously expressed in a letter to William Hayley, from late 1788 to early 1789, describing William Lane's attempt to purchase the copyright of *Ethelinde* (1789) after it had already been promised to Cadell. *Ibid.*, pp. 17–19.

Chapter 3

1 Mary Wollstonecraft, *A Vindication of the Rights of Woman*, reprinted in *The Works of Mary Wollstonecraft*, ed. Janet Todd and Marilyn Butler with Emma Rees-Mogg, 7 vols (London: William Pickering, 1989), V, p. 133. Subsequent references will be given in the text.

2 Mary Wollstonecraft, *The Collected Letters of Mary Wollstonecraft*, ed. Janet Todd (London: Allen Lane, 2003), p. 238. Subsequent references will be given in the text.

3 Charlotte Smith was, of course, Wollstonecraft's contemporary, a writer whose career was as indelibly informed by the political and cultural upheavals witnessed in the 1790s as was that of the author of *A Vindication of the Rights of Woman*. However as we have seen, Smith's treatment of work was framed by, and most commonly figured as, its author's personal story, even though the implications of her arguments about labour, gender and authorship were much more far-reaching than this observation might suggest. Wollstonecraft, by contrast, presented the question of women's work as a matter of *public* concern.

4 Barbara Taylor has identified the Female Philosopher as only one of several personae that Wollstonecraft adopted during her career, the others being 'the prissy moralist' of the early children's writing, 'the lyrical romantic of her letters from Sweden', the 'satirist, teacher, [and] melancholy *solitaire*'. *Mary Wollstonecraft and the Feminist Imagination* (Cambridge: Cambridge University Press, 2003), p. 31. My own reading of Wollstonecraft's self-styling both as a writer and as an intellectual suggests that the Female Philosopher was an ideal to which she aspired, to varying degrees, in each of her works.

5 For an overview of the 'cultural revolution' and its implications for women see Gary Kelly, *Women, Writing and Revolution, 1790–1827* (Oxford: Clarendon Press, 1993), particularly pp. 3–9.

6 Clifford Siskin, *The Work of Writing: Literature and Social Change in Britain, 1700–1830* (Baltimore and London: The Johns Hopkins University Press, 1998), p. 107. That the newly professional classes' claims to civic virtue and cultural authority were predicated upon their members' participation in the division of labour is explored by Harriet Guest in *Small Change: Women, Learning, Patriotism, 1750–1810* (Chicago and London: The University of Chicago Press, 2000). See particularly pp. 286–7.

7 Guest, *Small Change*, p. 286.

8 This is the provocative opening claim of Priscilla Wakefield's *Reflections on the Present Condition of the Female Sex; with Suggestions for its Improvement* (London: J. Johnson, 1798), p. 1.

9 Guest, *Small Change*, p. 285; p. 287. Guest goes on to argue that prostitution was the only profession 'available to define the position of women within the language of the division of labour', a fact that explains prostitution's centrality to 1790s feminists' critiques of the insidious link between the language of the division of labour and female abjection.

10 Wakefield, *Reflections*, pp. 1–2.

11 Priscilla Wakefield's projected division of labour was much more conservative than her opening assault upon Smith's *The Wealth of Nations* suggested it would be, particularly in relation to its views on class. For the purposes of the book, Wakefield divides women into four 'classes', for whom distinct employments are deemed fitting. For the first and second classes, for example, authorship and the arts are suggested as 'Lucrative Employments', while the third class are judged suitable for shopkeeping and farming. The fourth class consists principally of the poor and objects of charity.

12 Paul Keen, *The Crisis of Literature in the 1790s: Print Culture and the Public Sphere* (Cambridge: Cambridge University Press, 1999), p. 10.

13 *Ibid.*, pp. 76–99.

14 Gruffudd Aled Ganobcsik-Williams, 'The Sweat of the Brain: Representations of Intellectual Labour in the Writings of Edmund Burke, William Cobbett, William Hazlitt, and Thomas Carlyle' (unpublished PhD thesis: University of Warwick, 2001), p. 1.

15 Siskin, *The Work of Writing*, pp. 216–25. Keen, although judiciously sceptical of such arguments, on the grounds that they fail to take into account widespread contemporary anxieties about the 'demasculinization of literature' in the period, none the less subscribes in part to Siskin's narrative when he describes women writers, along with the those of the labouring classes and colonial subjects, as 'subaltern' others who existed at the collective 'beyond' of the republic of letters (*The Crisis of Literature*, p. 177; p. 137).

16 Mary Wollstonecraft, *A Vindication of the Rights of Men*, reprinted in *Works*, V, p. 15; p. 56. Subsequent references will be given in the text.

17 Mary Ann Radcliffe, *The Female Advocate; or, an Attempt to Recover the Rights of Women from Male Usurpation* (London: Vernor and Hood, 1799), p. 46; p. 73. Subsequent references will be given in the text.

18 This quotation is taken from the tenth letter of William Dodd's *The Magdalen, or the History of the First Penitent Received into that Charitable Asylum,* a novel published in 1783, but plagiarized from the first part of the earlier, and anonymous, *The Histories of Some of the Penitents in the Magdalen-House* (1760). The story, discussed briefly in Chapter 1, follows the demise of a young clergyman's daughter who is orphaned, put into service and subsequently seduced by her master. Following her seduction and abandonment, Emily strives in vain to support herself and her young child, before resorting to beggary and prostitution. Clearly, Radcliffe read Emily's story as the factual biography Dodd pretended it to be.

19 Mary Poovey has read this passage rather differently, not as a vision of female labour but as an idealized portrait of domestic life in which women's role is to facilitate the labours of men. She argues that Wollstonecraft presents women as the 'the invisible centre' of the domestic economy. Their 'actions epitomize indirection: they "soften" labour without working themselves . . . They are, in other words, textbook Proper Ladies.' Mary Poovey, *The Proper Lady and the Woman Writer: Ideology as Style in the Works of Mary Wollstonecraft, Mary Shelley, and Jane Austen* (Chicago and London: University of Chicago Press, 1984), p. 67. It is not clear, however, that women's role as providers of '[d]omestic comfort', here, is intended to signal their non-participation in other forms of labour. Women's domestic responsibilities, as Radcliffe maintained in *The Female Advocate* and as Wollstonecraft argued in a number of her works, were entirely compatible with economic production.

20 See, for example, Alice Clark, *The Working Life of Women in the Seventeenth Century* [1919] (New York: Augustus M. Kelley, rept. 1968). Ivy Pinchbeck, *Women Workers and the Industrial Revolution 1750–1850* [1930] (London: Virago, rept. 1985).

21 See Introduction, notes 70, 75.

22 Wollstonecraft's *Thoughts on the Education of Daughters* (1787), *A Vindication of the Rights of Woman* and *The Wrongs of Woman; or Maria*

are, for example, cited in Bridget Hill's *Women, Work and Sexual Politics in Eighteenth-Century England* (London: UCL Press, 1994). Ruth Perry similarly makes references to the work of Radcliffe, Wakefield and Wollstonecraft in her account of the late eighteenth-century labour market in Novel Relations: The Transformation of Kinship in English Literature and Culture, 1748–1818 (Cambridge: Cambridge University Press, 2004), p. 219.

23 Mary Ann Radcliffe, *The Memoirs of Mrs Mary Ann Radcliffe; in Familiar Letters to her Female Friend* (Edinburgh: Manners and Miller, A. Constable & Co., J. Anderson, Oliphant and Balfour; London: Longman, Hurst, Rees, Orme and Brown, 1810), p. 261. This edition reprinted *The Female Advocate* in its entirety.

24 Radcliffe writes that she could persuade herself to place an advertisement for work only because this particular method of securing employment shielded her from disrepute. Since advertisements were placed anonymously, 'no one would know from whence it originated'. Radcliffe, *Memoirs*, p. 252. The author had recourse to this method of seeking work on several occasions.

25 Taylor, *Mary Wollstonecraft and the Feminist Imagination*, pp. 240–1.

26 As Cora Kaplan has importantly argued, *A Vindication of the Rights of Woman* set up 'heartbreaking conditions for women's liberation – a little death, the death of desire, the death of female pleasure', 'Wild Nights: Pleasure/Sexuality/Feminism', in *Sea Changes: Essays on Culture and Feminism* (London and New York: Verso [1980], 1990), p. 39.

27 See 'Wild Nights', pp. 31–56; 'Pandora's Box: Subjectivity, Class and Sexuality in Socialist Feminist Criticism', in *Sea Changes*, pp. 147–76; and '"Like a Housemaid's Fancies": The Representation of Working-class Women in Nineteenth-century Writing', in *Grafts: Feminist Cultural Criticism*, ed. Susan Sheridan (London and New York: Verso, 1988), pp. 55–75.

28 Kaplan, '"Housemaid's Fancies"', p. 62, p. 65.

29 Kaplan, 'Wild Nights', p. 48.

30 Samuel Johnson, *Rambler* 85 (8 January 1751), reprinted in *The Yale Edition of the Works of Samuel Johnson*, 16 vols (New Haven and London: Yale University Press, 1969), IV, p. 85. For an excellent discussion of Johnson's complex attitudes towards labour and leisure see Sarah Jordan, *Anxieties of Idleness: Idleness in Eighteenth-century British Literature and Culture* (Lewisburg: Bucknell University Press; London: Associated University Presses, 2003), pp. 153–77.

31 Johnson, *Rambler* 85, p. 86.

32 On Johnson's influence on Wollstonecraft see James G. Basker, 'Radical Affinities: Mary Wollstonecraft and Samuel Johnson', in *Tradition in Translation: Women Writers and the Eighteenth-century Canon*, ed. Alvaro Ribeiro and James G. Basker (Oxford: Clarendon Press, 1996), pp. 41–55.

33 Johnson, *Rambler* 85, p. 82, p. 85.

34 *Ibid.*, p. 86.

35 Judith Frank, *Common Ground: Eighteenth-century Satiric Fiction and the Poor* (Stanford [CA]: Stanford University Press, 1997), p. 137.

36 Johnson, *Rambler* 85, p. 86.

37 Saba Bahar, *Mary Wollstonecraft's Social and Aesthetic Philosophy: An Eve to Please Me* (Basingstoke: Palgrave Macmillan, 2002), p. 174; p. 148. Focusing primarily on moments of cross-class encounter in the novels and *Letters Written During a Short Residence in Sweden, Norway and Denmark* (1796), Bahar rejects claims that Wollstonecraft's treatment of women of the lower ranks was characterized by anxious displacement, arguing instead that her work successfully imagined a new communal aesthetics between women of different classes, based on model of affective spectatorship adapted from that articulated in Adam Smith's *The Theory of Moral Sentiments* (1759).

38 Mary Wollstonecraft, *An Historical and Moral View of the Origin and Progress of the French Revolution; and the Effect it has produced in Europe* (1794), reprinted in Works, VI, p. 230. Subsequent references will be given in the text.

39 Adam Smith, *An Inquiry into the Nature and Causes of the Wealth of Nations*, ed. W. B. Todd, 2 vols (Indianapolis: Liberty Fund, 1981), I, p. 19.

40 Mary Wollstonecraft, *Mary: A Fiction*, reprinted in *Works*, I, p. 7. The prison warder Jemima in *The Wrongs of Woman: or, Maria* is similarly referred to as a 'machine'. See *Works*, I, p. 117. Subsequent references to both of these novels will be given in the text.

41 Taylor, *Mary Wollstonecraft and the Feminist Imagination*, p. 218.

42 Keen, *The Crisis of Literature*, p. 91.

43 As Guest explains, 'The most remarkable feature of this characterization is the suggestion that absorption in fashion and bargain-hunting, is more contemptible and degrading than the behaviour of the sexually voracious woman, who at least has "something more in view"'. *Small Change*, p. 278.

44 Lucinda Cole, '(Anti)Feminist Sympathies: The Politics of Relationship in Smith, Wollstonecraft, and More', *ELH*, 58: 1 (1991), p. 126.

45 *The Monthly Review*, new series, 8 (June 1792), pp. 208–9; p. 198.

46 *Ibid.*, p. 198.

47 *The Critical Review*, new series, 4 (April 1792), p. 397.

48 *Ibid.*, p. 390; p. 397.

49 *Ibid.*, p. 141.

50 *Ibid.*, p. 393.

51 Kaplan, '"Housemaid's Fancies"', p. 62.

52 John Barrell, *The Birth of Pandora and the Division of Knowledge* (Basingstoke: Macmillan, 1992), p. 92.

53 As Janet Todd and Marilyn Butler explain in their edition of *Young Grandison. A Series of Letters from Young Persons to their Friends*, Joseph

Johnson claimed in a manuscript note that Wollstonecraft 'almost re-wrote' this text. *Works*, II, p. 212. Subsequent references will be given in the text.

54 As Adriana Craciun argues, the emergence of the Female Philosopher, of which Wollstonecraft was arguably 'the preeminent example', remains an understudied phenomenon. Whereas 'other hostile formulations such as "unsex'd females" or "English Jacobins"' have remained 'current' in eighteenth-century and Romantic studies, the 'Female Philosopher' has not, which is 'regrettable', as Craciun observes, because of this designation's 'potential value to Romantic women writers' and to the scholarship dedicated to them. Sharing Craciun's interest in the recuperation of this figure, my focus, here, is more squarely upon Wollstonecraft's self-styling as a Female Philosopher, rather than upon the term's abuse by those who sought to discredit this figure. *British Women Writers and the French Revolution: Citizens of the World* (Basingstoke: Macmillan, 2005), pp. 27–8.

55 Smith, *Wealth of Nations*, II, p. 783.

56 There are three direct allusions to *The Theory of Moral Sentiments* in the *Vindication* alone: p. 127; p. 160; p. 261.

57 Angela Keane, *Women Writers and the English Nation in the 1790s* (Cambridge: Cambridge University Press, 2000), p. 121, p. 115.

58 Barrell, *The Birth of Pandora*, p. 91.

59 *Ibid.*, p. 92.

60 Kathryn Sutherland, 'Adam Smith's Master Narrative: Women and *The Wealth of Nations*', in *Adam Smith's Wealth of Nations: New Interdisciplinary Essays*, ed. Stephen Copley and Kathryn Sutherland (Manchester and New York: Manchester University Press, 1995), p. 97. Wollstonecraft is not included by Sutherland in her account of female interpreters of Smithian economics.

61 *Ibid.*, p. 97.

62 Keane, *Women Writers*, p. 121.

63 *Ibid.*

64 Wollstonecraft's embracing of this model of intellectual industry is evident not only in the works discussed in this chapter but also in the many reviews she wrote for Joseph Johnson's *Analytical Review*. For a more detailed account of this career and Wollstonecraft's significance as 'the first truly professional woman literary critic' see Mary A. Waters, *British Women Writers and the Profession of Literary Criticism* (Basingstoke: Palgrave Macmillan, 2004).

65 Mary A. Favret, *Romantic Correspondence: Women, Politics and the Fiction of Letters* (Cambridge: Cambridge University Press, 1993), p. 122.

66 Mary Wollstonecraft, *Letters Written During a Short Residence in Sweden, Norway and Denmark*, reprinted in *Works*, VI, p. 260; p. 266; p. 326. Subsequent references will be given in the text.

67 Bahar, for example, reads this episode as evidence of the effectiveness with which sympathy can efface the 'distance' between the spectator and spectacle (*Mary Wollstonecraft's Social and Aesthetic Philosophy*, p. 147).

68 Wollstonecraft to Everina Wollstonecraft, 24 December [17]92, *Collected Letters*, p. 215.

69 Wollstonecraft to Reverend Henry Dyson, 16 April 1787, *ibid.*, p. 149.

70 Favret, *Romantic Correspondence*, pp. 125–6.

71 As Keen notes in his study of non-fictional writing of this decade, '[p]rofessional authors' were able to turn the distinction between manual and intellectual work to their 'advantage by insisting on the need to earn a living as a positive social characteristic rather than a necessary evil, and by highlighting the fact that they did so by means of an intellectual rather than a manual vocation' (*The Crisis of Literature*, p. 91).

72 Sandra Sherman, *Imagining Poverty: Quantification and the Decline of Paternalism* (Columbus: Ohio State University Press, 2001).

73 *Ibid.*, pp. 253–70.

74 For a particularly compelling reading of these relationships see Claudia L. Johnson, *Equivocal Beings, Politics, Gender and Sentimentality in the 1790s* (Chicago: University of Chicago Press, 1995), pp. 47–58.

75 Taylor, *Mary Wollstonecraft and the Feminist Imagination*, p. 242.

76 Poovey, *The Proper Lady and the Woman Writer*, p. 104.

77 A notable exception is Hannah Primrose, the lower-class heroine of Elizabeth Inchbald's *Nature and Art* (1796). Hannah is seduced by a man of status and wealth, and bears a child without her lover's knowledge. After the illegitimate child's birth is discovered by her seducer's father, Hannah is forced to leave her place of residence to seek work. Eventually, she turns to prostitution and theft, for which latter crime she is condemned to death. Hannah's story is, in many ways, as powerful and as shocking as Jemima's, but lacks some of the force of its successor by being narrated in the third, rather than the first, person. Moreover, Hannah's experience of labour is framed, unlike Jemima's, in terms of the sentimental labour-as-fall plot. Hannah may be labouring class, but, as the child of uncommonly 'industrious' and virtuous parents, she harbours a quasi-genteel 'tenderness and delicacy' that means that feels 'reduced' by the work she obtains prior to her expulsion from her neighbourhood community. Elizabeth Inchbald, *Nature and Art*, ed. Shawn L. Maurer (Peterborough, Ontario: Broadview Press, 2005), p. 123. On the novel's displacement of questions surrounding labouring-class poverty see Sherman, *Imagining Poverty*, pp. 253–70.

78 Bahar, *Mary Wollstonecraft's Social and Aesthetic Philosophy*, p. 171.

79 Taylor, *Mary Wollstonecraft and the Feminist Imagination*, p. 244.

80 *Ibid.*, p. 240.

81 *Ibid.*, p. 241.

82 I am thinking particularly, here, of Kaplan's essays in *Sea Changes* and her 'Housemaid's Fancies', each of which argues for Wollstonecraft's central role in originating a complex narrative about gender, class and feminist politics that unfolds in the following centuries in the works of writers such as Elizabeth Barrett Browning and Virginia Woolf.

Chapter 4

1 David Williams, *Claims of Literature: The Origin, Motives, Objects, and Transactions, of the Society for the Establishment of a Literary Fund* (London: William Miller and W. Bulmer, 1802), pp. 22–3. Subsequent references will be given in the text.

2 Susan Wood to the Royal Literary Fund, 3 February 1819. *Archives of the Royal Literary Fund: 1790–1918*, 145 reels (London: World Microfilms Publications, 1981–84), reel 4, case 135. All references to Fund applications are taken from this archive and identified by reel and case number.

3 Gruffudd Aled Ganobcsik-Williams, 'The Sweat of the Brain: Representations of Intellectual Labour in the Writings of Edmund Burke, William Cobbett, William Hazlitt, and Thomas Carlyle' (unpublished PhD thesis: University of Warwick, 2001), p. 25.

4 Adam Smith, *An Inquiry into the Nature and Causes of the Wealth of Nations*, ed. W. B. Todd, 2 vols (Indianapolis: Liberty Fund, 1981), I, p. 330.

5 A similar critique of the impact of *The Wealth of Nations* on the profession of authorship can be found in *Calamities of Authors* (1812), a work authored by Fund supporter Isaac D'Israeli: 'I leave the whole school of Adam Smith to clam their calculating emotions concerning "that unprosperous race of men" (sometimes this Master-Seer calls them "unproductive") commonly called "*men of letters*", who are pretty much in the situation which lawyers and physicians would be in, were these, as he tells us, in that state when "*a scholar* and *a beggar* seem to have been very nearly *synonymous terms*" – and this melancholy fact that man of genius discovered, without the feather of his pen brushing away a tear from his lid – without one spontaneous and indignant groan! I turn from the leaden-hearted disciples of Adam Smith, and from all their vile vocabulary of "unproductive stock".' *Calamities of Authors; including some Inquiries Respecting their Moral and Literary Characters*, 2 vols (London: John Murray; Edinburgh: W. Blackwood; Dublin: J. Cumming, 1812), I, pp. 39–40.

6 Wood to Fund, [?] May 1818; 3 February 1815. It is unlikely that the 'moral and pious works' to which Wood alludes were ever published. Wood published *Literary Exercises* in her own name. No other entries for Susan Wood are to be found in the *NSTC* or in the British Library catalogue.

7 Wood to the Fund, 21 February 1803.

8 Wood's four successful applications were awarded £5 each. Compare this to the £25 awarded in recognition of a single application made by Robert Burns's widow, Jean, in 1796.

9 Wood to Fund, 3 February 1815; 3 February 1819; [?] May 1818.

10 Wood to the Fund, 21 February 1803.

11 Wood to the Fund, [?] May 1820.

12 Wollstonecraft's reviews for the *Analytical Review* reflect these new hierarchies of textual production and the female-authored novel's role as the amateur other against which works of genuine literary merit and industry were to be judged. Wollstonecraft's review of Fund applicant Eliza Norman's *The Child of Woe* (1789) remarked that it, like 'ninety-nine out of a hundred' novels written to 'amuse the fair', had 'no marked features to characterise it'. Comprised of '[u]nnatural characters, improbable incidents, sad tales of woe rehearsed in an affected half-prose, half-poetical style, exquisite double-refined sensibility, dazzling beauty, and *elegant* drapery' it was a 'truly feminine novel'. *Analytical Review*, 3 (1789), reprinted in *The Works of Mary Wollstonecraft*, ed. Janet Todd and Marilyn Butler, 7 vols (London: Pickering and Chatto, 1989), VII, p. 82.

13 Clifford Siskin, *The Work of Writing: Literature and Social Change in Britain, 1700–1830* (Baltimore and London: The Johns Hopkins University Press, 1998), pp. 218–25.

14 Mary Wollstonecraft was 'disgusted' by such declarations, which, in a letter to Mary Hays dated 25 November 1792, she referred to as 'vain humility'. *The Collected Letters of Mary Wollstonecraft*, ed. Janet Todd (London: Allen Lane, 2003), p. 210.

15 This phrase is taken from the first advertisement the Fund produced in order to solicit applications and subscriptions, and is quoted in Williams, *Claims*, p. 105.

16 David Williams's first work, *The Philosopher*, was published anonymously in 1771; his last, *Preparatory Studies for Political Reformers*, appeared in 1810. In his forty-year writing career, Williams authored works on religion, including his *Essays on Public Worship* (1773), and on literature, including *A Letter to Garrick* (1772). In addition, he produced influential works on education and politics and, in the 1803 *Egeria*, on political economy.

17 Anon., 'Institution of the Society for the Establishment of the Literary Fund' (n.d.), in 'The Minutes of the General Committee', *The Archives of the Royal Literary Fund*, reel 125.

18 David Williams, *Incidents in my Life Which Have Been Thought of Some Importance*, ed. Peter France (Brighton: University of Sussex Library, 1980), p. 45; p. 44.

19 E. I. Carlyle, 'Sydenham, Floyer (1710–87)', rev. Anna Chahoud, *Oxford Dictionary of National Biography* (Oxford University Press, 2004). <www.oxforddnb.com/view/article/26861>.

20 The charity's constitution was published under the following title: *Constitutions of a Society to Support Men of Genius and Learning in Distress; and to assist the widows and children of those who have any claims on publick gratitude or humanity, from literary merit or industry* (London: J. Nichols and L. Davis, 1788). The implications of the gendering of authorship, here, as male – women are seen as legitimate claimants of the charity only as the dependants of male authors – are teased out in more detail later in this chapter.
21 Williams, *Incidents*, p. 49.
22 Donna T. Andrew, *Philanthropy and Police: London Charity in the Eighteenth Century* (Princeton: Princeton University Press, 1989), pp. 138–46.
23 Earlier in *Claims*, Williams pushed this argument further, stating not only that the common rank of men could not cultivate genius simply by desire but also that such individuals should be actively discouraged from futilely attempting to do so. In a long diatribe against charity schools, which are accused of taking the 'children of peasants . . . from the bosom of their parent earth . . . and swell[ing] the idle and vicious classes of national population', Williams argued that such children should be 'consigned to farmers' where they could 'assist in producing the food they consume' and thus ensuring that 'the learned might be fed better and cheaper' (pp. 69–70).
24 Williams, *Incidents*, p. 38.
25 Smith, *The Wealth of Nations*, I, p. 330.
26 Penelope J. Corfield, *Power and the Professions in Britain 1700–1850* (London and New York: Routledge, 1995), p. 23; p. 26.
27 *Ibid.*, p. 26.
28 Anon., *An Account of the Institution of the Society for the Establishment of a Literary Fund* (London: John Nichols, one of their Registers, 1797), p. 5.
29 Paul Keen, *The Crisis of Literature in the 1790s: Print Culture and the Public Sphere* (Cambridge: Cambridge University Press, 1999), p. 85.
30 A similar argument was deployed by Isaac D'Israeli in *An Essay on the Manners and Genius of the Literary Character* (London: T. Cadell, 1795). Chapter 15 of D'Israeli's work makes the case for the establishment of 'an Academy of polite Literature' modelled on the Royal Academy.
31 The Fund's insistence upon utility, while clearly a response to the productive/non-productive binary that Williams intuits from *The Wealth of Nations*, was also no doubt linked to the charity's claims for authorship's professional status. As Corfield has indicated, all of the eighteenth-century professions were 'organized around a formal corpus of specialist knowledge with both a theoretical *and* a practical bearing' (emphasis added). Corfield, *Power and the Professions*, p. 25.
32 One of the difficulties posed by the archive is its relative one-sidedness. Although the voices of authors are heard loudly and clearly, those of

committee members are often all-but mute. The decisions made on individual cases (sums awarded or cases rejected) are noted on the individual case files and in the committee minutes. However, the justifications for such decisions are clear only in a limited number of cases, where, for example, a claimant was deemed ineligible for further awards because they had already been relieved once in the calendar year, or where a case was rejected because of lack of evidence. How the committee arrived at the sums awarded to individual claimants is unclear, although a number of credible reasons, as we shall see, can be inferred.

33 An additional 22 claims were made by female dependants of male authors in this same period.

34 W. C. Proby, the author of two favourably reviewed novels, *The Mysterious Seal* (1799) and *The Spirit of the Castle* (1800), also wrote a response to William Godwin's *Political Justice* entitled *Modern Philosophy and Barbarism* (1798). Alexander Bicknell, author of *The Benevolent Man* (1775) and *The History of Lady Anne Neville* (1776), was additionally the author of various histories and a grammar. He made sixteen applications to the Fund and was awarded £69 6s in a period of five and a half years.

35 These women were Ann Burke, Phebe Gibbes, Elizabeth Helme, Maria Hunter, Charlotte Lennox, Eliza Norman and Eliza Parsons. If we accept the probably spurious attribution of *Hermione, or the Orphan Sisters* (1791) to Lennox, Gibbes was the only one of these women not to work for Lane. However, Lennox is in many ways an exception to the rule of the Fund's treatment of female novelists. Lennox, who made her first application to the Fund in May 1792, made eleven applications over the next eleven years, all of which were successful and six of which resulted in awards in excess of £10. In July 1803 Lennox was, uniquely among the women writers discussed in this chapter, offered a regular allowance of a guinea a week.

36 In fact, referral to the Committee of Inquiry did not always mean that claimants would receive no future awards. Proby, for example, was deemed 'suspect' by the 1806 Committee, but received further awards of £10 and £15 in response to applications made in 1827 and 1830. Reel 3, case 89.

37 Notable exceptions to this rule include Deborah Anne McLeod's 'The Minerva Press' (unpublished PhD dissertation, University of Alberta, 1997) and Edward Copeland's *Women Writing About Money: Women's Fiction in England, 1790–1820* (Cambridge: Cambridge University Press, 1995).

38 Devendra P. Varma, 'Introduction' to Eliza Parsons, *The Mysterious Warning: A German Tale in Four Volumes*, ed. Devendra P. Varma (London: The Folio Press, 1968), p. viii.

39 Nigel Cross, *The Common Writer: Life in Nineteenth-century Grub Street* (Cambridge: Cambridge University Press, 1985), p. 171.

40 Andrew Elfenbein, *Romantic Genius: The Prehistory of a Homosexual Role* (New York: Columbia University Press, 1999), pp. 28–30.

41 Martha Woodmansee, 'The Genius and the Copyright: Economic and Legal Conditions of the Emergence of the "Author"', *Eighteenth-century Studies*, 17 (1984), p. 426.

42 *Ibid.*

43 Edward Young, *Conjectures on Original Composition. In a Letter to the Author of Sir Charles Grandison* (London: A. Millar and R. and J. Dodsley, 1759), p. 12.

44 Anon., *Papers and Documents Respecting the Society for the Management and Distribution of the Literary Fund* (London: John Nichols and Son, 1820), p. 10.

45 D'Israeli, *Calamities*, I, p. 45; p. 3.

46 Sonia Hofkosh, *Sexual Politics and the Romantic Author* (Cambridge: Cambridge University Press, 1998), p. 16.

47 Jean Burns to the Literary Fund, 30 August 1796. Reel 2, case 46. Burns's application resulted in a substantial award of £25. No other extant applications from Jean Burns are to be found in the archives, but in 1801 the charity apparently made enquiries into the financial situation of the Burns family and granted a further £20.

48 D'Israeli, *Essay*, p. 52. Phebe Gibbes rehearsed this common formulation in an application to the Fund dated 14 October 1804 in which she expressed her hopes that the committee would excuse her 'deficiencies' on the grounds that she, like all 'Literary persons' was 'unsuited . . . for other pursuits'. None the less, as explored in more detail in the following section, Gibbes maintained that her authorial career was entirely compatible with her domestic duties as a woman and as a writer. Reel 2, case 74.

49 Hofkosh, *Sexual Politics and the Romantic Author*, p. 16; p.18.

50 Anon., *Papers and Documents*, pp. 9–10.

51 As Christine Battersby has argued, most eighteenth-century accounts of genius assumed it to be a male characteristic, although the figure of the genius possessed a number of feminine traits. Women writers' critique of the effeminacy commonly associated with genius, and their efforts to claim this attribute for themselves, are discussed in more detail below. Christine Battersby, *Gender and Genius: Towards a Feminist Aesthetics* (Bloomington: Indiana University Press, 1989), and Elfenbein, *Romantic Genius*, particularly pp. 16–38.

52 Maria Julia Young to the Literary Fund, 28 March 1808. Reel 6, case 216. Young enclosed a list of publications with her application comprising seven original novels, two translations of novels (one from the French, one from the German), poems and sonnets, a biographical memoir and a translation of extracts of works by Voltaire.

53 *Ibid.*

54 Ann Burke to the Fund, 19 October 1795. Reel 1, case 35.

55 Burke to the Fund, 19 October 1795.

56 Minutes, 19 November 1795. Reel 125.

57 Burke to the Fund, 14 September 1799. An undated paper listing Burke's publications appears to have been sent to the Fund in 1805. The date can be surmised by the reference to Burke's *Secret of the Cavern* (1805) as currently in press. However, no claim accompanies the list and no mention is made of an application in the Fund Minutes.

58 A similar judgement was made of Elizabeth Helme, whose three daughters all applied to the Fund after their mother's death – only one, the children's writer Elizabeth Somerville, was an author herself. The family's third application was summarily dismissed, officially on the grounds that grants had already been given. Unofficially, the Fund felt that Helme's talents had more been more than adequately recompensed. In a rare surviving letter, Octavian Blewitt wrote to the referee who had applied to the charity on behalf of Helme's daughter Louisa Dalton, to explain that 'the sum granted altogether to the Family certainly now exceeds what would be considered an adequate reward for her literary claims' (3 July 1847, reel 3, case 97).

59 Minutes, 17 October 1799. Reel 125.

60 Eliza Parsons to the Fund, 30 May 1803. Reel 1, case 21.

61 Parsons to the Fund, 18 December, 1792.

62 Parsons to the Fund, 30 May 1803.

63 Parsons to the Fund, 7 July 1796.

64 Parsons to the Fund, 30 May 1803; 7 July 1796; 17 December 1792.

65 Parsons to the Fund 7 July 1796.

66 Parsons to the Fund, 30 May 1803.

67 Gérard Genette, *Paratexts: Thresholds of Interpretation*, trans. Jane E. Lewin (Cambridge: Cambridge University Press, 1997), p. 198; p. 209.

68 *Ibid.*, p. 198.

69 For an illuminating re-examination of Genette's work in relation to the prefaces of earlier eighteenth-century women writers see Cheryl L. Nixon, '"Stop a Moment at this Preface": The Gendered Paratexts of Fielding, Barker, and Haywood', *JNT: Journal of Narrative Theory*, 32: 2 (2002): 123–53.

70 Eliza Parsons, *The History of Miss Meredith: A Novel*, 2 vols (London: T. Hookham, 1790), I, p. ii. Subsequent references will be given in the text.

71 Jacqueline Pearson, 'Mothering the Novel: Frances Burney and the Next Generations of Women Novelists', *CW3: Corvey Women Writers on the Web*, 1 (2004). <www2.shu.ac.uk/corvey/CW3journal/issues/pearson.html>.

72 Genette, *Paratexts*, p. 198.

73 Frances Burney, *Evelina, or the History of a Young Lady's Entrance into the World*, ed. Edward A. Bloom and Lillian Bloom (Oxford: Oxford University Press, 1998), p. 7.

74 Parsons to the Fund, 7 July 1796.

75 Hofkosh makes a similar point when she notes in her discussion of *Biographia Literaria* that 'Prostitution serves in this period as a general metaphor for the debasement of literary practice into a promiscuous professionalism that renders authorship meaningful only by disempowering the author *as such*' (*Sexual Politics*, p. 23).

76 Clark Lawlor, *Consumption and Literature: The Making of the Romantic Disease* (Basingstoke: Palgrave, 2006). See particularly pp. 111–52.

77 *Ibid.*, p. 120.

78 D'Israeli, *Calamities*, I, p. 196.

79 Elfenbein, *Romantic Genius*.

80 Helen Deutsch, 'Symptomatic Correspondences: The Author's Case in Eighteenth-century Britain', *Cultural Critique*, 42 (1999), p. 56.

81 D'Israeli, *Essay on the Manners and Genius of the Literary Character*, p. 41.

82 On this paradox see Andrew Elfenbein, 'Mary Wollstonecraft and the Sexuality of Genius', in *The Cambridge Companion to Mary Wollstonecraft*, ed. Claudia L. Johnson (Cambridge: Cambridge University Press, 2002), pp. 235–7.

83 On the connections between male genius, textual production and consumption see Clark Lawlor and Akihito Suzuki, 'The Disease of the Self: Representing Consumption, 1700–1830', *Bulletin of the History of Medicine*, 74: 3 (2000): 458–95.

84 Mary Wollstonecraft, *Mary: A Fiction*, reprinted in *The Works of Mary Wollstonecraft*, I, p. 71.

85 Mary Wollstonecraft, *A Vindication of the Rights of Woman*, reprinted in *Works*, V, p. 129.

86 Catherine Bayley to the Literary Fund, 27 March 1815. Reel 9, case 317. Bayley was the author of *Vacation Evenings, or Conversations between a Governess and her Pupils* (1809), a translation of Voltaire's *Zadig and Astarte* (1810), several pieces for the *European Magazine* and a probably unpublished romance rejected by Longman and Co., the publishers of *Vacation Evenings*.

87 Elizabeth Macauley to the Literary Fund, [?] May 1812. Reel 8, case 278. In addition to her published poetry and miscellaneous works, Macauley claimed to have written a novel, completed during a ten-week period of confinement in debtor's prison. The title of the work and its fate are unknown.

88 Gibbes to the Literary Fund, 14 October 1804. In fact, Gibbes was of so 'withdrawing' a temper that she prejudiced her own case. Having published all of her novels anonymously, she struggled to prove her authorship and was forced to obtain a reference from Joseph Johnson, a rare surviving publisher of Gibbes's work, to prove that she had written at least one of the fictions to which she laid claim. Johnson wrote to the Fund on 15 October 1804 to confirm her status as a 'respectable woman' and to testify to her

authorship of *Elfrida* (1786), a novel that remains unattributed in the *ESTC*. Burke was likewise forced to ask George Robinson to confirm her authorship of her first two anonymous works.

89 Some male writers also adopted the feminine discourse of domesticity to defend their applications to the Fund. Bicknell, for example, a serial and highly successful Fund claimant, wrote in a letter dated 22 March 1791 that 'This Application, Gentlemen, is not the Consequence of Dissipation or Extravagance, the Person applying being a domestic, regular, & not intemperate Man' (Reel 1, case 6). Interestingly, however, Bicknell's applications, which include enthusiastic poems in praise of the Fund's beneficence, contain very little information about his publications or his own perception of his claims as a writer – he simply lets his works speak for themselves in a way that so many of Bicknell's female counterparts evidently felt unable to do.

90 Eliza Norman to the Literary Fund, 21 May 1802. Reel 1, case 36.

91 Mary Ann Newman to the Literary Fund, 8 March 1820. Reel 11, case 409.

92 Julie Kipp's *Romanticism, Maternity and the Body Politic* (Cambridge: Cambridge University Press, 2003) examines the maternal body's implication in wider political debates on the social structure and nationhood. Laurie Langbauer's 'An Early Romance: Motherhood and Women's Writing in Mary Wollstonecraft's Novels', in *Romanticism and Feminism*, ed. Anne Mellor (Bloomington: University of Indiana Press, 1988, pp. 208–19), explores the relationship between Wollstonecraft's treatment of the romance genre and her ambitions for women's writing through the creation of plot structures in which 'mothers and daughters enjoy a union and happiness denied . . . men' (p. 209). Jacqueline M. Labbe's 'The Romance of Motherhood: Generation and the Literary Text', *Romanticism on the Net*, 26 (May 2002), investigates a number of women writers' exploitation of the 'Romantic-period idealization of the mother' to produce a 'controlled' image of themselves to their children and to their readers (<www.erudit.org/revue/ron/2002/v/n26/005698ar.html>). Jane Spencer investigates the connections between maternity and textual production as part of an expansive notion of 'kinship', which she suggests was the 'organizing principle of literary history' and genealogy in the long eighteenth century in *Literary Relations: Kinship and the Canon, 1660–1830* (Oxford: Oxford University Press, 2005).

93 Susan Stanford Friedman, 'Creativity and the Childbirth Metaphor: Gender Difference in Literary Discourse', *Feminist Studies*, 13: 1 (1987), p. 65.

94 Friedman, 'Creativity and the Childbirth Metaphor', pp. 51; p. 65; p. 49.

95 On Smith's unhappy meeting with Lane see Chapter 2, note 95.

96 Charlotte Smith, *Desmond: A Novel*, ed. Stuart Curran, reprinted in *The Works of Charlotte Smith*, 14 vols (London: Pickering and Chatto, 2005–7), V, pp. 3–4.

97 Diane E. Boyd, '"Professing Drudge": Charlotte Smith's Negotiation of a Mother-writer Author Function', *South Atlantic Review*, 66: 1 (2001), p. 164.

98 Helme was among the most popular, and most critically maligned, of all the authors discussed in this chapter. She was the author of some 19 novels, children's books, translations and histories, although her husband, the teacher and author William Helme, would claim that he had co-authored or completed some of the works published under her name (including the posthumously published *Magdalen; or, the Penitent of Godstow* (1812) and *Modern Times or the Age in Which We Live* (1814)) when he applied to the Literary Fund. See William Helme's letter to the Literary Fund, 28 January 1815. Reel 8, case 295.

99 Elizabeth Helme, *Clara and Emmeline; or, the Maternal Benediction*, 2 vols (London: G. Kearsley, 1788), I, p. iv.

100 *The Critical Review*, 64 (1787), p. 480.

101 On Siddons and maternity see Jan McDonald, '"Acting and the Austere Joys of Motherhood": Sarah Siddons Performing Maternity', in *Extraordinary Actors: Essays on Particular Performers*, ed. Jane Milling, Martin Banham and Peter Thomson (Exeter: University of Exeter Press, 2004), pp. 57–70; and Laura J. Rosenthal, 'The Sublime, The Beautiful, "The Siddons"', in *The Clothes that Wear Us: Essays on Dressing and Transgressing in Eighteenth-century Culture*, ed. Jessica Munns and Penny Richards (Newark: University of Delaware Press, 1999), pp. 56–79.

102 Helme would adopt the dual role of mother to the reader and mother of the text throughout her career, notably in her children's book *Maternal Instruction; or, Family Conversations on Moral and Entertaining Subjects*, 2 vols (London: n. pub., 1802).

103 A similar manoeuvre is made by the Fund applicant and children's writer Charlotte Palmer who, in the preface to the children's book *It is and It is Not*, wrote of her 'FEAR' that she had not 'taught this little offspring of my imagination its duty, so far as to shield it from danger on its first entrance into the world' (I, p. v) and her hopes that 'those who have the honour to support the maternal character with exemplary prudence and virtue' will place it 'in the hands of their daughters'. *It is and It is Not*, 2 vols (London: Hookham and Carpenter, 1792), I, p. iv.

104 Laura L. Runge 'Churls and Graybeards and Novels Written by a Lady: Gender in Eighteenth-century Book Reviews', *CW3: Corvey Women Writers on the Web*, 1 (2004). <www2.shu.ac.uk/corvey/cw3journal/Issue%20one/runge.html>.

105 The discourse of feminine selflessness is embraced not only by writers who had children. Those who weren't mothers often figured themselves as dutiful daughters and siblings, positions which, owing to constraints of space, lie beyond the scope of this chapter. For example, the poet and

novelist Emily Frederick Clark, granddaughter of the writer and successful Fund claimant Colonel Frederick, explained that she wrote 'only in obedience to a friend of my mother', but implicitly cast herself as the mother of her publications when she described the 'tears' of pride she 'shed' when her first work was published, a work that enabled her 'to comfort the best of parents & [her] family'. Emily Frederick Clark to the Literary Fund, 18 January 1830. Reel 7, case 266. Clark's first application was dated 20 March 1811; her last was submitted on 3 March 1833.

106 Samuel Taylor Coleridge, *Biographia Literaria or Biographical Sketches of my Life and Opinions*, ed. James Engell and W. Jackson Bate, 2 vols (London: Routledge; and Princeton: Princeton University Press, 1983), I, p. 31.

107 Gibbes to the Fund, 18 April 1805; Gibbes to the Fund, 14 October 1804.

108 Mary Pilkington to the Literary Fund, 2 June 1811. Reel 7, case 256. Pilkington wrote several works of fiction, including *Celebrity: or, the Unfortunate Choice* (1815), and numerous books for children as well as *Memoirs of Celebrated Female Characters* (1804).

109 Ruth Perry, *Novel Relations: The Transformation of Kinship in English Literature and Culture, 1748–1818* (Cambridge: Cambridge University Press, 2004), pp. 337–8.

110 *Ibid.*, p. 366.

111 Perry discusses the significance of 'emblematic independent' women, such as *Evelina*'s Mrs Selwyn, who speak 'the author's mind' (p. 358), but omits the author's maternal role as the text's originator and guide.

112 Eliza Parsons, *The Convict, or, the Navy Lieutenant*, 3 vols (Brentford: P. Norbury, 1807), I, p. 140. Subsequent references will be given in the text.

113 Eleanor Ty, *Unsex'd Revolutionaries: Five Women Novelists of the 1790s* (Toronto, Buffalo and London: University of Toronto Press, 1993), pp. 60–72.

114 Mary Hays, *The Victim of Prejudice*, ed. Eleanor Ty (Peterborough, Ontario: Broadview, 1998), p. 71.

115 Mary Hays, *Memoirs of Emma Courtney*, ed. Marilyn L. Brooks (Peterborough, Ontario: Broadview, 2000), p. 66.

116 Langbauer, 'An Early Romance', pp. 211–12.

117 Anne K. Mellor, *Mothers of the Nation: Women's Political Writing in England, 1780–1830* (Bloomington and Indianapolis: Indiana University Press, 2000), p. 104.

118 Copeland, *Women Writing About Money*, p. 12.

119 *Ibid.*, p. 165.

120 Burke, for example, wrote to the Fund on 19 October 1795, requesting money 'to procure a few articles of furniture, and open a School, for which I am well calculated'. The novelist and children's writer Sarah Scadgell Wilkinson made a similar request in May 1819 and later worked in a 'Free

School', which she was forced to leave after developing cancer of the arm. Case 375, reel 10. Other writers, such as the novelist Anne Ker, more modestly requested funds simply to afford them decent clothes which might help them in their endeavours to obtain suitable employment. Ker to the Literary Fund, 2 January 1821. Case 424, reel 12.

121 Pilkington, who like the author Ann Burke, had worked as a governess, had published *Celebrity* with the Minerva Press, '[f]inding that Necessities were very pressing and that Mr Harris', her publisher of choice, 'was not inclined to purchase my Productions as fast as I could compose them'. Pilkington to the Fund, 7 February 1815.

122 April London, *Women and Property in the Eighteenth-century English Novel* (Cambridge: Cambridge University Press, 1999), p. 8; p. 7.

123 Eliza Parsons, *The Valley of St. Gothard*, 3 vols (Brentford: P. Norbury, 1799), I, p. 54.

124 Ann Burke, *Adela Northington: A Novel*, 3 vols (London: W. Cawthorne, 1796), I, p. 122.

125 Elizabeth Helme, *Instructive Rambles Extended in London, and the Adjacent Villages*, 2 vols (London: Samson Low and E. Newbery, 1800), II, p. 123. Subsequent references will be given in the text.

126 On the 'mutually informing and antagonistic' categories of georgic and pastoral in the literature of the period see London, *Women and Property*.

127 Elizabeth Helme, *The Farmer of Inglewood Forest: A Novel*, 4 vols (London: William Lane, 1796), I, p. ii; II, p. 184.

128 Copeland, *Women Writing about Money*, p. 190.

129 *Ibid*., p. 198.

Coda

1 Betty A. Schellenberg, *The Professionalization of Women Writers in Eighteenth-century Britain* (Cambridge: Cambridge University Press, 2005), p. 164.

2 Donna Landry, 'Picturing Benevolence Against the Commercial Cry, 1750–1798: or, Sarah Fielding and the Secret Causes of Romanticism', in *The History of British Women's Writing, Volume V, 1750–1830* (forthcoming, Palgrave Macmillan).

3 Eve Tavor Bannet's *The Domestic Revolution: Enlightenment Feminisms and the Novel* (Baltimore and London: The Johns Hopkins University Press, 2000) is perhaps one of the most notable exceptions to this rule, although its division of eighteenth-century feminist writers into two camps ('Matriarchal' feminists such as Fielding and Scott and 'Egalitarian' feminists such as Smith and Wollstonecraft) underscores difference as much as continuity.

4 Susan Staves's *A Literary History of Women's Writing in Britain, 1660–1789* (Cambridge: Cambridge University Press, 2006) gives plenty of food for thought in its fine, and ambitious, literary history, which counters a number of the organizing principles I allude to here. Staves's study is notable for many reasons, particularly, for its decentring of the novel, but also for its foregrounding of the many and varied works of women writers at mid-century. Her study's endpoint in 1789, however, leaves to other scholars the somewhat daunting task of tackling the nature and extent of these earlier women writers' legacies to those of subsequent generations.

5 Sarah Fielding, *The Adventures of David Simple and Volume the Last*, ed. Malcolm Kelsall (Oxford: Oxford University Press, 1987), p. 52.

Bibliography

Archival sources

Archives of the Royal Literary Fund: 1790–1918, 145 reels. London: World Microfilms Publications, 1981–84.

The Elizabeth (Robinson) Montagu Collection, Henry E. Huntington Library.

Primary sources

[Anon.], *An Account of the Institution of the Society for the Establishment of a Literary Fund.* London: John Nichols, one of their Registers, 1797.

Barker, Jane, *The Galesia Trilogy and Selected Manuscript Poems of Jane Barker*, ed. Carol Shiner Wilson. Oxford and New York: Oxford University Press, 1997.

Burke, Ann, *Adela Northington: A Novel*, 3 vols. London: W. Cawthorne, 1796.

Burney, Frances, *Cecilia; or Memoirs of an Heiress* (1782), ed. Peter Sabor and Margaret Anne Doody. Oxford: Oxford University Press, 1988.

— *The Early Journals and Letters of Fanny Burney. Volume III The Streatham Years: Part I, 1778–1779*, ed. Lars E. Troide and Stewart T. Cooke. Oxford: Oxford University Press, 1994.

—— *The Early Journals and Letters of Fanny Burney. Volume IV The Streatham Years: Part II, 1780–1781*, ed. Betty Rizzo. Oxford: Oxford University Press, 2003.

—— *Evelina, or the History of a Young Lady's Entrance into the World* (1778), ed. Edward A. Bloom and Lillian Bloom. Oxford: Oxford University Press, 1998.

—— *The Wanderer* (1814), ed. Margaret Anne Doody, Robert L. Mack and Peter Sabor. Oxford and New York: Oxford University Press, 1991.

Coleridge, Samuel Taylor, *Biographia Literaria, or Biographical Sketches of my Life and Opinions* (1817), ed. James Engell and W. Jackson Bate, 2 vols. London: Routledge; and Princeton: Princeton University Press, 1983.

D'Israeli, Isaac, *Calamities of Authors; including some Inquiries Respecting their Moral and Literary Characters*, 2 vols. London: John Murray; Edinburgh: W. Blackwood; Dublin: J. Cumming, 1812.

—— *An Essay on the Manners and Genius of the Literary Character*. London: T. Cadell, 1795.

Duck, Stephen, *The Thresher's Labour* (1730), reprinted in *The Thresher's Labour (Stephen Duck) and The Woman's Labour (Mary Collier)*. Introduction by Moira Ferguson. Los Angeles: William Andrews Clark Memorial Library, 1985.

[Anon.], *An Enquiry into the Nature and Origin of Literary Property*. London: William Flexney, 1762.

Fielding, Henry, *Joseph Andrews* (1742), ed. Thomas Keymer. Oxford: Oxford University Press, 1999.

Fielding, John, *A Plan for a Preservatory and Reformatory for the Benefit of Deserted Girls and Penitent Prostitutes.* London: R. Francklin, 1758.

Fielding, Sarah, *The Adventures of David Simple* (1742), ed. Malcolm Kelsall. Oxford: Oxford University Press, 1987.

—— *The History of the Countess of Dellwyn,* 2 vols. London: A. Millar, 1759.

Gisborne, Thomas, *An Enquiry into the Duties of the Female Sex*. London: T. Cadell and W. Davies, 1797.

—— *An Enquiry into the Duties of Men in the Higher and Middle Classes of Society in Great Britain, Resulting from their Respective Stations, Professions, and Employments*. London: B. and J. White, 1794.

Goldsmith, Oliver, *An Enquiry into the Present State of Polite Learning in Europe*. London: R. and J. Dodsley, 1759.

Hanway, Jonas, *A Plan for Establishing a Charity-House, or Charity-Houses for the Reception of Repenting Prostitutes to be Called the Magdalen Charity*. London: n. pub., 1758.

—— *Thoughts on the Plan for a Magdalen-House for Repentant Prostitutes*. London: James Waugh, 1758.

Hays, Mary, *Memoirs of Emma Courtney* (1796), ed. Marilyn L. Brooks. Peterborough, Ontario: Broadview, 2000.

—— 'Mrs Charlotte Smith'. *Public Characters of 1800–1801*. London: Richard Phillips, 1807.

—— *The Victim of Prejudice* (1799), ed. Eleanor Ty. Peterborough, Ontario: Broadview, 1998.

Helme, Elizabeth, *Clara and Emmeline; or, the Maternal Benediction*, 2 vols. London: G. Kearsley, 1788.

—— *The Farmer of Inglewood Forest: A Novel*, 4 vols. London: William Lane, 1796.

—— *Instructive Rambles Extended in London, and the Adjacent Villages*, 2 vols. London: Samson Low and E. Newbery, 1800.

—— *Maternal Instruction; or, Family Conversations on Moral and Entertaining Subjects*, 2 vols. London: n. pub. 1802.

[Anon.], *The Histories of Some of the Penitents in the Magdalen-House, As Supposed to be Related by Themselves* (1760), ed. Jennie Batchelor and Megan Hiatt. London: Pickering and Chatto, 2007.

Hume, David, *Selected Essays*, ed. Stephen Copley and Andrew Elgar. Oxford and New York: Oxford University Press, 1993.

Inchbald, Elizabeth, *Nature and Art* (1796), ed. Shawn L. Maurer. Peterborough [Ontario]: Broadview Press, 2005.

Johnson, Samuel, *The Yale Edition of the Works of Samuel Johnson*. Ed. W. J. Bate and Albrecht B. Strauss, 16 vols. New Haven and London: Yale University Press, 1969.

Lennox, Charlotte, *Henrietta* (1758), ed. Ruth Perry and Susan Carlile. Lexington: The University Press of Kentucky, 2008.

Locke, John, *Two Treatises of Government* (1690). London: A. Millar, 1764.

Mandeville, Bernard, *A Modest Defence of Publick Stews: or, An Essay upon Whoring*. London: A. Moore, 1724.

[Anon.], 'A New Method for making Women as useful and as capable as men of maintaining themselves, as the men are; and consequently preventing their becoming old maids, or taking ill Courses, By a Lady', *Gentleman's Magazine*, 9 (1739): 525–6.

Palmer, Charlotte, *It is and It is Not*, 2 vols. London: Hookham and Carpenter, 1792.

[Anon.], *Papers and Documents Respecting the Society for the Management and Distribution of the Literary Fund*. London: John Nichols and Son, 1820.

Parsons, Eliza, *The Convict, or, the Navy Lieutenant*, 3 vols. Brentford: P. Norbury, 1807.

—— *The History of Miss Meredith: A Novel*, 2 vols. London: T. Hookham, 1790.

—— *The Mysterious Warning: A German Tale in Four Volumes*, with an introduction by Devendra P. Varma. London: The Folio Press, 1968.

—— *The Valley of St. Gothard*, 3 vols. Brentford: P. Norbury, 1799.

Pennington, Lady Sarah, *An Unfortunate Mother's Advice to her Absent Daughters; In a Letter to Miss Pennington*. London: S. Chandler, 1761.

Radcliffe, Mary Ann, *The Memoirs of Mrs Mary Ann Radcliffe; in Familiar Letters to her Female Friend* and *The Female Advocate; or, an Attempt to Recover the Rights of Woman from Male Usurpation*. Edinburgh: Manners and Millar, A. Constable & Co., J. Anderson, Oliphant and Balfour; London: Longman, Hurst, Rees, Orme and Brown, 1810.

Ralph, James, *The Case of Authors by Profession or Trade* (1758), reprinted with *The Champion* (1739–40), with an introduction by Philip Stevick. Gainesville, FL: Scholars' Facsimiles and Reprints, 1966.

Richardson, Samuel, *Clarissa, or, the History of a Young Lady* (1747–48), ed. Angus Ross. Harmondsworth: Penguin, 2004.

Scott, Sarah, *A Description of Millenium Hall and the Country Adjacent* (1762), ed. Gary Kelly. Peterborough [Ontario]: Broadview, 1995.

—— *The History of Cornelia* (1750), with an introduction by Caroline Franklin. London: Routledge/Thoemmes Press, 1992.

—— *The History of Sir George Ellison* (1766), ed. Betty Rizzo. Kentucky: The University of Kentucky Press, 1996.

—— *A Journey through Every Stage of Life* (1754), ed. Gary Kelly. *Bluestocking Feminism: Writings of the Bluestocking Circle, 1738–1785*. Gen. Ed. Gary Kelly. London: Pickering and Chatto, 1999, V.

Scott, Sir Walter, *Miscellaneous Prose Works of Sir Walter Scott*, 28 vols. Edinburgh: Robert Cadell; E. Whittaker and Co., 1834–36.

Seward, Anna, *The Letters of Anna Seward written between the Years 1784 and 1807*, 6 vols (New York: AMS Press, 1995).

Smith, Adam, *An Inquiry into the Nature and Causes of the Wealth of Nations* (1776), ed. W. B. Todd, 2 vols. Indianapolis: Liberty Fund, 1981.

Smith, Charlotte, *The Collected Letters of Charlotte Smith*, ed. Judith Phillips Stanton. Bloomington and Indianapolis: Indiana University Press, 2003.

—— *The Old Manor House* (1793), ed. Jacqueline Labbe. Peterborough, Ontario: Broadview, 2002.

—— *The Poems of Charlotte Smith*, ed. Stuart Curran. Oxford and New York: Oxford University Press, 1993.

—— *The Works of Charlotte Smith*, gen. ed. Stuart Curran. 14 vols. London: Pickering and Chatto, 2005–7.

Steuart, James, *An Inquiry into the Principles of Political Economy: Being an Essay on the Science of Domestic Policy in Free Nations*, 2 vols. London: A. Miller and T. Cadell, 1767.

Wakefield, Priscilla, *Reflections on the Present Condition of the Female Sex; with Suggestions for its Improvement*. London: J. Johnson, 1798.

Williams, David, *Claims of Literature: The Origin, Motives, Objects, and Transactions, of the Society for the Establishment of a Literary Fund*. London: William Millar and W. Bulmer, 1802.

—— *Incidents in my Life Which Have Been Thought of Some Importance* (1802), ed. Peter France. Brighton: University of Sussex Library, 1980.

Wollstonecraft, Mary, *The Collected Letters of Mary Wollstonecraft*, ed. Janet Todd. London: Allen Lane, 2003.

—— *The Works of Mary Wollstonecraft*, ed. Janet Todd and Marilyn Butler with Emma Rees-Mogg, 7 vols. London: Pickering and Chatto, 1989.

Young, Edward, *Conjectures on Original Composition. In a Letter to the Author of Sir Charles Grandison*. London: A. Millar and R. and J. Dodsley, 1759.

Secondary sources

Andrew, Donna T., *Philanthropy and Police: London Charity in the Eighteenth Century*. Princeton: Princeton University Press, 1989.

Armstrong, Nancy, *Desire and Domestic Fiction: A Political History of the Novel*. New York and Oxford: Oxford University Press, 1987.

Bahar, Saba, *Mary Wollstonecraft's Social and Aesthetic Philosophy: An Eve to Please Me*. Basingstoke: Palgrave Macmillan, 2002.

Bannet, Eve Tavor, *The Domestic Revolution: Enlightenment Feminisms and the Novel*. Baltimore and London: The Johns Hopkins University Press, 2000.

—— 'Lives, Letters and Tales in Sarah Scott's *Journey through Every Stage of Life*'. *Age of Johnson*, 17 (2006): 233–59.

Barker, Hannah, *The Business of Women: Female Enterprise and Urban Development in Northern England, 1760–1830*. Oxford: Oxford University Press, 2006.

Barrell, John, *The Birth of Pandora and the Division of Knowledge*. Basingstoke: Macmillan, 1992.

—— *The Dark Side of the Landscape: The Rural Poor in English Painting, 1730–1840*. Cambridge: Cambridge University Press, 1980.

—— *English Literature in History 1730–1780: An Equal, Wide Survey*. London, Melbourne, Sydney, Auckland, Johannesburg: Hutchinson, 1983.

Basker, James G. 'Radical Affinities: Mary Wollstonecraft and Samuel Johnson', in *Tradition in Translation: Women Writers and the Eighteenth-century Canon*, ed. Alvaro Ribeiro and James G. Basker. Oxford: Clarendon Press, 1996, pp. 41–55.

Bataille, Georges, 'The Notion of Expenditure', in *Visions of Excess: Selected Writings, 1927–1939*, ed. Allan Stoekl and trans. Allan Stoekl with Carl Lovitt and Donald M. Leslie Jr. Minneapolis: University of Minnesota Press, 1985.

Batchelor, Jennie, 'The Claims of Literature: Women Applicants to the Royal Literary Fund, 1790–1810'. *Women's Writing*, 12: 1 (2005): 505–21.

—— *Dress, Distress and Desire: Clothing and the Body in Eighteenth-century Literature*. Basingstoke: Palgrave Macmillan, 2005.

—— '"Industry in Distress": Reconfiguring Femininity and Labour in the Magdalen House'. *Eighteenth-century Life*, 28: 1 (2004): 1–20.

Battersby, Christine, *Gender and Genius: Towards a Feminist Aesthetics*. Bloomington: Indiana University Press, 1989.

Baudino, Isabelle, Jacques Carré, Cécile Révauger, eds. *The Invisible Woman: Aspects of Women's Work in Eighteenth-century Britain*. Aldershot: Ashgate, 2005.

Berg, Maxine, *The Age of Manufactures, 1700–1830*. New York and Oxford: Oxford University Press, 1985.

—— 'What Difference Did Women's Work Make to the Industrial Revolution?' *History Workshop Journal*, 35 (1993): 22–44

Binhammer, Katherine, 'Revolutionary Domesticity in Charlotte Smith's *Desmond*', in *Women, Revolution and the Novels of the 1790s*, ed. Linda Lang-Peralta. East Lansing: Michigan State University Press, 1999, pp. 25–46.

Blakey, Dorothy, *The Minerva Press, 1790–1820*. Oxford: The Bibliographical Society at the University Press, 1938.

Bourdieu, Pierre, *The Logic of Pratice*. Trans. Richard Nice. Cambridge: Polity Press, 1990.

Bowditch, Phebe Lowell, *Horace and the Gift Economy of Patronage*. Berkeley and London: University of California Press, 2001.

Boyd, Diane E., '"Professing Drudge": Charlotte Smith's Negotiation of a Mother-writer Author Function'. *South Atlantic Review*, 66: 1 (2001): 145–66.

—— 'Working Fictions: Representations of Middle-class Working Women in Eighteenth-Century Fiction'. Unpublished PhD thesis, Auburn University, 2002.

Bradley, Harriet, *Men's Work, Women's Work: A Sociological History of the Sexual Division of Labour*. Cambridge: Polity, 1989.

Carretta, Vincent, 'Utopia Limited: Sarah Scott's *Millenium Hall* and *The History of Sir George Ellison*'. *The Age of Johnson*, 5 (1992): 303–26.

Christmas, William J., *The Lab'ring Muses: Work, Writing and the Social Order in English Plebeian Poetry*. Newark: The University of Delaware Press, 2001.

Cixous, Hélène, 'Sorties: Out and Out: Attacks/Ways Out/Forays', in Hélène Cixous and Catherine Clément, *The Newly Born Woman*, trans. Betsy Wing. Minneapolis: University of Minnesota Press, 1987.

Clark, Alice, *The Working Life of Women in the Seventeenth Century* [1919]. New York: Augustus M. Kelley, rept. 1968.

Clarke, Norma, *The Rise and Fall of the Woman of Letters*. London: Pimlico, 2004.

Clery, E. J., *The Feminization Debate in Eighteenth-century England: Literature, Commerce and Luxury*. Basingstoke: Palgrave Macmillan, 2004.

Cole, Lucinda, '(Anti)Feminist Sympathies: The Politics of Relationship in Smith, Wollstonecraft, and More'. *ELH*, 58: 1 (1991): 107–40.

Collier, Mary, *The Woman's Labour*, in *The Thresher's Labour (Stephen Duck) and The Woman's Labour (Mary Collier)*, with an introduction by Moira Ferguson (Los Angeles: William Andrews Clark Memorial Library, 1985).

Copeland, Edward, *Women Writing About Money: Women's Fiction in England, 1790–1820*. Cambridge: Cambridge University Press, 1995.

Corfield, Penelope J., *Power and the Professions in Britain 1700–1850*. London and New York: Routledge, 1995.

Craciun, Adriana, *British Women Writers and the French Revolution: Citizens of the World*. Basingstoke: Macmillan, 2005.

Cross, Nigel, *The Common Writer: Life in Nineteenth-century Grub Street*. Cambridge: Cambridge University Press, 1985.

Curran, Stuart, 'Charlotte Smith and British Romanticism'. *South Central Review*, 11: 2 (1994): 64–78.

Davidoff, Leonore, and Catherine Hall, *Family Fortunes: Men and Women of the English Middle Class, 1780–1850*. London: Routledge, 1995.

Derrida, Jacques, *Given Time. 1. Counterfeit Money*, trans. Peggy Kamuf. Chicago: University of Chicago Press, 1992.

Deutsch, Helen, 'Symptomatic Correspondences: The Author's Case in Eighteenth-century Britain', *Cultural Critique*, 42 (1999): 40–103.

Donoghue, Frank, *The Fame Machine: Book Reviewing and Eighteenth-century Literary Careers*. Stanford, CA: Stanford University Press, 1996.

Doody, Margaret Anne, *Frances Burney: The Life in the Works*. Cambridge: Cambridge University Press, 1988.

Earle, Peter, *The Making of the English Class: Business, Society and Family Life in London, 1660–1730*. London: Methuen, 1989.

Eger, Elizabeth, Charlotte Grant, Clíona Ó Gallchoir and Penny Warburton, eds. *Women, Writing and the Public Sphere, 1700–1830*. Cambridge: Cambridge University Press, 2001.

Eilenberg, Susan, 'Copyright Rhetoric and the Problem of Analogy in the British Eighteenth Century Debates', in *Romanticism and the Law*, ed. Michael Macovski. Romantic Circles Praxis Series: March 1999. <www.rc.umd.edu/praxis/law/eilenberg/sebg.htm>.

Elfenbein, Andrew, 'Mary Wollstonecraft and the Sexuality of Genius', in *The Cambridge Companion to Mary Wollstonecraft*, ed. Claudia L. Johnson. Cambridge: Cambridge University Press, 2002, pp. 228–45.

—— *Romantic Genius: The Prehistory of a Homosexual Role*. New York: Columbia University Press, 1999.

Ellinghausen, Laurie, *Labour and Writing in Early Modern England, 1567–1667*. Aldershot and Burlington, VT: Ashgate, 2007.

Elliott, Dorice Williams, *The Angel out of the House: Philanthropy and Gender in Nineteenth-century England*. Charlottesville and London: University Press of Virginia, 2002.

Favret, Mary A., *Romantic Correspondence: Women, Politics and the Fiction of Letters*. Cambridge: Cambridge University Press, 1993.

Fletcher, Loraine, *Charlotte Smith: A Critical Biography*. Basingstoke: Palgrave Macmillan, 2001.

Frank, Judith, *Common Ground: Eighteenth-century Satiric Fiction and the Poor*. Stanford, CA: Stanford University Press, 1997.

Friedman, Susan Stanford, 'Creativity and the Childbirth Metaphor: Gender Difference in Literary Discourse'. *Feminist Studies*, 13: 1 (1987): 49–82

Fry, Carrol L. *Charlotte Smith: Popular Novelist.* New York: Arno Press, 1980.

Gadeken, Sara, '"A Method of Being Perfectly Happy": Technologies of Self in the Eighteenth-century Female Community'. *The Eighteenth-century Novel* (2001): 217–35.

Gallagher, Catherine, *Nobody's Story: The Vanishing Acts of Women Writers in the Marketplace, 1670–1820*. Berkeley and Los Angeles: University of California, 1994.

Ganobcsik-Williams, Gruffudd Aled, 'The Sweat of the Brain: Representations of Intellectual Labour in the Writings of Edmund Burke, William Cobbett, William Hazlitt, and Thomas Carlyle'. Unpublished PhD thesis, University of Warwick, 2001.

Genette, Gérard, *Paratexts: Thresholds of Interpretation*, trans. Jane E. Lewin. Cambridge: Cambridge University Press, 1997.

Goodridge, John, *Rural Life in Eighteenth-century English Poetry*. Cambridge: Cambridge University Press, 1995.

Griffin, Dustin, *Literary Patronage in England, 1650–1800*. Cambridge: Cambridge University Press, 1996.

Guest, Harriet, *Small Change: Women, Learning, Patriotism, 1750–1810*. Chicago and London: The University of Chicago Press, 2000.

Hill, Bridget, *Women, Work and Sexual Politics in Eighteenth-century England*. London: UCL Press, 1994.

Hoeveler, Diane Long, *Gothic Feminism: The Professionalization of Gender from Charlotte Smith to the Brontës*. University Park, PA: The University of Pennsylvania Press, 1998.

Hofkosh, Sonia, *Sexual Politics and the Romantic Author*. Cambridge: Cambridge University Press, 1998.

Holmes, Geoffrey, *Augustan England: Professions, State and Society, 1680–1730*. London: George Allen and Unwin, 1982.

Honeyman, Katrina, *Women, Gender and Industrialisation in England, 1700–1870*. Basingstoke: Macmillan, 2000.

Hunt, Margaret, *The Middling Sort: Commerce, Gender and the Family in England, 1680–1780*. Berkeley and London: The University of California Press, 1996.

Hyde, Lewis, *The Gift: Imagination and the Erotic Life of Property*. London: Vintage, 1999.

Ingrassia, Catherine, *Authorship, Commerce, and Gender in Early Eighteenth-century England: A Culture of Paper Credit*. Cambridge: Cambridge University Press, 1998.

Irigaray, Luce, 'Women on the Market', in *This Sex Which Is Not One*, trans. Catherine Porter with Carolyn Burke. Ithaca: Cornell University Press, 1985.

Johns, Alessa, *Women's Utopias of the Eighteenth Century*. Urbana and Chicago: University of Illinois Press, 2003.

Johnson, Claudia L., *Equivocal Beings, Politics, Gender and Sentimentality in the 1790s*. Chicago: University of Chicago Press, 1995.

Jones, Vivien, 'Placing Jemima: Women Writers of the 1790s and the Eighteenth-century Prostitution Narrative'. *Women's Writing*, 4: 2 (1997): 201–20.

Jordan, Sarah, *Anxieties of Idleness: Idleness in Eighteenth-century British Literature and Culture*. Lewisburg: Bucknell University Press; London: Associated University Presses, 2003.

Joyce, Patrick, ed., *The Historical Meanings of Women's Work*. Cambridge: Cambridge University Press, 1987.

Justice, George, *The Manufacturers of Literature: Writing and the Literary Marketplace in Eighteenth-century England*. Newark: University of Delaware Press, 2002.

Kaplan, Cora, "Like a Housemaid's Fancies": The Representation of Working-class Women in Nineteenth-century Writing', in *Grafts: Feminist Cultural Criticism*, ed. Susan Sheridan. London and New York: Verso, 1988, pp. 55–75.

—— *Sea Changes: Essays on Culture and Feminism*. London and New York: Verso [1980], 1990.

Keane, Angela, 'The Market, the Public, and the Female Author: Anna Laetitia Barbauld's Gift Economy'. *Romanticism: The Journal of Romantic Culture and Criticism*, 8: 2 (2002): 161–78.

—— *Women Writers and the English Nation in the 1790s*. Cambridge: Cambridge University Press, 2000.

Keen, Paul, *The Crisis of Literature in the 1790s: Print Culture and the Public Sphere*. Cambridge: Cambridge University Press, 1999.

Kelly, Gary, *Women, Writing and Revolution, 1790–1827*. Oxford: Clarendon Press, 1993.

King, Kathryn R., 'Of Needles and Pens and Women's Work'. *Tulsa Studies in Women's Literature*, 14:1 (1995): 77–93.

Kipp, Julie, *Romanticism, Maternity and the Body Politic*. Cambridge: Cambridge University Press, 2003.

Klekar, Cynthia, '"Her Gift Was Compelled": Gender and the Failure of the "Gift" in *Cecilia*'. *Eighteenth-century Fiction*, 18: 1 (2005): 107–26.

Klekar, Cynthia, and Linda Zionkowski, eds, *The Culture of the Gift in Eighteenth-century England*. New York and Basingstoke: Palgrave Macmillan, 2009.

Kord, Susanne, *Women Peasant Poets in Eighteenth-century England, Scotland and Germany: Milkmaids on Parnassus*. Rochester, NY, and Woodbridge: Camden House, 2003.

Kowaleski-Wallace, Elizabeth, *Consuming Subjects: Women, Shopping, and Business in the Eighteenth Century*. New York: Columbia University Press, 1997.

Labbe, Jacqueline, ed., *Charlotte Smith in British Romanticism*. London: Pickering and Chatto, 2008.

—— *Charlotte Smith: Romanticism, Poetry and the Culture of Gender*. Manchester and New York: Manchester University Press, 2003.

—— 'Metaphoricity and the Romance of Property in *The Old Manor House*'. *Novel: A Forum on Fiction*, 32 (2001): 216–31.

—— 'The Romance of Motherhood: Generation and the Literary Text', *Romanticism on the Net*. 26 (May 2002). <www.erudit.org/revue/ron/2002/v/n26/005698ar.html>.

—— 'Selling One's Sorrows: Charlotte Smith, Mary Robinson, and the Marketing of Poetry'. *The Wordsworth Circle*, 25 (1994): 68–71.

Landry, Donna, *The Muses of Resistance: Laboring-class Women's Poetry in Britain, 1739–1796*. Cambridge: Cambridge University Press, 1990.

—— Picturing Benevolence Against the Commercial Cry, 1750–1798: or, Sarah Fielding and the Secret Causes of Romanticism', in *The History of British Women's Writing, Volume V, 1750–1830*. Basingstoke: Palgrave Macmillan, forthcoming.

Langbauer, Laurie, 'An Early Romance: Motherhood and Women's Writing in Mary Wollstonecraft's Novels', in *Romanticism and Feminism*, ed. Anne Mellor. Bloomington: University of Indiana Press, 1988, pp. 208–19.

Langford, Paul, *A Polite and Commercial People: England, 1727–1783*. Oxford: Oxford University Press, 1989.

Lanser, Susan Sniader, *Fictions of Authority: Women Writers and Narrative Voice*. Ithaca and London: Cornell University Press, 1992.

Lawlor, Clark, *Consumption and Literature: The Making of the Romantic Disease*. Basingstoke: Palgrave, 2006.

Lawlor, Clark, and Akihito Suzuki, 'The Disease of the Self: Representing Consumption, 1700–1830'. *Bulletin of the History of Medicine*, 74: 3 (2000): 458–95.

London, April, *Women and Property in the Eighteenth-century English Novel*. Cambridge: Cambridge University Press, 1999.

Lutz, Alfred, 'Commercial Capitalism, Classical Republicanism, and the Man of Sensibility in *The History of Sir George Ellison*', *SEL*, 39: 3 (1999): 557–74.

McDonald, Jan, '"Acting and the Austere Joys of Motherhood": Sarah Siddons Performing Maternity', in *Extraordinary Actors: Essays on Particular Performers*, ed. Jane Milling, Martin Banham and Peter Thomson. Exeter: University of Exeter Press, 2004, pp. 57–70.

McDonegal, Julie, 'The Tyranny of Gift Giving: The Politics of Generosity in Sarah Scott's *Millenium Hall* and *George Ellison*'. *Eighteenth-century Fiction*, 19: 3 (2007): 291–306.

McDowell, Paula, *The Women of Grub Street: Press, Politics, and Gender in the London Literary Marketplace, 1678–1730*. Oxford: Clarendon Press, 1998.

McLeod, Deborah Anne, 'The Minerva Press'. Unpublished PhD dissertation, University of Alberta, 1997.

Mauss, Marcel, *The Gift: The Form and Reason for Exchange in Archaic Societies*, trans. W. D. Halls. London and New York: Routledge, 1990.

Mellor, Anne K., *Mothers of the Nation: Women's Political Writing in England, 1780–1830*. Bloomington and Indianapolis: Indiana University Press, 2000.

Nixon, Cheryl L., '"Stop a Moment at this Preface": The Gendered Paratexts of Fielding, Barker, and Haywood'. *JNT: Journal of Narrative Theory*, 32: 2 (2002): 123–53.

Peace, Mary, '"Epicures in Rural Pleasures": Revolution, Desire and Sentimental Economy in Sarah Scott's *Millenium Hall*'. *Women's Writing*, 9: 2 (2002): 305–16.

Pearson, Jacqueline, 'Mothering the Novel: Frances Burney and the Next Generations of Women Novelists'. *CW3: Corvey Women Writers on the Web*, 1: 2004. <www2.shu.ac.uk/corvey/CW3journal/issues/pearson.html>.

Perry, Ruth, 'Bluestockings in Utopia', in *History, Gender, and Eighteenth-century Literature*, ed. Beth Fowkes Tobin. Athens: University of Georgia Press, 1994, pp. 159–78.

—— *Novel Relations: The Transformation of Kinship in English Literature and Culture, 1748–1818*. Cambridge: Cambridge University Press, 2004.

Phillips, Nicola, *Women in Business, 1700–1850*. London: The Boydell Press, 2006.

Pinch, Adela, *Strange Fits of Passion: Epistemologies of Emotion, Hume to Austen*. Stanford: Stanford University Press, 1996.

Pinchbeck, Ivy, *Women Workers and the Industrial Revolution 1750–1850*. London: Virago, [1930] 1985.

Poovey, Mary, *The Proper Lady and the Woman Writer: Ideology as Style in the Works of Mary Wollstonecraft, Mary Shelley, and Jane Austen*. Chicago and London: University of Chicago Press, 1984.

Rizzo, Betty, *Companions Without Vows: Relationships Among Eighteenth-century British Women*. Athens and London: University of Georgia Press, 1996.

Rose, Mark, *Authors and Owners: The Invention of Copyright*. Cambridge [MA] and London: Harvard University Press, 1993.

Rosenthal, Laura J., 'The Sublime, The Beautiful, "The Siddons"'. In *The Clothes that Wear Us: Essays on Dressing and Transgressing in Eighteenth-century Culture*. Ed. Jessica Munns and Penny Richards. Newark: University of Delaware Press, 1999, pp. 56–79.

Runge, Laura L., 'Churls and Graybeards and Novels Written by a Lady: Gender in Eighteenth-century Book Reviews' *Corvey CW3 Journal*, 1 (2004). <www2.shu.ac.uk/corvey/cw3journal/Issue%20one/runge.html>.

Schellenberg, Betty A., *The Professionalization of Women Writers in Eighteenth-century Britain*. Cambridge: Cambridge University Press, 2005.

Schofield, Mary Anne, '"The Witchery of Fiction": Charlotte Smith, Novelist', in *Living by the Pen: Early British Women Writers*, ed. Dale Spender. New York: Teachers College Press, 1992, pp. 72–88.

Sharpe, Pamela, *Adapting to Capitalism: Working Women in the English Economy, 1700–1850*. Basingstoke: Palgrave Macmillan, 1996.

—— 'Continuity and Change: Women's History and Economic History in Britain', *Economic History Review*, 48 (1995): 353–69.

—— ed. *Women's Work: The English Experience 1650–1914*. London, New York, Sydney and Auckland: Arnold, 1998.

Sherman, Sandra, *Imagining Poverty: Quantification and the Decline of Paternalism*. Columbus: Ohio State University Press, 2001.

Sherman, Stuart, *Telling Time: Clocks, Diaries and English Diurnal Form, 1660–1785*. Chicago and London: The University of Chicago Press, 1996.

Siskin, Clifford, *The Work of Writing: Literature and Social Change in Britain, 1700–1830*. Baltimore and London: The Johns Hopkins University Press, 1998.

Skinner, Gillian. *Sensibility and Economics in the Novel, 1740–1800: The Price of a Tear*, Basingstoke: Palgrave Macmillan, 1999.

Smail, John, *The Origins of Middle-class Culture: Halifax, Yorkshire, 1660–1780*. Ithaca: Cornell University Press, 1994.

Smith, Johanna M., 'Philanthropic Community in *Millenium Hall* and the York Ladies' Committee'. *Eighteenth Century: Theory and Interpretation*, 36: 3 (1995): 266–82.

Snell, K. D. M., *Annals of the Labouring Poor*. Cambridge: Cambridge University Press, 1988.

Spencer, Jane, *Literary Relations: Kinship and the Canon, 1660–1830*. Oxford: Oxford University Press, 2005.

—— *The Rise of the Woman Novelist: From Aphra Behn to Jane Austen*. Oxford: Blackwell, 1986.

Staves, Susan. *A Literary History of Women's Writing in Britain, 1660–1789*. Cambridge: Cambridge University Press, 2006.

Still, Judith, *Feminine Economies: Thinking Against the Market in the Enlightenment and the Late Twentieth Century*. Manchester and New York: Manchester University Press, 1997.

Straub, Kristina, *Divided Fictions: Fanny Burney and Feminine Strategy*. Lexington: The University Press of Kentucky, 1987.

Sutherland, Kathryn, 'Adam Smith's Master Narrative: Women and *The Wealth of Nations*', in *Adam Smith's Wealth of Nations: New Interdisciplinary Essays*, ed. Stephen Copley and Kathryn Sutherland. Manchester and New York: Manchester University Press, 1995, pp. 97–121.

—— 'Fictional Economies: Adam Smith, Walter Scott and the Nineteenth-century Novel', *ELH*, 54 (1987): 97–127.

—— 'Writings on Education and Conduct: Arguments for Female Improvement', in *Women and Literature in Britain, 1700–1800*. Cambridge: Cambridge University Press, 2000.

Tauchert, Ashley, *Mary Wollstonecraft and the Accent of the Feminine*. Basingstoke: Palgrave Macmillan, 2001.

Taylor, Barbara, *Mary Wollstonecraft and the Feminist Imagination*. Cambridge: Cambridge University Press, 2003.

Tenger, Zeynep, and Paul Trolander, 'Genius versus Capital: Eighteenth-century Theories of Genius and Adam Smith's *Wealth of Nations*'. *Modern Language Quarterly*, 55 (1994): 169–89.

Thompson, James, *Models of Value: Eighteenth-century Political Economy and the Novel*. Durham [NC]: Duke University Press, 1996.

Todd, Janet, *Mary Wollstonecraft: A Revolutionary Life*. New York: Columbia University Press, 2000.

—— *The Sign of Angellica*. London: Virago, 1989.

Turner, Cheryl, *Living by the Pen: Women Writers in the Eighteenth Century*. London: Routledge, 1992.

Ty, Eleanor, *Unsex'd Revolutionaries: Five Women Novelists of the 1790s*. Toronto, Buffalo and London: University of Toronto Press, 1993.

Valenze, Deborah, *The First Industrial Woman*. New York and Oxford: Oxford University Press, 1995.

Van Sant, Ann, 'Crusoe's Hands'. *Eighteenth-century Life*, 32: 2 (2008): 120–37.

Vickery, Amanda, *The Gentleman's Daughter: Women's Lives in Georgian England*. New Haven and London: Yale University Press, [1998] 2003.

Wallech, Steven, '"Class Versus Rank": The Transformation of Eighteenth-century English Social Terms and Theories of Production'. *Journal of the History of Ideas*, 47: 3 (1986): 409–31.

Waters, Mary A., *British Women Writers and the Profession of Literary Criticism*. Basingstoke: Palgrave Macmillan, 2004.

Weber, Max, *The Protestant Ethic and the Spirit of Capitalism*, trans. Talcott Parsons. London: George Allen and Unwin, 1930.

Woodmansee, Martha, *The Author, Art, and the Market: Rereading the History of Aesthetics*. New York: Columbia University Press, 1994.

—— 'The Genius and the Copyright: Economic and Legal Conditions of the Emergence of the "Author"'. *Eighteenth-century Studies*, 17 (1984): 425–48.

Zimmerman, Sarah, 'Charlotte Smith's Letters and the Practice of Self-presentation'. *Princeton University Library Chronicle*, 53: 1 (1991): 50–77.

Zionkowski, Linda, *Men's Work: Gender, Class, and the Professionalization of Poetry, 1660–1784*. New York and Basingstoke: Palgrave, 2001.

Index